WITHDRAWN

PO
CL
AND VOTE

POINT, CLICK, AND VOTE

The Future of Internet Voting

R. Michael Alvarez

Thad E. Hall

BROOKINGS INSTITUTION PRESS
Washington, D.C.

ABOUT BROOKINGS

The Brookings Institution is a private nonprofit organization devoted to research, education, and publication on important issues of domestic and foreign policy. Its principal purpose is to bring knowledge to bear on current and emerging policy problems. The Institution maintains a position of neutrality on issues of public policy. Interpretations or conclusions in Brookings publications should be understood to be solely those of the authors.

Library of Congress Cataloging-in-Publication data
Alvarez, R. Michael, 1964–
Point, click, and vote : the future of Internet elections / R. Michael Alvarez and Thad E. Hall.
p. cm.
Includes bibliographical references and index.
ISBN 0-8157-0368-6 (cloth : alk. paper) —
ISBN 0-8157-0369-4 (pbk. : alk. paper)
1. Internet voting—United States. 2. Elections—United States.
I. Hall, Thad E., 1936– II. Title.
JK1985.A58 2004
324.6'5'02854678—dc22

2003020964

9 8 7 6 5 4 3 2 1
The paper used in this publication meets minimum requirements of the American National Standard for Information Sciences—Permanence of Paper for Printed Library Materials: ANSI Z39.48-1992.

Typeset in Sabon

Composition by OSP, Inc.
Arlington, Virginia

Printed by R. R. Donnelley
Harrisonburg, Virginia

Contents

Preface

Like many things in life, this project was largely due to a fortunate coincidence. Early one morning in a nondescript office park right next to the Baltimore/Washington international airport, the two authors-to-be entered an unmarked office building at roughly the same time. As each of us introduced himself to the security guard inside the door, we realized that both of us were there for the same purpose—to attend the "peer review" of the 2000 Voting Over the Internet project of the Federal Voting Assistance Program (FVAP).

Over the course of the next year, we continued our discussions about our experiences in Baltimore and began to work with FVAP as it planned a successor Internet voting project for the 2004 elections. We talked at professional meetings and on a number of occasions in Washington when Alvarez was testifying before Congress and meeting with congressional staff regarding federal election reform legislation (the Help America Vote Act). Each time we talked it was evident that both of us could see the need for a clear discussion of the pros and cons of Internet voting. From those discussions sprang this book.

Along the way we have benefited from our interactions with colleagues and friends working in many different fields. We both thank Carol Paquette of FVAP, without whom we probably would never have found our common interests. We also wish to thank others associated with the FVAP's Internet voting projects, who in various ways have shaped our thinking about Internet voting and electoral reform: Polli Brunnelli, Nicole Forlano, and Richard Schum. We thank Carl Almond, Peter Meulbroek, and Ned

Rynearson for their comments on specific chapters of this book, Simon Wilkie for discussions about FCC policy, and Sonya Hoo for helping us edit the manuscript. Last, Mary Sikora has been a wonderful editor and friendly presence during our collaboration on this project, and Chris Kelaher and Eileen Hughes at the Brookings Institution Press helped us improve the manuscript and guided it through the publication process.

Alvarez has been involved in various ways with the study of Internet voting since 1999. He thanks Jonathan Nagler for his collaboration on their early paper on Internet voting. He also thanks California's former secretary of state, Bill Jones, and two of Jones's staff members, Alfie Charles and Beth Miller, who gave him the opportunity to participate on the California Internet Voting Task Force. His colleagues on the Caltech/MIT Voting Technology Project also helped sharpen his interest in this topic, and the research and advocacy efforts of the project members have allowed him to learn a great deal about how elections are run in America. He would also like to thank the Carnegie Foundation of New York and the John S. and James L. Knight Foundation for their support of the Voting Technology Project's research in this area.

Hall would like to thank David King, whose recommendation led to his attending the VOI peer review in the first place, and the Georgia Tech Research Institute, which hosted a conference on Internet voting in 2002 that provided a forum for testing some of our early thinking about this project. Conny McCormack—along with Kris Heffron, Jennifer Collins-Foley, and others—spent a week showing him the ins and outs of how elections work in a big city like Los Angeles, and Steve Katsurinis, with the city of Alexandria, Virginia, helped show him how elections are run in a smaller locality. His work on the professional staff of the National Commission on Federal Election Reform helped shape his views on election administration. Finally, he would like to thank his colleagues at the Century Foundation for their support in this effort, which does not necessarily reflect the views of the foundation.

Both authors realize how amusing this book will be to their children, Sophia Alvarez and Ethan Hall, when each votes for president in the 2020 election using some wireless hand-held device that we haven't even thought of. We dedicate this book to them and hope that our research will help produce better ways for young people to vote in the future.

POINT,
CLICK,
AND **VOTE**

CHAPTER 1

The Past and Future
of Internet Voting

During the recount of votes in Florida in the 2000 presidential election, one of the most heated debates was over how military ballots should be counted. Under a 1982 federal consent decree between the U.S. Department of Justice and the state of Florida, ballots from overseas voters are to be accepted up to ten days after an election.[1] As the nation watched and the presidential election hung in the balance, election supervisors and canvassing boards met to determine which overseas votes would count and which would not.

The canvassing boards often rejected as many or more ballots from overseas voters as they accepted. Orange County—home of the tourist magnet Disneyworld—rejected 117 overseas ballots and accepted only thirty. But in Escambia County—home of the Pensacola Naval Air Station—the canvassing board rejected 112 ballots and accepted 147. Across the state, election officials estimated that 40 percent of overseas ballots were rejected in the initial 2000 election count—about as many as were rejected in 1996.[2]

Thousands of individuals—many of them men and women in the United States armed forces, military dependents, or civilians serving the nation in nonmilitary capacities—went to great lengths to procure an absentee ballot and vote in the 2000 election, only to have their ballot not included in the final count. In the end, their votes were disregarded for reasons that occur in election after election. The absentee ballots of many voters were rejected because the ballot lacked a signature or witness. In many other cases, the rejection of the ballot was not due to a mistake of the voter; while the Pentagon has rules specifying that all mail is to be postmarked, military mail clerks sometimes fail to do so in order to get the mail into bags and onto waiting airplanes or boats headed for the United States. As Pat Halloran, the election supervisor in Okaloosa County, noted, "Postmarks were never a problem before; we never accepted [ballots without postmarks] before, and we didn't accept them this time."[3]

The experience of overseas voters in the 2000 election raises fundamental questions about the election process: Can technology facilitate voter registration and voting? Can registration and voting from remote locations be done easily and accurately, so that voters do not have to worry about whether they are eligible to vote or whether their ballot will be counted? For many, the answer seems simple: Internet voting.

The 2000 election was a historic event. Of course, most people view it as being historic for the obvious reason: it was one of the closest presidential elections in the history of the United States, and for thirty-seven days, it was unclear who would be elected president. The nation received a crash course in election administration, learning about voting procedures, voting equipment, pregnant and dimpled "chads," military and absentee voting, and the rules for counting and recounting ballots. In the end, the decision of the U.S. Supreme Court in *Bush* v. *Gore*, by halting the Florida recounts, made the story that much more compelling.

However, the controversy surrounding the 2000 presidential vote in Florida was not the only thing that made the election historic. History also was being made on election night because hidden among the tens of millions of ballots being counted across the country were eighty-four ballots that were unique in the history of U.S. presidential elections. These ballots were cast over the Internet by citizens overseas, the first online ballots ever counted in a presidential general election. Moreover, earlier in the year, online voting had come to the primary process in two states: in a straw poll of Alaska Republicans and in the Arizona Democratic presidential primary, when Arizona became first state to use the Internet as a mode of voting.

For many, Internet voting seems natural. Ever since the Netscape Navigator software made the World Wide Web easy to use, the Internet has been touted as a revolutionary force in American society. Indeed, in many ways, it has been revolutionary. In just four years, Internet use in the United States skyrocketed: while only 18 percent of households had an Internet connection in 1997, by 2000 almost 42 percent of households were online and more than half of all households had a personal computer.

For young people, Internet availability is even more ubiquitous—almost 95 percent of white school children and approximately 80 percent of minority students have access to the Internet at school.[4] An entire generation of kids will soon enter adulthood with no memory of a world without instant messaging, web surfing, and e-mail.

The revolutionary nature of the Internet has carried over to the political realm, as Internet savvy politicians have realized how this technology can be used to further their interests. Consider the following examples from the past several years:

Presidential candidates in the 2000 election used the Internet in every aspect of their campaigns. Steve Forbes declared his candidacy in an online web cast.[5] Senator John McCain raised $810,000 in campaign contributions over the Internet in forty-eight hours after winning the New Hampshire primary; 40 percent of the donors were first-time political contributors and 34 percent were under the age of forty.[6] Candidates posted speeches, policy positions, and attacks and counterattacks on their websites at a frantic pace as they competed to control the flow of information during the campaign.

Unconventional political activists also have found the Internet to be a revolutionary tool. As Juliette Beck, an activist in the antiglobalization movement, told the *New York Times*, "The events and the nonviolence training and the political theater—the Internet made it possible. . . . We have lots of Lilliputians all acting autonomously and at the same time connected."[7] With the Internet, disparate groups of activists share information, coordinate activities, rally supporters, and develop strategies without ever meeting face to face. Wireless technology is expanding the opportunities for such activities, allowing political dissidents and other actors to communicate on the fly, as events occur.[8]

Because of the difficulty of controlling the flow of information online, the Internet often is touted as the medium that will promote democracy around the world. As President Bill Clinton said, "In the new century, liberty will spread by cell phone and cable modem. . . . We know how much the Internet has changed America, and we are already an open society. Imagine how much it could change China. Now, there's no question China has been trying to crack down on the Internet—good luck. That's sort of like trying to nail Jell-O to the wall."[9]

Finally, governments across the United States and around the world are developing "e-government" initiatives designed to connect the public to the government through the Internet.[10] In addition to offering direct e-mail connections to government staff, e-government allows the public to access a variety of services online. For example, the federal government hopes to have 80 percent of taxpayers file their tax returns electronically by 2007; in fiscal year 2002, 20.7 percent of all tax returns were filed electronically.[11] Millions of Americans use the Internet every day to get information from the government, and there is growing demand for more online government services.[12]

Internet Voting: A Good Idea?

With the Internet being used for a variety of different political activities—from collecting information to collecting political contributions—it is only a small leap to asking why the Internet cannot be used for voting as well. President Clinton asked just that question well before the 2000 presidential election; in a memorandum dated December 17, 1999, he directed the National Science Foundation to study the potential for Internet voting.[13] Some would argue that Internet voting could be a panacea for what ails our political system.

But before we launch deeply into the debate over Internet voting, we need to clarify our use of the term. When we write about Internet voting in this book we are discussing what has been defined as "remote Internet voting."[14] Remote Internet voting is voting by using a computer that is not under the physical control of election officials; the ballot is cast over an Internet connection. It is important to distinguish remote Internet voting, or what we refer to in this book as Internet voting, from three other types of Internet voting:

—*Kiosk Internet voting.* Voting is done at certain locations by using a computer under the physical control of election officials to cast a ballot over the Internet.

—*Polling place Internet voting.* Voting done at any valid polling place by using a computer under the physical control of election officials to cast a ballot over the Internet.

—*Precinct Internet voting.* Voting that is identical to polling place Internet voting except that the voter can vote only at his or her own precinct polling place.

Despite the four types of Internet voting, unless otherwise indicated, when we say Internet voting we mean remote Internet voting, although in practice a jurisdiction may use any combination of the four types in an election. In addition, our use of the term "voting" includes both registration and voting; thus when we write about Internet voting systems in this book, we are talking about an integrated remote Internet registration and voting system.[15]

Proponents of Internet voting make several arguments in its favor. First, Internet voting may make it easier for voters to participate in an election because every computer that has an online connection becomes a potential polling site. Internet voting also might lower the cost of voting for the entire electorate, and it has the potential to eliminate problems such as those that might have kept millions of voters from participating in the 2000 presidential election.[16] No longer would voters have to trudge down to a school, church, or community center in order to vote. No longer would factors like bad weather, long lines, or confusion over the location of polling places impede voter participation. Instead—in the comfort of their home or office, a public library, or an Internet café—individuals could log on and vote without having to make a special effort. The Internet also could be used to register voters and to allow them to check the status of their registration, thus reducing problems that often plague the first steps in the electoral process.[17]

Internet voting could especially lower the cost of participation for certain special populations. Consider, for example, four types of voters. First, imagine a soldier overseas or a sailor on a nuclear submarine. Both are serving their country, yet their ability to vote is limited because of the logistics of obtaining an absentee ballot and getting it back in time to be counted. In the last presidential election, military personnel encountered numerous problems in the voting process.[18] With the Internet, they could vote from anywhere in the world, confident that their vote would be received and counted.

Second, consider voters confined to a wheelchair. They want to participate in the electoral process like everyone else, but in most of the United States that is difficult for them to do. According to a General Accounting Office study conducted during the 2000 presidential election, more than 80 percent of polling places across the nation had some barrier that prevented citizens in a wheelchair from accessing the poll site.[19] With Internet voting, disabled voters could cast their ballot from their own home without having to navigate the myriad of obstacles that await them at the polling place.

Third, imagine an executive who travels frequently or a working single parent. Both might want to vote on election day but find it difficult or impossible to do so because of events beyond their control. For example, the executive may have to take an unexpected trip out of town the day before the election or the single parent may have to work longer than usual on Election Day and then rush to get his or her children from the daycare center. Under current election procedures, these potential voters generally cannot obtain an absentee ballot on short notice. In each case, with Internet voting, these individuals could find it easier to vote because they could do so without having to make a trip to the polls.

Finally, Internet voting might pull the hardest-to-reach voters—those between the ages of eighteen and twenty-five—into the political process. As noted, younger Americans typically are well-versed in using the Internet. They have a tremendous amount of experience in surfing the Net and like the idea of using new, cutting-edge technologies. Internet voting could help increase voting among this group, which historically has voted at very low rates. The Internet also could help many young people who are attending college away from home to vote without having to make a special trip home or request an absentee ballot.

Proponents also note that even without the Internet, alternative voting methods have become more pervasive since the early 1970s.[20] The most extreme version of alternative voting is found in Oregon, which now holds all of its elections by mail. The state has no poll site voting at all; instead, all voters receive a ballot by mail that they can cast anytime after they receive it through election day. Oregon's system often is presented as analogous to Internet voting because it is a truly remote system designed to lower the cost of voting by making it easier to vote. According to that argument, Internet voting would not be much different from voting in Oregon: everyone votes from home; they just use the technologically superior Internet instead of the mail.

Internet voting also could have a positive effect on other factors that are difficult to quantify. Proponents of Internet voting have asserted that it could increase the quality of votes cast. It is easy to imagine a voter opening one browser window on her computer to display the ballot, opening a second window to display a voter guide with information about candidates and ballot measures, and opening two or three other windows to candidate, party, or other election-oriented websites. The voter could then spend more time becoming informed about the choices she faces, in the convenience of her home or office, increasing the quality of her vote. Internet voting systems could also be programmed to help voters avoid common mistakes, such as casting more votes than allowed in a certain race.

Imagine moreover a system of Internet voting in which voters can access their ballot weeks before the election, make their choices then, but revise their votes until 8:00 p.m. on election day. Such a system could dramatically alter the dynamics of contemporary political campaigns, in which a decision to mount a negative attack on the opposition often is made in the final days of the campaign, when (as has occurred in recent California elections) as many as 25 percent of votes already have been cast in the vote-by-mail process.[21] Such a system could change the incentives for using last-minute negative attacks: voters, alienated by a harsh end-of-campaign personal attack by a candidate, might reconsider their earlier vote for that candidate.

...Or a Recipe for Disaster?

Just as some people see Internet voting as the solution to many of the problems facing the U.S. electoral system, others see it as sowing the seeds of disaster. Most opponents point first to the issue of online security. Over the past several years, there have been numerous high-profile cases of Internet viruses and attacks on Internet portals that have shut down the websites of major corporations and government agencies. In February 2000, computer hackers brought down five highly prominent websites: Amazon.com, Buy.com, CNN.com, eBay, and Yahoo.com. The hackers used a "denial-of-service" attack, which flooded the servers with fake messages, to bring down the servers.[22] In 2001 several computer "worms" and e-mail viruses spread across the Internet, often causing havoc. In July 2001, the "Code Red" worm attacked more than a quarter-million computers and forced the Department of Defense to block access to many of its public websites in order to install a prophylactic device to stop future attacks.[23]

Most of these Internet attacks have been carried out by young hackers. However, the Internet is also vulnerable to more sophisticated attacks carried out by national governments. At congressional hearings held after the 2000 denial-of-service attacks, two terrorism experts noted that many nations and terrorist organizations were developing plans for cyberterrorism. As one expert noted, denial-of-service attacks "could be used on a much more massive scale at the nation-state level to generate truly damaging interruptions to the national economy and infrastructure."[24] These attacks can be quite problematic because they can be staged from anywhere in the world where an individual can log on to the Internet. The

CIA has argued that "the foreign cyber threat constitutes a means to harm U.S. national interests in a nontraditional way using nontraditional attacks. It is transnational in origin, transcends geographic limitations, and is wholly independent of military intervention."[25]

A second major concern about Internet voting is whether such a system would favor some voters at the expense of others. Individuals who connect to the Internet at home tend to be white, wealthy, well educated, male, and Republican.[26] Similarly, white-collar workers are more likely to have Internet access at work than are blue-collar and retail workers. The gap between those who have convenient Internet access and those who do not is called the digital divide. With Internet voting, the digital divide would create a situation in which one group of voters could access the polls easily, while another group would have fewer avenues for gaining access. Even more problematic, the voters who would be likely to have an advantage are those who typically vote at higher-than-average rates, while the voters who probably would be disadvantaged generally vote at lower-than-average rates. Thus the interaction of the digital divide and the factors that lead some voters to participate at higher rates than others might exacerbate current inequities in political representation.

A second type of digital divide is now becoming a concern to observers of Internet development: the growth of significant differences in the quality of Internet access. Urban, wealthy, and typically white areas of the United States have access to relatively inexpensive, high-speed Internet service, either in the form of a digital subscriber line (DSL) or cable modem access. In 2000 less than 20 percent of Internet users had such high-speed connections.[27] The remainder of the Internet-using population had either 28.8K or 56.6K dial-up modem access, both of which are considerably slower in downloading today's multimedia Internet content. This new manifestation of the digital divide could become a significant obstacle to Internet voting if it requires broadband access.

The digital divide also could create a legal barrier to wide-scale Internet voting. In a seminal study conducted following the 2000 election, the California Institute of Technology and the Massachusetts Institute of Technology found that some voting technologies are more effective than others in ensuring that votes are counted.[28] The digital divide may create a situation in which the ballots of Internet voters are more likely to be counted than those of non-Internet users. Because Internet voting is likely to be more accurate than other forms of voting, its use could be problematic. Even more problematic is the fact that this new technology may not be as available to groups that historically have been victims of both intentional and unintentional discrimination—especially poor and minority voters. Particularly in light of the Supreme Court's decision in *Bush* v. *Gore*—and laws such as the Voting Rights Act and its amendments— these two factors make Internet voting a likely target of litigation for some time to come.

A third criticism of Internet voting is that it could further the disintegration of civic life in the United States. As Robert Putnam found in his study of civic involvement, there was a marked decline in participation over the last half of the twentieth century, with fewer people engaging in political or civic activities. Instead of being part of a group, Americans now tend to "bowl alone."[29] Internet voting could exacerbate this problem, allowing individuals to participate in one of the most important civic duties—voting—in isolation. Internet voting is the antithesis of the community-based electoral process that many believe is desirable. Norm Ornstein eloquently described this process before the National Commission on Federal Election Reform:

> Voting at the polls on Election Day is an act of community, balanced with individual freedom. . . . It is done just as voters choose, from a common pool of available information, with prompt counting and verification of results, and with a critical zone of privacy surrounding that vote. . . . [V]oting at the polls really is an important link to citizenship. It is an exquisitely balanced act where you go and congregate with your fellow citizens, showing that you are a community, but then you move into a private booth, draw a curtain, and perform a supremely private act, an enormous act expressing the freedom of choice that exists in a democracy.[30]

Our Argument

Both sides in the debate over Internet voting make compelling arguments. Internet voting could expand the opportunities to vote for many citizens, especially those who have a hard time getting to the polls. As much as U.S. soldiers in Afghanistan or Iraq may want to do their civic duty at a polling place in their hometown, the Defense Department is not going to fly them back to the United States to vote. The Internet could allow active-duty military personnel to vote from the front lines or at sea, and they could be assured that their vote would be counted. If Internet voting can mobilize and attract hard-to-reach voters—like young people, who typically vote at very low rates but often are tech-savvy—then it could benefit U.S. democracy. Of course, if the critics are correct in claiming that a teenaged hacker or a foreign agent can affect the outcome of an election through cyberterrorism, then the election fiasco of 2000 might look like a picnic. An election tainted by widespread fraud and uncertainty over whether votes submitted online accurately reflect the preferences of the voters who submitted them could completely undermine public confidence in the electoral process.

Our argument is very straightforward:

There is no way to know whether any argument regarding Internet voting is accurate unless real Internet voting systems are tested, and they should be tested in small-scale, scientific trials so that their successes and failures can be evaluated.

The debate over Internet voting will continue to rely on heated but often poorly informed arguments about its potential benefits and problems. What is needed, however, are facts about its actual pros and cons, and those facts will come to light only if serious scientific testing of Internet voting is undertaken. Unfortunately, the field of election administration has not been known for developing and testing products in an orderly, systemic manner. The existing standards and testing procedures focus primarily on technical requirements for voting machinery, not on how voters actually interact with voting machines or on how voting systems perform in real-world settings.[31]

Many of the problems that occurred in Florida during the 2000 presidential election can be traced to lack of testing or failure to use the scientific method of investigation. Imagine, for instance, that the Palm Beach election administrator had tested the butterfly ballot in a random sample of voters before using it on election day and compared the voting experience of the experimental group to a control group that used some more traditional ballot format. If the experiment was set up correctly, it is likely that the problems with the butterfly ballot design would have been revealed and that it would not have been used in Palm Beach County.

Even today, after the 2000 elections illustrated the problems that voters have with almost every type of voting technology, from punch cards to optical scan ballots, localities across the country are buying new voting technologies without conducting field tests to determine how well the technologies will work for the types of voters who live in their area. For example, the Florida legislature passed election reform legislation in 2000 that allowed communities across the state to purchase optical scan equipment, even though it has been asserted that optical scan voting was the source of a tremendous number of voting errors in the 2000 presidential election in the state of Georgia.[32] If a locality adopts a new technology without first running tests to determine how effectively it works with the voters who will actually use it, there is no way of knowing whether it will solve problems such as overvoting or undervoting in a specific community or whether it will cause new problems.

Pilot testing can be an effective means of learning about the efficacy of a voting system. For example, Los Angeles County pilot tested a touch-screen voting system during early voting for the 2000 general election. The test allowed the county to determine whether touch-screen voting effectively served the county's entire population—which includes concentrations of elderly, disabled, and language-minority voters—as well as to examine administrative issues, such as poll worker training and the simple logistics associated with the use of electronic equipment.[33] Small-scale pilot testing can effectively and inexpensively provide a great deal of data on how new voting technologies work in specific settings, without forcing election officials to make logistical commitments or a massive financial investment in an unproven system. Small-scale testing of any new voting system, especially an Internet system, will also minimize risks when things do not work as expected. Experiments do fail, and experiments with new voting systems will be no exception; however, as much, and maybe more, can be learned from failed experiments as from successful ones. It is only through experimentation, on a small scale, that the advantages and disadvantages of Internet voting will become apparent.

With that in mind, a strong argument can be made for pilot testing Internet voting systems in real elections. Three small-scale tests of Internet voting technology already have been conducted, and Congress is interested in seeing such a system tested for overseas and military voters in the 2004 general election. We argue that limited testing, followed by appropriate evaluation, would allow for thorough examination of many of the points raised by both sides in the debate. Only productive experimental data from pilot projects, coupled with government and privately funded research on Internet security, can provide the scientific data that policymakers and the public need to make intelligent decisions regarding the electoral process and the future of Internet voting in the United States.

Plan of the Book

The remainder of the book addresses specific issues related to Internet voting and concludes with an analysis of how it may fit into the American electoral landscape. Chapter 2 presents a careful examination of academic and policy reviews of Internet voting conducted in recent years. Of particular concern for our work are two major policy studies, one by the California Internet Voting Task Force and the other by the National Science Foundation. These two reports, which were conducted by task forces of social and computer scientists, policymakers, and election officials, have set the agenda for the broad debate on Internet voting. As one of the authors of this book participated in both projects, we have a unique perspective on the process behind both studies and the logic behind the cautious conclusions reached in each report.

Chapter 3 examines the basic problems of voting systems and the digital divide and how both affect political representation. One of the important results of the 2000 presidential election has been a much deeper appreciation of the impact of different voting systems on how people cast their ballots and on the ease with which they participate in the political process. For Internet voting to be effective in a democratic society, all members of that society must have access to similar voting technologies. If some groups of people—for example, the rich—have extensive access to the Internet but other groups—such as low-income citizens or members of certain ethnic minorities—do not have access or have different types of access, some groups of voters may have more influence in the electoral process than others. If a digital divide exists between classes of voters, Internet voting could promote a biased instead of democratic representation of the people's will.

Chapter 4 explores how the Internet fits into the broader political dynamic, such as online political debate, interactive policymaking, and e-government. As many will recall, in 1992 presidential candidate Ross Perot presented a vision of American deliberative democracy in which voters would educate themselves on various issues and then vote directly, in an instant referendum, on the policy choices before them. This is a vision of a return to Greek democracy, in which the rule of the majority of eligible voters determined the outcome of every issue, with the public directly selecting the policy it wants over the Internet. We offer two critiques of this vision. First, we examine the reality of the debate that occurs in referendums and consider whether electronic communication would facilitate a more informed debate or lead instead to the coarsening and narrowing of debate. Second, referring to the literature on communitarianism and representative democracy and applying our understanding of the arguments put forth by the nation's founders, we question the political efficacy of this approach. We consider the reasons why we live in a republican society and how instant online referendums could have a negative impact on the ability of the government to function effectively.

Chapter 5 examines the issue of online security—for many observers, the 500-pound gorilla of Internet voting. We frame the discussion within the broader debate over election fraud and security. Cases of vote fraud, such as in the 1997 Miami mayoral election, compromise the integrity of the electoral process. American history contains examples of electoral fraud perpetrated through all forms of voting: individuals have stuffed ballot boxes, manipulated lever machines, and cast illegal absentee votes. Internet voting, like any voting system, is susceptible to fraud, although Internet vote fraud is obviously different because of its potentially greater magnitude. Consider, for instance, how using the Internet to vote differs from using the Internet to make a purchase. The failure of a website because of a denial-of-service attack inconveniences both buyers and sellers, but transactions can be completed once the problem is corrected. But because elections are conducted on a specific day between specific hours, a similar problem on an election website would disenfranchise voters, who have a right to choose the people who will represent them. Similarly, data show that a small but significant percentage of Internet transactions are fraudulent. That is not a significant problem for most merchants or buyers, as most transactions are insured in some way. Similar levels of fraud in an election could undermine public confidence in the outcome, and it could be quite costly if an election had to be repeated. We discuss how market pressures and government intervention are likely to improve Internet security in the near future.

Chapter 6 presents analogies to Internet voting that provide a basis for gauging the potential impact of Internet voting on the U.S. electoral process. The most direct analogy is Oregon's vote-by-mail system, which we examine to determine whether it increases voter turnout and whether it affects turnout differently among different categories of voters. We also consider analogous reforms, such as general expansions of absentee voting and early voting, to see whether they do in fact increase voter turnout and representation, and we use recent polling data to consider whether these reforms properly identify the potential benefits that may accrue from

Internet voting. New technologies, especially the Internet, have energized and excited younger generations of Americans. We therefore ask whether Internet voting will make younger Americans—who do not participate frequently in elections—more excited about politics and more likely to vote in future elections.

Chapter 7 examines recent tests of Internet voting in the United States—such as the Republican straw poll in Alaska, the Democratic primary in Arizona, and the use of the Internet by the Federal Voting Assistance Program (FVAP) in the 2000 general election—and the use of the Internet in public elections overseas. Each of these cases illustrates both the potential of Internet voting and the myriad of problems associated with it, and they all point to the need for additional small-scale, controlled experiments.

Chapter 8 presents a series of policy recommendations for bringing Internet voting into the electoral realm. The United States is becoming a highly wired society, and as citizens use the Internet more to perform routine activities, pressure is likely to increase on the government to use the Internet for voting. We describe a process for slowly, deliberately, and gradually integrating Internet voting into the existing election system. We contend that during this process, several different reforms could and should occur that would facilitate a gradual transition to Internet-based voting.

First, a series of well-planned, controlled experiments testing the feasibility of Internet voting should be conducted. The FVAP, whose clients have special reasons for voting over the Internet, will conduct the first such experiment in 2004, under a congressional mandate to allow military voters to vote over the Internet in the next presidential election.[34] We believe that additional small-scale experiments are likely to occur in the near future that will further test the effectiveness of Internet voting.

Second, the federal government should play a key role in facilitating these types of experiments. It should initiate a program that gives grants to states to implement well-designed Internet voting pilot projects. These state projects should become laboratories for studying the impact of Internet voting on the electoral process—for learning what works well and what does not.

Third, a transitional process should be developed that leads from the way elections are conducted today to full-blown Internet registration and voting in the future. That transition cannot, and should not, occur overnight. There must be a deliberate strategy, involving experimentation and research, that moves along a rational path to Internet voting.

Fourth, the transitional process should include efforts to promote a different, robust, and interactive form of democracy over the Internet that avoids the trap of instant referendums and to encourage government at all levels to make better use of the Internet to provide information and services. The Internet should become a forum in which political rhetoric and debate produce meaningful contributions to policy discussions, and we later discuss ways in which political rhetoric and debate can be improved.

Fifth, Internet security issues must be studied more effectively. We propose that the government help fund deliberate efforts to develop solutions to known security problems.

Sixth, study must begin on the legal and regulatory changes needed to make Internet voting a reality in every state. Election law in America is a patchwork quilt of laws and regulations at the state, county, and local levels, and it is likely that hundreds or perhaps thousands of laws and regulations will have to be changed to make Internet voting possible.

Seventh, the digital divide must be narrowed, so that all voters will have a more equal opportunity to vote over the Internet. We discuss various reforms aimed at eliminating the digital divide.

The remainder of the book addresses specific issues related to Internet voting and concludes with an analysis of how Internet voting may fit into the American electoral system. This book is not about the technology for conducting Internet voting. The technology—the code to create such a system and the computers and servers to host it—is well known and has been tested numerous times. In addition to the Internet voting trials that have been conducted in public elections, many private elections are held online. Shareholders file online proxy votes, union members and university faculty cast online ballots, and teenagers "vote" for their favorite artists or sports figures in online popularity contests. There is no question that an Internet voting system can be constructed. We focus instead on how such a system will affect the electoral landscape for voters and the administrative landscape for election officials.

CHAPTER 2

Conventional Wisdom about Unconventional Voting

The debate over using the Internet for voting is relatively new; not until the late 1990s did academics or policymakers make any serious efforts to study the possibility.[1] Of the major policy statements about Internet voting that have come out in the past few years, all have been decidedly negative. With the exception of the Federal Voting Assistance Program's report detailing their successful implementation of an Internet voting system in the 2000 presidential election, none of the major reports on the feasibility of Internet voting has endorsed its use in contemporary public elections, nor did any major report on election reform arising from the 2000 presidential election advocate the immediate use of Internet voting.

Whenever the subject of Internet voting arises, two major reports on the topic generally are cited: the California Internet Voting Task Force report and the Report of the National Workshop on Internet Voting.[2] Both reports focused on similar discussions, and both were heavily influenced and written by roughly the same group of individuals. Furthermore, both reports generated a great deal of media attention, and they have since been relied on in policy discussions of Internet voting. These two reports are important in our discussion of Internet voting because, as we explain in later chapters, we advocate a different approach to the development of Internet voting in the United States. Both reports, especially the California task force report, argue that Internet voting currently is not feasible, primarily for security reasons. Both reports argue for a phased-in, gradual transition to electronic voting in which it first is implemented in secure locations and then implemented remotely for large-scale, public elections.

We do not believe that the gradual, phased-in approach advocated in these reports is the best way to implement Internet voting in the United States. Instead, Internet voting should be used today for certain types of elections and certain classes of voters; only then can studies be done of how Internet voting influences voting behavior and election administration. We therefore advocate a controlled and incremental process that is different from either approach presented in these two reports. Internet voting can be implemented and studied *now* in meaningful, although limited and controlled, efforts before it is used in major statewide or national elections. We advocate this alternative approach because there are groups of voters who need the remote access to the electoral process that only Internet voting can provide. We also advocate our approach because only by studying the implementation of Internet voting in real elections—using real voters and real election administrators—in carefully controlled settings can researchers learn how Internet voting affects the electoral process, in both positive and negative ways.

The California Internet Voting Task Force

In many ways, California should be an ideal place for Internet voting to begin. In 2001, 55.3 percent of California households had Internet access, well above the national average of 50.5 percent.[3] Much of the technology behind the explosion in computer and Internet use has come from California, from Silicon Valley in the north to Los Angeles, Orange County, and San Diego, with their many Internet-related businesses. Also, much of the population of California lives in densely populated urban areas, where the use of high-speed, or broadband, Internet access is relatively high.[4] Furthermore, some surveys of Californians have found support for the idea of Internet voting: in a 1999 survey by the Public Policy Institute of California, 47 percent of respondents said that they favored "a system that allowed Californians to vote in elections over the Internet," while 48 percent were opposed and 5 percent said that they had no opinion. Given the choice between voting at the ballot box, by mail, or over the Internet, 46 percent favored the ballot box, 30 percent the Internet, and 23 percent the mail; 1 percent had no opinion.[5]

Politically, Internet voting could easily be adopted in California. In the last decade, Californians have demonstrated a remarkable willingness to initiate and support significant electoral reforms when given the chance to vote on such propositions. For example, Californians voted to dramatically change their primary system, from closed to open (Proposition 198 in 1996); to limit campaign contributions (Proposition 208 in 1996); and most recently to fund the purchase of new voting systems (Proposition 41 in 2002). Armed with a few million dollars, an individual or group interested in Internet voting probably would be able to qualify a ballot measure that, if it won a majority of votes, would force implementation of Internet voting. Given the amount of money that could be made by hardware and software companies if a large state were to shift to Internet-only elections, there is a good chance that an initiative to push Internet voting may arise in the very near future in California. In fact, in 2000 a ballot measure was floated that would have made digital signatures legal for some purposes in California electoral politics, most especially for election petitions, but the measure did not qualify for the ballot. Because the financial stakes are so high, it is not unreasonable to think that other ballot measures that might lead to Internet voting may surface soon in California.

But well before the idea of a ballot measure on digital signatures was floated, in 1996 the California legislature passed Assembly Bill 44—The Digital Electoral System Act—that would have required the state to set up a California Internet voting task force to study the creation of a digital electoral system, focusing especially on the development and use of digital signature technologies in elections. Governor Pete Wilson vetoed the bill, largely because of concerns over potential voter fraud. The secretary of state of California, Bill Jones, a Republican from the conservative Central Valley of California, decided to study the issue of electronic elections after the governor vetoed the legislation. Bill Jones had run for the position of secretary of state in 1994 in the afterglow of his celebrity as the coauthor of California's "three strikes" crime legislation. He based his 1994 campaign on a twelve-point plan for fighting voter fraud, including strong antifraud measures that would purge voter registration rolls periodically, require photo identification and Social Security numbers for voter registration, and create a voter fraud investigation unit. Jones won office, and he made voter fraud and the security of elections a central theme of his service as secretary of state. This provides an important context for the approach taken in California to study electronic elections under Jones's direction, as the security of Internet voting became the paramount concern.

The California Internet Voting Task Force was established in March 2000 and charged with assessing the feasibility of Internet voting in California. The task force was chaired by Alfred Charles, from the secretary of state's office, and it had two subcommittees: the technical issues committee, chaired by David Jefferson (then of Compaq Computers), and the practical issues committee, chaired by Linda Valenty of San Jose State University. The task force had thirty-four members: fifteen representatives from the private sector, primarily from computer, software, and technology companies; three academics from California universities; two representatives from voting rights organizations; four representatives from the California state legislature; and ten members from the secretary of state's office or a variety of county election offices.[6]

The task force and the two subcommittees held periodic meetings, circulating draft reports during the process. The final report of the task force, issued on January 18, 2000, flatly rejected the idea that Internet voting could be used to completely replace the statewide election procedures then in place. Its conclusion was based on four important points:

—Internet voting would require some form of statewide digital identification.

—It would require an Internet-based voter registration system.

—It would require Internet-based petition and referendum signature systems.

—It would require equity in Internet access for all voters in the state.

Given the impossibility or infeasibility of meeting those requirements, the task force argued that Internet voting could not replace the existing voting systems for statewide elections in California anytime in the near future. Instead, the task force made two recommendations. First, it recommended that any short-term use of Internet voting in California be based on the current absentee voting process—that is, if Internet voting was to be used, it should be used in a process in which a voter requests an electronic ballot in advance of an election by submitting some form of signed paper application. In the eyes of the task force, that stipulation resolved two of the problems that must be confronted to implement Internet voting. By obtaining a signature on paper, county election officials could verify the voter's identity by using traditional signature verification procedures, eliminating the need for digital identification. And, like the current vote-by-mail system, Internet-based absentee voting would be optional. In the view of the task force, that would remove legal and political constraints arising from the digital divide.

The second recommendation outlined an incremental, two-step approach for phasing in true Internet voting in California. The first step would involve developing Internet voting systems in environments that could be closely monitored by election officials, using computers under their physical control. In this supervised step, Internet voting stations would be installed in traditional polling places, replacing the current voting system. After this step was successfully implemented, Internet voting could be expanded by allowing voters to vote from an Internet voting station at any polling place in the state, not just the site assigned to them on the basis of their residence. The critical aspects of this phase were that Internet voting stations would be subject to tight electronic and physical security and that voters could be identified by traditional means.

The second step in this incremental approach would lead to true remote Internet voting by directly addressing the issues of ballot security and voter identification. This step would attack the problem of identification through what has been termed kiosk Internet voting. Here, voters would come to a centrally located kiosk—which would be physically and electronically secured by county election officials—and use a previously provided password or digital signature to verify their identify in order to vote. Once the kiosk model had been successfully implemented, it would be possible to go to full-blown remote Internet voting. Then, Internet voting would be allowed from any Internet-connected device, as long as the operating system and web browser of the device were secured. The task force recommended that each voter be provided with a single-use operating system and web browser for voting.

The California Internet Voting Task Force thus devised a very cautious approach to adopting remote Internet voting for California's statewide elections. The paramount concerns of the task force were voter identification and computer security, as can be seen in the deliberate steps of the suggested development process: permit Internet voting in situations in which security can be ensured and voters can be identified using current procedures, and then allow research and development to proceed so that voter identification can be handled electronically, security can be ensured, and real remote Internet voting facilitated.

Unfortunately, the task force report is silent on exactly how election officials in California can and should attempt to phase in Internet voting. The report also is silent on exactly how the research and development needed to make Internet voting a reality is to be financed and conducted. While these issues are outside the limited scope of the task force's mandate, they are vital to the development of Internet voting in California. By failing to map out a plan of action—especially on the critical issue of research and development—the task force did not produce any momentum toward addressing the important barriers to Internet voting that it identified. The office of the secretary of state has not moved to begin phasing in Internet voting, and there is no indication that the task force's recommendations are being followed by state election officials. It is unclear whether the failure to advance a research or policy agenda for moving Internet voting forward is a result of the lack of a better roadmap in the task force report, the perceived difficulty of implementing the recommendations, a lack of political will, or a lack of financial resources.

The task force report has been interpreted as stating that Internet voting is not feasible for the foreseeable future. It is true that the report's executive summary concluded, "At this time, it would not be legally, practically or fiscally feasible to develop a comprehensive remote Internet voting system that would completely replace the current paper process used for voter registration, voting, and the collection of initiative, referendum and recall petition signatures."[7] However, the report did not address the issue of whether Internet voting could be implemented successfully in other environments, such as in smaller-scale projects for special populations of voters. As we show, the task force report has set the agenda for subsequent academic and policy discussions about Internet voting, despite what we argue are shortcomings in the task force's conceptualization of a development path for Internet voting.

The National Workshop on Internet Voting

On December 17, 1999, just as the presidential campaign season was beginning to heat up and with the first round of presidential primaries for the 2000 election only weeks away, President Bill Clinton issued a memorandum on electronic government. This memorandum grew out of the "reinventing government" initiative spearheaded by Vice President Al Gore, and it aimed to help citizens gain one-stop access to government information and services; to improve government services; and to increase government accountability to citizens.[8]

The sixth directive of this memorandum stated that "the Director of the National Science Foundation, working with appropriate Federal agencies, shall conduct a 1-year study examining the feasibility of online voting."[9] There also was congressional interest in Internet voting in the fall of 1999. Representative Jesse L. Jackson Jr. (D-Ill.) introduced the Digital Democracy Study Act, which would "direct the President to conduct a study of issues relating to the incorporation of online and Internet technologies in the voting process."[10] It is somewhat ironic that, as the soon-to-be-infamous 2000 election season was just beginning, President Clinton and congressional Democrats were clamoring for studies of Internet voting.

Following the president's directive, the National Science Foundation (NSF) awarded a $95,000 grant to the Internet Policy Institute (IPI), in Washington, D.C., to study the feasibility of Internet voting. Working in collaboration with the University of Maryland, the IPI developed an executive committee chaired by University of Maryland president C. D. Mote and a workshop of panelists drawn from academia, the private sector, and government. The workshop was held in October in Washington, and the IPI issued a report, drafted by David Cheney and Richard Schum, on its findings in March 2001.

A wide variety of opinions and positions regarding the feasibility of Internet voting were presented during the workshop sessions.[11] In addition, there was a great deal of discussion of how the NSF might structure a research agenda designed to identify problems with Internet voting and develop research-based solutions to those problems.

The workshop's agenda regarding the feasibility of Internet voting was established largely by the California task force report. David Jefferson provided the workshop audience with a summary of the task force procedures, report, and recommendations. The IPI workshop adopted the general nomenclature favored by the California task force, differentiating remote Internet voting from poll site and kiosk Internet voting. Furthermore, the workshop largely framed the feasibility issue in similar terms: while the California task force investigated the feasibility of Internet voting for a California statewide election, the IPI workshop concerned itself largely with whether Internet voting was currently feasible for use in a national election.

Given the foundation provided by the California Internet Voting Task Force report, it is not surprising that the IPI workshop report reached the same basic conclusions regarding the feasibility of Internet voting. The IPI report summarized the workshop's findings on feasibility as follows:

—Poll site Internet voting systems offer some benefits and could be responsibly fielded within the next several election cycles.

—Remote Internet voting systems pose significant risk to the integrity of the voting process, and should not be fielded for use in large-scale public elections until substantial technical and social science issues are addressed.

—Internet-based voter registration poses significant risk to the integrity of the voting process, and should not be implemented until an adequate authentication infrastructure is available and adapted.[12]

The "significant risk" cited by the report arises from the possibility of attacks on the client computer (the one the voter uses), the server (the one the election office uses to provide the ballot, authenticate the voter, and tabulate the votes), and the network (the path of communication between the voter's computer and the election office's computer). The report also cited as ancillary risks the possibility of Internet voting system failure and issues regarding ballot secrecy.

The IPI workshop report also presented a lengthy social science–oriented research agenda for Internet voting, raising important questions such as the following:

—How would Internet voting affect voter access and participation and the quality of the information voters bring to bear in making their decision?

—How might Internet voting improve voter registration systems and influence deliberation, representation, and "social capital"?

—What legal issues are associated with attempting to implement Internet voting in the near future?

The workshop report outlined these topics, arguing that the NSF should fund studies of all of them. Unfortunately, to date, there has been no clear commitment by the NSF or any other research funding agency to follow up on the recommendations in the report. Although one of the NSF's stated multidisciplinary research goals is information technology research, including topics such as technology development and the social impact of new technologies, the NSF has made no investment in research on Internet voting.[13] A search of projects funded under the NSF's Digital Government program reveals only one grant for Internet voting, the grant that produced the IPI workshop report.[14]

Computer Scientists Sound Off

The basic criticisms of Internet voting that have arisen in both the California Internet Voting Task Force report and the IPI report revolve around concerns over access and security. Both of these questions are explored in detail in later chapters. Here we briefly review the concerns of a small but strident group of computer scientists who have issued strong criticisms of Internet voting. While some of these individuals were involved in the two policy reports, they also have released independent studies that make strong arguments against implementing Internet voting.

One of these computer scientists is Avi Rubin, now of Johns Hopkins University. His 2001 study, "Security Considerations for Remote Electronic Voting over the Internet," concludes that "[g]iven the current state of widely deployed computers in people's homes, the vulnerability of the Internet to denial-of-service attacks, and the unreliability of the Domain Name Service, we believe that the technology does not yet exist to enable remote electronic voting in public elections."[15] He calls for further research into a new generation of personal computers that will have hardware for preventing unwanted intrusions in transactions between networked computers. Until these new personal computers are in wide use, Rubin's position appears to be that Internet voting for public elections should not be attempted.

Lorrie Faith Cranor echos his security concerns but reaches a slightly different conclusion regarding Internet voting. Cranor argued in 1996 that "[a]lthough electronic governmental elections may be a long way off, professional and social organizations have already started to conduct surveys and elections electronically. While most of these elections currently ignore privacy concerns, advances in e-mail and Web browser software that can easily interface with cryptography software should pave the way for secure and private electronic elections in the near future."[16]

More recently, following the 2000 election, Cranor again stated that "Internet voting may be a good solution for non-governmental elections. . . . These elections generally are less interesting targets for hackers, involve smaller numbers of voters, and sometimes have less stringent secret ballot requirements than governmental elections."[17] Cranor argues that Internet elections are fine for small-scale, private elections but that until advances in crypography are made, remote Internet voting is not feasible.

An even stronger criticism of Internet voting comes from the dissertation of Rebecca Mercuri. There, she uses very strong language to condemn Internet voting:

> Computer-based voting offers the promise of easy access and speedy tabulation in exchange for a variety of risks that were either not pres-

ent or are far worse than ones found in manual balloting systems. Some problems, such as those involving large-scale fraud, denials of service, and the incompatibility of anonymous balloting with audit trails, [are] inherently unresolveable. . . . Certain technologies, such as Internet voting and remote voter authorization, are particularily vulnerable to these risks, as well as other sociological problems (like vote selling and coercion), and should not be used at all.[18]

This computer science trio clearly is concerned about the feasibility of Internet voting. What is interesting about their stances is the stark differences in their long-term views on Internet voting. Cranor takes the least restrictive position: in her opinion, Internet voting can and should be used for small-scale, private elections now but be put on hold until cryptographic advances make its widespread use in public elections possible. Rubin takes a slightly stronger position, arguing that widespread Internet voting should await the development and implementation of new computer hardware protocols that will make stronger network security possible. Mercuri takes the strongest possible stance, asserting that Internet voting should not be used for public elections.

Testing the Critiques

The critiques of Internet voting coming from the computer science community—from independent experts and those participating in various task forces—are important and call for serious thought about its basic feasibility. However, the critiques are problematic in two ways. First, they cannot be tested, or they are framed in such a way that they are very difficult to test. For example, consider Mercuri's critique. She argues that Internet voting should not be implemented; however, she does not offer any hypotheses that could be tested in the field to determine if, in fact, her argument is correct. Consider also the oft-cited example of Internet voting being susceptible to a Trojan horse software attack, whereby a remote user places a piece of software on an Internet voter's computer and changes the vote or steals the voter's information (user name, password, and so forth). If this is a major problem, there should be data on Trojan horse attacks in other venues, especially online banking and commerce, which offer a financial incentive for mounting such attacks. The use of these attacks in various settings can be tested. Without data, the arguments are only philosophical.

Second, these computer scientists are too restrictive in how they frame the debate. Each begins by assuming that the basic choice is between an absolute ban on Internet voting or total implementation of Internet voting in all public elections in the United States. This is, simply put, the wrong way to frame the issue of Internet voting. In our opinion, Cranor (and the California task force report) comes closest to articulating the development strategy that we advocate. Instead of thinking about the implementation of Internet voting in stark, either/or terms, a gradual, phased development and implementation strategy should be created.

Cranor and Rubin offer ideas about the software and hardware that should be developed before widespread use of Internet voting occurs, but neither lays out a clear strategy for moving from current technology to the future technology that they argue is necessary. This also is a major issue with the California Internet Voting Task Force report, which also lacks a plan for implementing Internet voting. It is one thing to lay out essential requirements for Internet voting systems, but it is an altogether different thing to develop a research and policy agenda that leads to the development of those systems. We think that the computer scientists have put the cart before the horse; only when demand is created for new technologies will public and private actors make the effort to develop the technologies. A clear agenda for research on and testing of Internet voting systems in public elections should be developed now, because as Internet voting is gradually implemented, it will help to increase demand for new and better technologies.

Whither the Policy Debate?

For better or worse, these two policy reports and the other critiques of the use of the Internet for public elections have set the rules of the current popular debate. On the positive side, both the California task force and IPI workshop reports contain important statements about how Internet voting systems can be developed and studied; both reports articulated the same basic progression from poll site to kiosk to remote Internet voting. The IPI workshop report even went one step further by identifying critical areas where scientific research needs to be conducted so that Internet voting can eventually be implemented successfully.

Unfortunately, despite calls for a research, development, and implementation agenda, little has emerged from either the public or the private sector. Despite the outlines of a research agenda for Internet voting in the

IPI workshop report, there has been little commitment from any public or private funding agency to provide the investment necessary to study the issue. Calling for research and development is one thing; developing and financing the required research and development programs is another. In chapter 8, we outline a new research and development agenda. However, for these efforts to get off the ground and develop the momentum necessary to resolve the pressing issues raised by the critics of Internet voting, limited experimental trials of Internet voting in public elections must begin.

The Internet voting debate has been framed the wrong way, whether unintentionally or in a deliberate attempt to keep people from seriously considering its implementation. Regardless of the motive, the choices on Internet voting are not as stark as they have been made out to be. The question is not whether the Internet should be used for elections, but when. It seems to us inevitable: Internet voting is the future of voting in the United States. Nor is the question one of whether there should be wholesale implementation of Internet voting in the next presidential election or the next statewide election in a large state like California. Rather, the question should be how Internet voting can be implemented in upcoming elections in limited and controlled circumstances, either by allowing specific groups of voters to use the Internet to cast their ballots when such a change would greatly increase their ability to participate in the political process, or by allowing Internet voting in limited electoral settings—for example, local municipal or school board elections. Only by conducting Internet voting experiments can the pros and cons of Internet voting be clarified and the resources necessary for research and development be made available.

In the wake of the 2000 presidential elections, some now see a "third way" for Internet voting. We agree with this third-way assessment, which was articulated in a Caltech/MIT Voting Technology Project report released in June 2001. The report stated that "Internet voting is here" and further argued that "Internet voting does hold immediate promise for lowering the obstacles experienced by some voters. Technology today presents very significant obstacles to special classes of voters—most notably blind people (who cannot see visual systems and who also have difficulty with transportation) and overseas military personnel (who cannot get to the polls and for whom traditional registration and absentee procedures are very difficult)."[19]

Other studies have reached similar conclusions, the most interesting a study of the potential for Internet voting in the United Kingdom, which noted that "[t]he vision of e-voting is not one of a sudden switch over to a single technology. Rather, the vision is one of a phased move to multi-channel elections in which voters are offered a range of means by which to cast their vote and choose the mechanism that most suits them."[20]

Developing a third way for Internet voting is needed because the reality is that Internet voting already has occurred in one presidential election and is going to occur in the future. While the IPI report on Internet voting was being drafted, the Federal Voting Assistance Program was allowing a small but significant group of voters to cast the first Internet votes ever in a general election. Moreover, in 2001 Congress enacted the National Defense Authorization Act, which requires the FVAP to conduct an Internet voting demonstration project in an upcoming federal election (this project will occur in 2004). Money has been allocated for the development of a system, which the FVAP will test on up to 100,000 voters in a number of states during the 2004 primary and general elections.

While overseas military personnel and blind individuals might benefit from improved access if they could use an Internet voting system, there are other important benefits for both groups. Currently, both have difficulty casting a private, secure ballot. Many military personnel in recent elections have cast their ballot by faxing it—in the open, neither securely nor privately—to the election office. Furthermore, to cast a ballot on most current voting systems requires a blind voter to obtain the assistance of a friend or polling place worker. In either situation, the voter is forced to cast a ballot that is not private.[21]

Other special classes of voters might benefit greatly from an Internet voting system. First, a variety of American citizens reside overseas, either permanently or for long periods of time, including people who are overseas for business reasons; college students; retirees; and government employees. Currently, most rely on foreign mail service to obtain and return their registration and absentee ballots. This can be a significant impediment to registering and voting. Because many overseas citizens also have Internet access—especially students, business people, and government employees—they are excellent candidates for Internet voting. Second, young people, who are among the least likely to vote, often are away from home at college during most election seasons. Since most college students have Internet access at school, they too are good candidates for Internet voting. Third, voters who have great difficulty making it to a polling place, like elderly or physically disabled voters, might find Internet voting a more secure and reliable means of casting their ballot than the traditional vote-by-mail process. For example, a computer kiosk at a nursing home could serve as a portable election booth.

Clearly, certain groups of American voters could benefit from immediate implementation of Internet voting systems. For some of these voters—especially overseas military personnel and those who are blind—the need for Internet voting is pressing. These individuals have great access problems, and currently they often cannot cast a private or secure vote. For others—such as college students or the physically disabled—the need is perhaps not quite as severe since they can use the current vote-by-mail system. However, a well-designed Internet voting system could make the process more accessible and more secure for these voters as well.

Given that Internet voting can significantly improve access and privacy for some American voters, we feel that it is imperative that Internet voting systems be developed and fielded for those voters. Just as the Food and Drug Administration (FDA) now expedites drug approval for desperately ill patients when there are positive indications of a drug's effectiveness in preliminary trials, the government should offer Internet voting to those in desperate need of access and privacy in order to vote. The FDA process also provides a helpful analogous mechanism for developing such systems. In drug trials, drugs are tested in relatively small but scientifically rigorous tests that have real-life consequences and risks. Internet voting trials for special populations also can and should be conducted by using rigorous, quasi-experimental designs, including test and control voters, to determine the factors that make Internet voting effective. The results of these small-scale trials then can be used to determine how to make large-scale Internet voting a reality in the future. It is only through scientific testing that an effective Internet voting system can be developed.

If Internet voting becomes a reality for these target groups of citizens, two important dynamics could be set in motion. First, there would be greater government investment in Internet voting and security systems. If the federal government decided to adopt Internet voting for all American voters overseas and committed the necessary funding to developing Internet security and voting systems, it could produce important innovations that might mitigate, if not entirely reduce, many current security concerns. The security of Internet voting is likely to improve dramatically over the next decade because of increased federal investment in cybersecurity in light of the terrorist attacks of September 11, 2001. Because the nation's computer networks and the Internet are so important for its economic well-being, corporations and the federal government will feel continued pressure to improve online security. This technological agenda must also include Internet voting.

Second, as the general voting public becomes aware that Internet voting works—as family members and friends successfully cast ballots over the Internet—the demand for expansion of Internet voting systems will increase. Increased demand will increase pressure for funding research and procurement, prompting further innovation and development. Again, the federal government could play a key role in giving private corporations incentives to develop improved online security systems. In a variety of policy areas—most notably, environmental policy—the federal government has created benchmark standards and provided economic incentives to ensure that they are met. For example, the Clean Air Act and its amendments set high standards for air quality, which many thought were unattainable. However, providing incentives to corporations and governments ensured that the standards were attained. There is no reason why similar incentives could not be provided to help ensure that the nation's online systems are made more secure and more accessible for Internet voting.

CHAPTER **3**

Representation and the Digital Divide

The 2000 presidential election clearly illustrated that small differences in the way elections are conducted can have important ramifications. They can affect the ability of voters to participate meaningfully in the electoral process; more important, they can create burdens that often are not shared equally by different groups of voters. As many recent studies have documented,

—some types of voting system have higher rates of uncounted or spoiled ballots than other types.

—minority voters often have more difficulty using punch-card voting systems than do white voters.

—disabled voters often are inadvertently kept away from polling places by lack of special parking, no wheelchair access, or voting equipment that does not accommodate them.

—long lines, inaccurate voting lists, and failure to provide a provisional balloting option (which allows individuals who are not on the certified voting list to cast a ballot pending verification of their registration status) make voting generally more burdensome than it should be and often keep potential voters from voting at all.[1]

Such problems in the American electoral system lead to voter disenfranchisement. Before the 2000 presidential election, the exact extent of the problems, especially in terms of the sheer number of voters who cannot participate or whose votes are not counted, was unknown.

The Caltech/MIT study estimated that in the 2000 presidential election between 4 and 6 million votes of the roughly 100 million votes cast were "lost" and that millions more were "lost" in other races on the ballot throughout the nation in the same election.[2] The study found that between 1.5 and 2 million votes were lost because of faulty equipment and confusing ballots. Another 1.5 to 3 million votes were lost because of problems with voter registration systems, and as many as 1 million votes were lost because of polling place problems. The massive number of votes lost, especially in a very close presidential election, led to calls for greater use of modern technology in elections and for other reforms to reduce or eliminate lost votes. In fact, the Caltech/MIT Voting Technology Project (of which one of the authors is still an active member) was born of the belief of the presidents of Caltech and MIT that together the two universities could produce technological solutions to the problems that plagued the 2000 election. That some of the best minds in social science, computer science, and engineering have yet to announce the development of a voting technology that will immediately "fix" the lost-vote problem demonstrates the complexity of the task.

More generally, the history of voting in the United States is littered with examples of both overt and subtle efforts to keep specific groups of voters from voting.[3] At various times, poor people, women, African Americans, and younger Americans have been kept from voting by legal or extralegal measures. In many cases, state laws ensured that such voters could not vote. However, even when voters were enfranchised through a constitutional amendment—such as the Fifteenth Amendment, which prohibits states from denying the right to vote to citizens on the basis of race—other methods were used to disenfranchise voters, such as poll taxes or all-white primary elections.

This history of electoral discrimination has made many interest groups sensitive to any changes in elections mechanisms or procedures that could disenfranchise voters, as can be seen by the lawsuits filed after the 2000 presidential election.[4] Especially in this environment, all classes and categories of voters must have similar access to Internet voting technologies. If some groups of people (for example, the rich) have extensive access to the Internet, but other groups (such as low-income Americans or members of certain ethnic minorities) do not, some groups of voters will have more influence in the electoral and subsequent policy process than others.[5]

This is an important legal issue. Internet voting cannot violate the Voting Rights Act. It is also an important political issue, because even if Internet voting systems pass muster under the Voting Rights Act, subtle differences in Internet access could have important effects on political representation. Understanding both the legal and political consequences of Internet voting requires understanding the parameters of the so-called digital divide between Americans with Internet access and those without. However, we argue that the intersection between Internet access and political participation—and between the quality of Internet access and political participation—should be examined. Understanding who has Internet access, who has high-quality Internet access, and who participates in politics is critical to determining which voters might be better represented under Internet voting. If a digital divide exists between classes of voters, the Internet could promote biased representation rather than extend the benefits of democracy to everyone.

Representation

When the nation's founders drafted the Constitution, they spent much of their time debating how to structure the federal government so that it would represent all Americans.[6] One mechanism they devised was conducting popular elections for members of the House of Representatives; they believed that allowing people to elect their own representatives would help ensure that those representatives would be responsive to their constituencies. As Hamilton notes in *Federalist 35*, "Is it not natural that a man who is a candidate for the favor of the people, and who is dependent on the suffrages of his fellow-citizens for the continuance of his public honors, should take care to inform himself of their dispositions and inclinations and should be willing to allow them their proper degree of influence on his conduct?"[7] The close representation of their constituents is recognized as a keystone of the work done by members of the House.[8]

If all voters are not equally able to vote, then elected representatives do not have to be as attentive to the concerns of those who are less able. John Stuart Mill summed up the problem when he described the way in which the British Parliament addressed the needs of working-class voters, who were denied the right to vote: "Does Parliament ever for an instant look at any question with the eyes of a workingman? When a subject arises in which the laborers as such have an interest, is it regarded from any point of view but that of employers of labor?"[9] Because laborers could not vote but the owners of businesses could, Parliament was responsive only to the needs of the owners. This example illustrates that quite often there is a strong link between the preferences of people who are eligible to vote and the policy decisions made by a legislative body. For Internet voting to be viable, it should not disrupt the current links between voters and their representatives or provide certain voters with an advantage over others in their ability to connect with their representatives. Rather, Internet voting should strengthen those links.

Robert Dahl has noted three indicators of a society's degree of democratic representation: whether people have equal and effective opportunities to make their views known to the people who represent them; whether they have equal and effective opportunities to vote; and whether their votes have equal weight.[10] When these criteria are met, effective representation is possible. Representation can take two forms: descriptive or substantive.[11] Both descriptive and substantive representation refer to a situation in which voters are represented by someone who is like them, but the basis of this "likeness" differs. Descriptive representation requires only that representatives look like their constituents: they have the same racial, ethnic, or socioeconomic background or are of the same gender. The presumption behind descriptive representation is that people who look alike think alike, because their life experiences have been the same. Substantive representation suggests that representatives will reflect the collective opinion of their constituents on important matters of policy. A more precise form of substantive representation is called "policy responsiveness." This notion of representation, derived largely from formal political science, looks at how closely representatives reflect their constituents' opinions in terms of roll call votes or other legislative actions.

The connection between representative and voter, whether descriptive or substantive, has a more practical and political dimension. To whom do representatives look for information about their constituents' opinions or to determine what larger concerns to take into consideration in policymaking? Richard Fenno, in his classic book *Home Style*, argued that representatives play to four different audiences, each nested within the next: the geographic constituency, the reelection constituency, the primary constituency, and the personal constituency. Representatives pay the most attention to the people in their personal constituency and the least to the people in their geographic constituency.

Fenno's ideas about political representation are important in studying Internet voting. Some groups of Americans rarely participate in politics, and they make up the audience that representatives pay the least attention to. Technological changes in the conduct of U.S. elections could alter the composition of the reelection and primary constituencies of many or all legislators. If Internet voting makes it easier or more interesting for younger Americans to participate in politics, then younger Americans will be seen by their representatives as being an important component of their reelection constituency rather than as less important members of their geographic constituency. Changing the way in which elections are conducted thus can change the views represented in policymaking.

Electoral systems play a key role in ensuring that elections result in effective representation, whether geographic, descriptive, or substantive. The historical example of the African American experience in the South makes the point. It was not until passage of the Voting Rights Act that African Americans could vote in large enough numbers to elect representatives to Congress who reflected their views. In addition, some have argued that with the creation of majority-minority voting districts in the South, African Americans achieved better representation in Congress.[12] When large numbers of African Americans could vote, white Southern Democrats in Congress paid more attention to the issues of importance to them. Studies have examined the voting behavior of many Southern Democrats and found that they became more liberal as a result of these legislative changes; in their votes on key issues, members tried harder to reflect the preferences of their new constituents.[13]

The advent of Internet voting could affect election outcomes and the representation that various populations of voters receive. If there are meaningful subsequent increases in participation among some voters or depressed turnout among others, that could be evidence that the new technology effected the change. If more votes were counted from groups with higher rates of lost votes, then those groups might see better representation. But before such changes can be measured, it is first necessary to have a baseline understanding of the voting and registration systems now in place and the rate of political participation among different demographic groups.

Differences in Representation: Voting and Registration Systems

The idea of political representation is based on the assumption that voters have preferences on policy or other issues, that voters favor one candidate over another because that candidate comes closer to reflecting the voters' preferences, and that when voters step into the voting booth and cast their ballot, their preferences are translated directly into a vote for their preferred candidate. This process should work identically for every voter, whether Democrat or Republican, white or black, new or experienced, using a decades-old punch-card voting system or a brand-new ATM-style touch-screen system. The property of a democratic election that ensures that voters' preferences are translated into counted votes in a way that is not biased by the attributes of the voter or by the voting or registration system used is commonly called the "transparency" of the voting process.

When the requirement for transparency is violated, the fundamental tenets of democracy are violated. If the registration system establishes conditions that are more difficult for certain classes of citizens to meet; if the voting system produces a fraction of ballots that cannot be counted; or if certain classes of voters do not understand how to use a particular voting system, the basic democratic principles of equality and fairness are violated. Furthermore, these problems can occur even when election officials, polling place workers, and voters have the best of intentions; voters can be disenfranchised without anyone trying to produce a voting or registration system that is biased in any way.

In the much-disputed results of the 2000 presidential election in Florida, examples abound. Consider Gadsden County. It has a total population of 45,087, of which 57.1 percent is African American. In the 2000 presidential election, 16,812 total votes were cast, of which 14,727 were counted in the presidential race; 2,085 ballots, or 12.4 percent, of ballots cast for the presidential race were either blank or spoiled.[14] Gadsden County voters used optical scan ballots, which were taken to a centralized location to be scanned and tabulated.

Columbia County is about the same size as Gadsden County, with a population of 56,513, of which 17 percent is African American. In the 2000 presidential race, 19,206 ballots were cast, and 18,513 were counted. Thus there were only 693 uncounted or spoiled ballots in Columbia County, a rate of 3.61 percent. The voting system used in Columbia County was different from that used in Gadsden County. In Columbia County voters used optical scan ballots, which were scanned for errors in the precincts, permitting voters to correct errors on their ballot. Voters in Gadsden County did not have their ballots scanned for errors in the precinct and thus could not as easily fix obvious errors.

Voters in these two smaller Florida counties both cast their ballots on optically scanned pages. However, whether the ballots were scanned in the precinct or in a central location made an enormous difference in the proportion of spoiled or uncounted ballots, in what was a very close election. It demonstrates the impact that the voting system used can have on elections in the United States. As long as differences in uncounted ballots like those pointed out in Gadsden and Columbia Counties exist and as long as the voting systems in the United States are not uniform, future elections will continue to be plagued with inaccurate results.

The problem of lost or missing votes arises not only from the voting system used and the way people use it; problems also arise from the nature of voter registration systems and the geographical nature of U.S. elections. After each federal election, the U.S. Census Bureau appends to its monthly Current Population Survey responses to a set of questions about registration and voting called the Voting and Registration Supplement. Respondents who say that they were registered to vote but did not are asked why they did not vote. In November 2000, 7.4 percent of respondents who were registered voters but did not vote gave "registration problems" as the reason. The exact nature of these problems was not given, but they likely included problems re-registering after moving and incorrect voter registration rolls. There were about 156 million registered voters in the United States in 2000, and 106 million of them voted in the presidential election. If 7.4 percent of the 50 million registered voters who did not vote failed to vote because they had a registration problem, then registration problems were responsible for 3.7 million lost votes. Had these voters been able to cast a ballot, voter turnout in the 2000 presidential election could have been as high as 53 percent of the voting-age population—instead of the actual turnout of 51 percent. Whether such a large increase in voter turnout might have altered the outcome of the 2000 presidential election and other elections throughout the county is unknown.

The geographical nature of elections in the United States also impedes voter turnout and political representation. Political representation is almost always equated with geographic location: states are split into geographic legislative districts, cities into geographic city council districts, school systems into geographic districts, and so on. All of these districts are then subdivided further, into registration and voting precincts. In a typical election voters can cast their ballot only in a single precinct in their geographic vicinity. The only exceptions to this rule exist in jurisdictions that have liberal vote-by-mail or early-voting systems.

The extent to which the geographical nature of elections affects voting can be seen in the Current Population Survey's Voting and Registration Supplement for the 2000 presidential election. It gave nonvoting registered respondents the opportunity to say whether being "out of town or away from home," "transportation problems," "bad weather," or "inconvenient polling place or hours or lines too long" kept them from voting. Being out of town or away from home prevented 11.1 percent of registered respondents from voting, transportation problems prevented 2.6 percent, and bad weather prevented 0.7 percent; polling place problems kept another 2.8 percent from turning out. Together, these four reasons kept 17.2 percent of registered nonvoting respondents—an estimated 8.6 million voters total—from participating in the 2000 presidential election. If these people had voted in 2000, turnout could have been as high as 55 percent in the 2000 presidential election. Problems associated with the geographic nature of the voting process make it difficult for many to vote and so have a significant impact on political representation.

Socioeconomic factors also influence participation. Not surprisingly, individuals who participate in politics tend to be wealthier, better educated, older, and white. This trend can be seen in table 3-1, which shows data from the U.S. Census Bureau's *Current Population Reports* on voter registration and turnout in both presidential and off-year congressional elections in selected races over the past two decades.[15] The data show a consistent pattern of differences in participation. Whites vote at higher rates than do African Americans and at twice the rate of Hispanics, although the gap between whites and African Americans has closed somewhat since the 1980 presidential race. Women are slightly more likely to vote than men, although the size of this gap tends to close in off-year congressional elections.

Although race and gender are important factors in determining who votes, the biggest differences in participation are based on factors such as education, income, and age. As a general rule, citizens with high socioeconomic status are much more likely than citizens with lower socioeconomic status to participate in various aspects of the political process. They are more likely to vote, to contribute to and participate in campaigns, and to lobby their representatives through both direct and indirect means.[16] Individuals who have attended college are approximately two times more likely to vote than individuals without a high school education, while unemployed people vote at much lower rates than do individuals with jobs. People also are more likely to vote as they get older: individuals over the age of forty-five vote at twice the rate of individuals under the age of twenty-five, and a large jump in participation appears when the voting rates of people under forty-five and those of people over forty-five are compared.

Table 3-1. *Percentage of Registered Voters and of Registered Voters Who Voted, Selected Years*

Demographic characteristic	Percent registered				Percent voted			
	1980	1986	1994	2000	1980	1986	1994	2000
Age								
18–20	44.7	35.4	37.2	40.5	35.7	18.6	16.5	28.4
21–24	52.7	46.6	45.5	49.3	45.7	22.0	19.2	24.2
25–34	62	55.8	51.5	54.7	54.6	35.1	32.2	43.7
35–44	70.6	67.9	63.3	63.8	64.4	49.3	46.0	55.0
45–64	75.8	74.8	71.0	71.2	69.3	58.7	56.0	64.1
65+	74.6	76.9	75.6	76.1	65.1	60.9	60.7	67.6
Gender								
Male	66.6	63.4	60.8	62.2	59.1	45.8	44.4	53.1
Female	67.1	65.0	63.2	65.6	59.4	46.1	44.9	56.2
Race								
White	68.4	65.3	64.2	65.6	60.9	47.0	46.9	56.4
Black	60.0	64.0	58.3	63.6	50.5	43.2	37.0	53.5
Hispanic	36.3	35.9	30.0	34.9	29.9	24.2	19.1	27.5
Education								
8 years or less	53	50.5	40.1	36.1	42.6	32.7	23.2	26.8
1–3 years high school	54.6	52.4	44.7	45.9	45.6	33.8	27.0	33.6
4 years high school	66.4	62.9	58.9	60.1	58.9	44.1	40.5	49.4
1–3 years college	74.4	70.0	68.4	70.0	67.2	49.9	49.1	60.3
4+ years college	84.3	77.8	76.3	77.3	79.9	62.5	63.1	72.0

Source: U.S. Bureau of the Census, "Voting and Registration," *Current Population Survey*, November 2000 (www.census.gov/ population/www/socdemo/voting.html [October 1, 2003]).

The differences in turnout among various demographic groups illustrate a key issue in efforts to reform the electoral process: reforms must help to attenuate, not exacerbate, those differences. Effective reforms will increase turnout among all voters, but especially among the young, the less educated, and individuals with lower socioeconomic status. Because of the differences between voters and nonvoters across various demographic categories, it is quite likely that reforms would benefit the more disadvantaged groups, but that is not guaranteed.

Of course, in the aftermath of the 2000 presidential election, many proposals have been made for "fixing" the multitude of problems in the U.S. electoral system that we have discussed and that have been documented elsewhere. However, most of these proposed reforms have been piecemeal in nature; it is not unusual to see calls for elimination of the punch-card voting system, national adoption of provisional voting, and development of state-administered computerized voter registration lists in the same reform package. In fact, this basic set of reform proposals is featured in the Help America Vote Act, passed in 2002. Other reform proposals have included calls for a whole assortment of changes, such as making election day a holiday, allowing felons who have completed their sentences to vote, and eliminating the electoral college.

Internet voting could resolve many of the problems with the current voting and registration systems in place throughout the United States. First, Internet voting could lead to much more uniformity among voting systems than currently exists. With the development of appropriate voting standards, states could easily field a uniform Internet voting system for all state elections; a uniform national Internet voting system for federal elections also is a possibility.[17] Standardization of Internet voting systems could go a long way toward eliminating huge differences in the number of uncounted ballots among otherwise similar geographic locations.

Second, Internet voting systems—and more generally, other electronic voting systems, like touch-screen voting—could and should be developed to eliminate most forms of voter error. Obviously, Internet voting would eliminate the problem of "hanging" and "dimpled" chads, but more generally it would remove any subjectivity from the postelection counting of ballots. Once cast, votes would be stored electronically, and as long as they were stored in a secure location, they would always add up to the same totals. Furthermore, Internet voting systems could easily be programmed to make it impossible for voters to overvote and to inform voters if they have undervoted or skipped a certain race. Last, Internet voting systems could provide a redundant recording of the vote, as called for by some observers, like the Caltech/MIT Voting Technology Project. An electronic recording of the vote could be transmitted through the Internet and a recording made on some other medium (paper, removable electronic media) that would be provided to election officials to produce an independent rendering of the voter's intentions. Internet voting systems should produce a much more accurate reflection of voter intentions than many existing voting systems.

Third, true remote Internet voting would eliminate many of the constraints imposed on participation by the geographic organization of the U.S. voting process. Internet voting could be the realization of anytime, anywhere voting—if a voter from Rhode Island found herself in Hawaii on election day, she could from there vote on an Internet-connected device. Participation rates among voters overseas could be much improved, and bad weather, transportation problems, and even poor health should cease to be major impediments to voting.

Internet voting has great potential to reduce or eliminate many of the differences in participation caused by problems with the voting and registration systems now in place. Designed appropriately, an Internet voting system could lead to a much more transparent voting process, reducing the possibility for errors, imposing uniformity, and facilitating access. Obviously, Internet voting poses important and in many ways new problems for the conduct of elections in the United States. Perhaps the largest problem is the digital divide, which must be addressed before widespread Internet voting can be adopted.

Factors Influencing Differences in Participation: Registration

One reason that there are large gaps between the participation rates of different groups of voters is that voting is costly. For example, effective voting requires knowing something about the candidates and their positions so that the voter can weigh the differences between them and make an informed choice.[18] Voters also have to make time in their day to vote, which can be difficult in states that have limited poll hours.[19] When poll hours are short or inconvenient, individuals often have a difficult time fitting voting into their schedule. Work, children's after-school care and activities, and similar obligations can easily get in the way of voting.

Of course, the most costly component of the voting process is not getting to the polls or deciding which candidate to vote for, it is being allowed to vote to begin with. Historically, voter registration has been the most difficult and disenfranchising component of the electoral process. Widespread pre–election day voter registration requirements have been in place since the Civil War.[20] The purpose of voter registration laws was to deter fraud and disruptions at the polls, especially in large urban areas, where they were used to control political machines. Often there also were partisan motives behind voter registration requirements; ideally, only members of the "correct" party could easily register. Some states required voters to appear in person during a very narrow time frame before an election and to renew their voter registration every year. Many voter registration requirements, such as poll taxes, were designed as a legal means of disenfranchising voters on the basis of their race or class. Thus, the repeal of poll taxes in the South during the first half of the twentieth century was important in enfranchising poor whites; African Americans remained disenfranchised through other means.

Not surprisingly, new registration requirements led to a precipitous decline in turnout, a decline that hit poor and minority voters harder than wealthy, white, and well-educated voters. The classic examination of the effects of modern registration laws on voter turnout was conducted by Steven Rosenstone and Raymond Wolfinger in the 1970s.[21] They found that having to register to vote before election day is the greatest barrier to increased turnout. When the registration deadline is a month before the election—currently the deadline in a majority of states—the likelihood that an individual will vote is decreased by between 3.3 and 6.7 percent.[22] As the deadline moves closer to election day, turnout is more likely to increase. It has been estimated that if all states had same-day voter registration—or no voter registration—turnout might increase by between 3 and 6 percent.[23]

Even today, registration remains a significant barrier to high voter turnout. As table 3-1 shows, in 2000 less than two-thirds of all voters said that they were registered to vote when questioned by the U.S. Census Bureau. That number is quite low, especially when considering that in response to a survey, some individuals, especially those with high socioeconomic status, do not admit to not being registered in order to give what they believe is the socially appropriate answer. Fewer than half of all individuals with only a high-school diploma are registered to vote, and the same is true of individuals under the age of forty-four. As with voting, there are large differences in rates of registration depending on age, education, and socioeconomic status and smaller gaps based on race and ethnicity.

Reforms to the electoral process that would close such gaps in registration rates could be an important way of closing the gaps in voting rates. In 1993, Congress passed the National Voter Registration Act (NVRA), which was designed to make the registration process easier. The NVRA required every state to allow individuals to register to vote when they applied for a driver's license and also to provide voter registration services at all state and local government offices, including those that provide public assistance, unemployment compensation, and disability services, and at armed forces recruitment offices. People also could register by mail.[24] The new system was designed to reduce the burden of registration for voters, especially those with lower educational attainment, by streamlining the process and making voter registration part of the services provided by the government agencies with which people frequently interact.[25] With voter registration forms available at a variety of locations, including places like the driver's license office, everyone would have an easy opportunity to register to vote.

As with voting, it is easy to imagine reforms to the system that could improve or hinder registration and turnout in elections. Consider the case of statewide voter registration. In most states, voter registration is handled at the local level by county administrators. Under such a system, whenever individuals move out of their voting precinct, they have to re-register to vote. This is quite a burden, considering that in any year between 16 and 17 percent of the U.S. population—just over 40 million Americans— move. Just over half of the moves are within the same county, but 20 percent are interstate moves, and over the past decade there has been a trend toward moves of longer distances. In addition, moving occurs most frequently among those least likely to register and vote: people who are young (especially between twenty and twenty-nine years of age), low-income, and nonwhite.[26] A statewide voter registration system (especially one with a unique identifier for each voter) that is linked to other databases would be able to track mobile voters more effectively than a county system. For example, in Michigan, individuals who change their address at the department of motor vehicles automatically have their voter registration updated without having to fill out additional forms. Such a system can keep records up to date and keep voters from being negatively affected by a simple act like moving.

Even when the government attempts to make voter registration and voting as simple and easy as possible, differences in participation based on class, race, and socioeconomic status persist. The United States has the lowest voter turnout in the western world, in part because voters are required to take the initiative to register, unlike in other western countries, where the government is responsible for creating a universal, permanent registry of voters.

Using the Internet for voter registration could minimize or eliminate many of the hurdles imposed by the current paper-based registration system. Imagine a system that allows an individual to simply fill out an online form to register to vote. Once the citizen submits the form, the data contained in it can be first checked against a statewide computerized voter registration database to determine whether the citizen is already registered in the state. The voter's information can then be authenticated by querying other databases, like the state driver's license database. Once the voter is authenticated and registered, the information goes into the statewide voter registration database, which the voter can then access to verify his or her registration status or to get information about upcoming elections, all over the Internet. Internet voter registration thus could simultaneously offer improved security and better citizen access.

The Digital Divide

The debate over the digital divide is relatively new, but divides in access to technology in American society are quite old. In the nineteenth century, there was a divide between cities and towns with telegraph connections and those without. In the twentieth century, there was a divide between people who had electricity and those who did not, between those who had telephone service and those who did not, and between those who had clear television reception and those who did not.[27] Many of those gaps, though much reduced, remain today: according to the Census Bureau, only 87 percent of households had telephone service in 1970, and more than 5 percent of households still do not have it today.[28] Gaps often exist in the early years following the introduction of a new technology but close quickly. In 1980, only 1 percent of households owned a videocassette recorder, but by 1990, 63 percent of households did. Today, more than 84 percent of households have one.[29]

Similar technology divides exist today with the computer and the Internet, but they also are shrinking. When the Census Bureau first started collecting data on computer ownership in 1984, 8.2 percent of households had a computer; today, 51 percent of households have one.[30] The rate of growth in the percentage of households with a computer is increasing as well: from 1984 to 1989, just under 7 percent of all households that had not had a computer acquired one; between 1997 and 2000, that figure rose to just over 14 percent. Even more impressive, the number of households with Internet access doubled over the same period: almost 42 percent of households had an Internet connection in 2000, compared with just 18 percent only three years earlier. These data reveal that the gap between those who have a computer and those who do not is closing, as is the gap between those who have an Internet connection and those who do not. Personal computer ownership in the United States has gone from zero to 50 percent in less than two decades. This rate is slower than that for VCRs; however, a computer is a much more expensive item.

The overall increase in the percentage of households with personal computers is quite impressive. However, the overall growth masks differences in the rates at which different types of households are acquiring computers. As table 3-2 shows, from 1997 to 2000, white, non-Hispanic households with personal computers had a larger percentage point gain, 14.9 points, than did African American or Hispanic households, which had 13.5 and 14.3 percentage point gains respectively. Of course, the overall rate of growth is faster for African American and Hispanic households, but they are starting from a much lower baseline figure: twice as many white households had computers in 1997. Even in 2000, 67 percent more white households than African American or Hispanic households had computers. Table 3-3 shows the digital divide that existed in 2000 by various demographic characteristics.

These data illustrate that the percentage of households with computers is increasing and doing so across racial and ethnic populations, but the gains are coming at slightly different rates. African American and Hispanic households are acquiring computers at a faster rate, but the overall percentage point gain is larger for white households. Similar findings hold true when comparing wealthy and poor households. In 2000, 87 percent of households with incomes over $75,000 had a computer, and 75 percent of households with incomes over $50,000 had one. Ownership rates for households below the median income are much lower: 28.2 percent for households with incomes under $25,000 and 47.1 percent for households with incomes between $25,000 and $34,999. The percentage point gains in computer ownership for upper-income households are comparable to those for lower-income households, even though the rate of growth among lower-income households is much faster. Because computer ownership is becoming nearly universal among upper-income households, the gap between the two will likely close more rapidly in the future, although lower-income households will remain behind for some time.

The divide between households with Internet connections and those without mirrors the divide in computer ownership. In 2000, 42.5 percent of white, non-Hispanic households had an Internet connection, compared with 20.5 percent of African Americans and 17.5 percent of Hispanics. The rate of Internet connectivity increased at relatively constant increments, with 11.3 percent of households with incomes under $15,000 being connected to the Internet, 26 percent of households with incomes

Table 3-2. *Percentage of Households with Computers, 1997–2000*

Demographic characteristic	October 1997	August 2000	Change	Percent change
Race				
White	40.8	55.7	14.9	36.5
Black	19.3	32.8	13.5	70.0
Hispanic	19.4	33.7	14.3	73.7
Asian/ Pacific Islander		65.1		
Total household income				
< $25,000	15.6	28.1	12.5	80.3
$25,000–50,000	38.8	55.0	16.2	41.7
$50,000–75,000	60.6	75.1	14.5	23.9
> $75,000	75.9	87.8	11.9	15.7

Source: U.S. Bureau of the Census, "Home Computers and Internet Use in the United States," *Current Population Survey*, August 2000 (www.census.gov/population/www/socdemo/computer.html [October 1, 2003]).

between $25,000 and $34,000, and 66.5 percent of households with incomes over $75,000. Income plays a key role in determining who can access the World Wide Web, with low-income households trailing far behind their rich neighbors. As the U.S. General Accounting Office (GAO) reported, "Internet users [are] more likely to be white and well educated and to have higher-than-average household incomes."[31]

Not only are there differences between those who have and who do not have connections to the Internet, but all Internet connections are not created equal. The traditional method of connecting to the Internet over a telephone line provides a serviceable but limited narrowband connection through which data are transmitted at relatively slow speeds. In contrast, a broadband connection allows for high-speed data transmission over a cable modem line or digital subscriber line (DSL).

In a study conducted by the GAO in 2001, 87.5 percent of individuals had a dial-up telephone connection to the Internet, while 3.2 percent had a DSL connection and 8.9 percent had a cable modem connection.[32] Just over 50 percent of Americans live in localities that provide broadband access, and one-quarter of respondents reported living in an area where both DSL and cable modem access were available; another quarter lived where either one or the other technology was available. Broadband access tends to be less available in rural areas and more available in areas where the poverty rate is low and household income and median home value are high.[33] Broadband service also tends to be expensive compared with nar-

Table 3-3. *Computer Ownership and Internet Access by Demographic Characteristic, 2000*
Percent

Demographic characteristic	Home computer	At-home Internet access
Age		
18–24	57.7	41.5
25–34	58.8	43.9
35–44	65.6	45.5
45–54	64.9	43.8
55–64	50.9	30.5
65+	28.4	12.8
Gender		
Male	56.8	38.5
Female	54.1	36.2
Race		
White	57.7	39.5
White, non-Hispanic	60.8	42.5
Black	37	20.5
Asian/Pacific Islander	66	43.7
Hispanic	35.3	17.5
Education		
Less than high school	23.3	8.4
High school/GED	46.1	25.9
Some college	66	46.5
Bachelor's degree or higher	78.4	62.4
Family income		
<$15,000	23.8	11.3
$15,000–19,999	30.6	14.7
$20,000–24,999	34.2	18.1
$25,000–34,999	46.4	26
$35,000–49,999	61.2	37.4
$50,000–74,999	74.5	50.9
$75,000+	87.4	66.5
Not reported	48.9	28.8

Source: U.S. Bureau of the Census, "Home Computers and Internet Use in the United States," *Current Population Survey,* August 2000 (www.census.gov/population/www/socdemo/computer.html [October 1, 2003]).

rowband service, and cost is the primary reason that individuals have narrowband service.

That only certain areas of the country—and thus only certain citizens—have broadband Internet access is a looming problem for Internet voting. As Internet access in U.S. households continues to increase, at some point simple Internet access will be nearly universal. However, the speed and quality of access might be very uneven, and those differences could become the next serious concern for proponents of widespread Internet voting. If Internet voting systems require broadband access, either because of their graphics and interactivity or because of their demand for a high level of security, citizens with narrowband access might be left behind.

Participation, Political Representation, and the Digital Divide

The data presented in table 3-4 illustrate the participation and digital divides that currently exist among various demographic groups in the United States. The obvious question is, quite simply, Would Internet voting serve to exacerbate the divides that already exist in the American political process? If these divides interact, they could have a fundamental impact on political representation. As discussed earlier, political representation breaks down into two types: descriptive and substantive. If Internet voting creates a situation in which certain demographic groups gain an advantage over others, it could easily affect descriptive representation in government and would likely affect substantive representation as well.

Consider how Internet voting might affect descriptive representation. Table 3-4 presents four columns of data from a 1999 poll conducted by CBS News.[34] The data in the first column—American adults—include the entire sample of survey respondents. The data in the second column consist of survey respondents who voted in the 2000 presidential general election. The third column presents data on individuals who stated that they had access to the Internet. The fourth column consists of individuals who both voted in the 2000 election and had access to the Internet.

The CBS News polling data suggest how voters differ from the general public. Respondents who voted in the 2000 election were slightly more likely to be white, male, better educated, older, and wealthier than the larger sample. For example, African Americans made up 11.6 percent of the overall sample, but just 10.3 percent of those who voted. Females constituted 56.3 percent of the overall sample, but only 55 percent of those who voted. And while individuals under the age of twenty-five made up 8.1 percent of the overall sample but just 5.4 percent of those who

Table 3-4. *The Digital Divide: Percentage of the U.S. Population by Selected Demographic Characteristics*

Demographic characteristic	All American adults	Voter in 2000	Internet access	Voter in 2000 with Internet access	Difference between voters in 2000 and voters with Internet access
Race					
White	77.9	81.4	83.3	83.4	2.0
Black	11.6	10.3	6.8	7.4	-2.9
Asian	1.8	1.6	1.9	2.1	0.5
Other	8.7	6.7	8.0	7.1	0.4
Gender					
Male	43.7	45.0	45.9	46.9	1.9
Female	56.3	55.0	54.1	53.1	-1.9
Education					
No high school	10.0	6.2	3.1	2.2	-4.0
High school	49.7	45.8	43.9	39.3	-6.5
Some college	9.3	9.3	9.6	9.2	-0.1
College	20.7	25.3	27.6	31.1	5.8
Postgraduate	10.2	13.4	15.9	18.1	4.7
Age					
18–24	8.1	5.4	9.8	7.0	1.6
25–29	7.4	5.7	8.1	6.6	0.9
30–39	21.7	20.1	24.3	24.4	4.3
40–49	21.6	22.1	25.4	26.0	3.9
50–59	17.9	20.7	20.0	22.0	1.3
60–69	10.7	11.5	7.6	8.8	-2.7
70+	12.5	14.4	4.8	5.3	-9.1
Income					
<$15,000	15.2	10.6	6.4	4.0	-6.6
$15,000–34,999	24.6	23.9	17.8	16.9	-7.0
$35,000–49,999	15.7	14.9	15.9	14.8	-0.1
$50,000–74,999	21.3	23.6	26.2	28.0	4.4
$75,000–94,999	10.2	11.6	14.3	15.4	3.8
$95,000–149,999	9.2	11.0	13.8	14.8	3.8
$150,000–199,999	2.8	3.3	4.1	4.6	1.3
$200,000+	0.9	1.1	1.3	1.5	0.4
Party					
Republican	25.1	28.9	29.7	30.7	1.8
Democrat	34.5	36.0	29.2	31.5	-4.5
Independent	40.4	35.1	41.1	37.8	2.7
Orientation					
Liberal	24.2	25.2	25.7	25.5	0.3
Moderate	35.2	33.1	31.2	31.9	-1.2
Conservative	40.6	41.7	42.7	42.6	0.9

Source: CBS Market Watch, CBS News Internet Poll (www.cbs.marketwatch.com [January 1999]).

voted, individuals aged seventy and over constituted only 12.5 percent of the total sample but 14.4 percent of those who voted. These findings are not surprising, and they are consistent with previous analyses of voting behavior.

What is troubling is that these biases tend to become more pronounced from left to right across the four columns. One comparison that is critical to appreciating the potential impact of Internet voting is that between the second column, which includes respondents who voted in the 2000 election, and the fourth column, which includes respondents who voted in 2000 and also had an Internet connection—those we call potential Internet voters. This comparison clearly shows that Internet voting could be disadvantageous for women, African Americans, the less well-educated, individuals who do not have a college education, and individuals whose household income is below the national median.

Briefly consider the potential impact of Internet voting on each of these demographic groups. There is a 2.9 percentage point decline in the percentage of African American potential Internet voters compared with the percentage of African American respondents who voted in 2000. In contrast, Internet voting could largely benefit whites, who show a 2 percentage point increase when the percentage of white respondents who voted in 2000 is compared with the percentage of white potential Internet voters. There is a similar 2 percentage point increase when the percentage of male respondents who voted in 2000 is compared with the percentage of male potential Internet voters.

What about education and income variables? There was a strong decrease in the number of potential Internet voters compared with respondents who voted in 2000 as respondents moved down the income and education ladder. Respondents with household incomes of between $15,000 and $35,000 constituted 23.9 percent of those who voted, but they made up only 16.9 percent of potential Internet voters. By contrast, those with incomes over $50,000 would be likely to benefit greatly from Internet voting. Similarly, respondents with a high school education were less likely to be potential Internet voters than individuals with a college degree. High school graduates constituted 45.8 percent of respondents who voted in 2000, but they made up only 39.3 percent of potential Internet voters. In contrast, respondents who were college graduates made up 25.3 percent of those who voted but 31.3 percent of potential Internet voters.

Just as there could be clear deleterious effects on descriptive representation if the nation moved to Internet voting today, there also could be changes in substantive representation. Specifically, there are meaningful changes in partisanship when respondents who voted in 2000 are compared with the potential Internet voting population, and there are slight changes in political orientation as well. Democrats are the big losers when we compare respondents who voted in the 2000 election with those who also had an Internet connection. Democratic respondents made up 36 percent of those who voted in the 2000 election but only 31.5 percent of the potential Internet voting population. While the Democrats lost 4.5 percentage points, Republicans and Independents gained 1.8 percentage points and 2.7 percentage points respectively. When moving from respondents who voted in 2000 to potential Internet voters, there is also a slight decline in the percentage of individuals who describe themselves as moderates. Conservatives benefit from this change slightly more than do liberals.

Conclusion: Internet Voting and Political Representation

The existence of digital divides has been widely cited as an important reason for delaying any implementation of Internet voting. However, as we have shown in this chapter, the important question is not just whether the differences between users and nonusers of the Internet are sufficient to keep Internet voting from becoming a reality in the near future. Equally important is the question of how Internet voting will affect who participates in the political process and how effectively they participate—and thereby how it will affect the representation of the American people's interests.

At present, we can only speculate on what impact widespread Internet voting might have on political representation. As documented above, were Internet voting used in a national election today, the intersection between people with Internet access and those who routinely participate in politics might change the interests that are expressed through voting and political behavior and thus alter political outcomes and policymaking. For example, the party affiliations of the electorate could change if Internet voting were introduced today: the survey data show that Internet-using, politically active individuals are more likely to be Republican and Independent than is the current electorate. These small changes in partisanship could produce large changes in the partisan balance among elected officials, from state legislators and members of Congress to governors and the president. Remember that in the 2000 election, five states were decided by a combined total of 17,500 votes. Moreover, in every election cycle some competitive congressional race commonly is decided by as little as 1 percentage point. If Internet voting affected who voted, then it clearly would affect who was elected.

Internet voting could change political representation in other ways as well. One profound observation about the current digital divide is that more younger Americans have an Internet connection than older Americans, although there is evidence that the difference is shrinking. The current generation of eighteen- to twenty-five-year-olds is certainly a new digital generation, but the unfortunate reality is that it is also among the age groups least likely to participate in politics.[35] If these young, wired potential voters had access to a voting system that they can understand and relate with, that provides them with information that they need and can use, and that they can easily interact with, the act of voting could become more interesting to them—and to the well-wired generations just behind them. Recent research conducted in March 2002 by the Center for Information and Research in Civic Learning and Engagement (CIRCLE) indicates that young adults are not politically engaged: 49 percent said that voting is only a little important or not at all important, only 53 percent said that government and elections address the needs and concerns of young adults, and 48 percent said that political leaders pay some attention to the concerns of young people. The CIRCLE research also indicates that young adults are not convinced that they have an impact on solving community problems or that they have a real impact on politics.[36] Young adults who have low opinions of their political efficacy are not likely to participate in politics. Thus one important benefit of Internet voting is that it could bring Americans who are currently poorly represented—especially the younger generations—into the political process if it can increase their perceptions of political effectiveness.

Obviously, the potential benefits of Internet voting for younger Americans should not come at the expense of other voters, especially minority voters and those with less education and income. Internet voting can be implemented throughout the nation for a federal election only after the problem of unequal Internet access is addressed—and implementing Internet voting may become a goal that prods policymakers to develop better strategies for making sure that a permanent, unconnected underclass is not created in the United States.

But the rationale for moving toward Internet voting is strong. While many argued that the uncertainty surrounding the outcome of the 2000 presidential election for weeks after election day undermined the legitimacy of the U.S. democratic system, it is important to remember that the problems encountered in the 2000 election brought with them a better understanding of other pressing problems that exist in the electoral process. As discussed in this chapter, the current electoral system does not transparently translate voter preferences into counted ballots uniformly for all citizens. Quite simply, paper systems with punch cards and optical scan ballots fail to capture votes in a manner that underrepresents minority voters and people with disabilities, making it impossible to know with certainty the voters' underlying preferences. The poll site voting model also disenfranchises those who cannot get to their voting precinct on a Tuesday because of work or family obligations or because the site is inaccessible. In addition, many eligible citizens do not register because of difficulties associated with the voter registration process. Internet voting has the potential to resolve many if not all of these problems; that is why it must be fully studied.

Even with the need to mitigate the problems associated with the digital divide, we believe that it is wrong to conclude that experiments with Internet voting cannot be conducted until those problems are addressed. In fact, the digital divide issue has led people to think about Internet voting in the wrong context. Most of the writing on the digital divide and Internet voting argues that as long as important differences in Internet access exist between socioeconomic groups, Internet voting cannot be implemented for national or statewide elections. We think that there is a better way to view the problem. Instead of thinking about implementing Internet voting for the entire national electorate or for an entire state, implementing Internet voting should be considered for certain groups of voters, specifically those for whom Internet connectivity is not an impediment but who have difficulty participating in elections through traditional means.

CHAPTER 4

Internet Voting, Political Debate, and Policymaking

During his 1992 presidential campaign, Ross Perot laid out a radical vision for a new form of direct democracy in America—the electronic town hall. His idea was simple: take an important public policy issue, present the costs and benefits of various proposals for addressing the issue, and let the public register their views about which solutions would be more effective. The public's views would then be made available to public officials (such as members of Congress, the president, and state governors), something that Perot viewed as being a form of democratic pressure politics. He argued that "if we ever put the people back in charge of this country and make sure they understand the issues, you'll see the White House and Congress, like a ballet, pirouetting around the stage and getting things done in unison."[1] As Perot saw it, the electronic town hall (ETH) would short-circuit the interest group process in Washington by empowering ordinary citizens to express their views to policymakers through a structured medium. The ETH also would provide an opportunity to educate voters about the issues and to help them make informed choices about the government policies that govern their lives.

Perot expounded his vision of the ETH before there was widespread use of the Internet. Today, many think that the Internet is exactly the right mechanism for allowing the public to express its views on important issues and to engage in the "deliberative democracy" that Perot had in mind a decade ago. The Internet is a fully interactive medium, allowing voters to view information and to respond in real time about a given policy. Moreover, Internet users have access to a world of information, larger than ever before in human history. Today, a person can go online and read newspapers from cities across the country and around the world. In Los Angeles, it is just as easy to read the *Washington Post*, the *Times of India*, or the *Times* of London as it is to read the *Los Angeles Times*. All major government agencies, politicians, and interest groups have a website where they publicize their mission. These sites may include detailed policy positions, audio and video clips, transcripts of major speeches, and mechanisms for channeling participation—especially memberships and fund-raising. And of course there are countless chat rooms, e-mail discussion lists, and "web logs" where people can interact and discuss politics on the Internet.

With all of the informational advantages available to a "wired" person, it is hard to imagine how easy access to huge quantities of information could be detrimental to American democracy. More information and citizen involvement should be good, shouldn't it? And if more information and involvement is good, the Internet can become another tool to improve American democracy. We examine this issue carefully, considering both the benefits and the costs associated with using the Internet in the political process. First we examine the benefits that voters can get from the increased amount of information available. We then consider whether the Internet can become a mechanism for promoting grassroots democracy—bringing back the New England town hall—or if it might produce the majoritarian democratic politics that the nation's founders feared, or even something worse.

The debate about the impact of the Internet on American democracy is divisive. On one side are its tireless, optimistic advocates, who point out how the Internet is even now reshaping and improving our democratic debates and decisions. One of the loudest advocates is Dick Morris, former pollster, presidential adviser, Internet entrepreneur, and founder of vote.com. Morris argues in his book *Vote.com* that "[t]he incredible speed and interactivity of the Internet will inevitably return our country to a de facto system of direct democracy by popular referendum. The town-meeting style of government will become a national reality." In his opinion, "Whether Internet democracy is good or bad is, however, quite beside the point. It is inevitable. It is coming and we had better make our peace with it."[2]

On the other side of the debate are those who see dangers that the Internet poses for democratic discourse and deliberation. Cass Sunstein, author of *Republic.com*, has become a prominent critic of the idea that the Internet necessarily improves the quality of democratic discourse. The core of Sunstein's argument is that "there are serious dangers in a system in which individuals bypass general interest intermediaries and restrict themselves to opinions and topics of their own choosing."[3] Sunstein argues that because the Internet allows much more selective filtering of information and permits people to bypass any intermediate interpretation of new information, the Internet will promote deeper social and political fragmentation and the rapid and dangerous transmission of rumors, innuendo, and incorrect information.

The key question therefore is whether the debate that actually occurs in a deliberative environment serves to facilitate a more informed debate or instead coarsens and narrows it. We begin by considering the wealth of information that is available online and the benefits that voters can gain from using the Internet. We then examine deliberative democracy and draw a distinction between two different forms: iterative deliberative democracy and direct voting democracy. The first is a vision of online, infrequent, participatory deliberation that informs policy debates and decisions, while the second is a vision of frequent and direct online voting on policy issues. We argue that using the Internet to promote an iterative deliberative policy debate may lead to better-informed policy decisions, but that direct and frequent voting on the Internet is a bad idea. While Internet voting should increase participation and might lead to better-informed voting, implementation of Internet voting need not lead to the type of electronic town hall that was such a large part of Ross Perot's vision for American democracy.

Information, Voting, and the Internet

Proponents of the Internet note that it brings a wealth of information to the user's fingertips. Using a search engine, a voter can find out about almost any candidate, issue, or interest group with the click of a few keys. Individuals can sign up to receive information updates by e-mail from their favorite candidate, newspaper, political party, or interest group. Clearly, the Internet can make it easier to become a better-educated participant in the political process.

However, this view begs a fundamental question: how informed do voters need to be to make reasonable choices and cast an effective ballot? Do people need to possess encyclopedic knowledge of an issue in order to cast a well-informed vote, or are there informational cues that voters can use to understand complex policy issues with little trouble? If people now need vast amounts of information to cast a meaningful vote, the Internet may be an important new tool. If not, the Internet may be important, but no more so than the information already available from the evening news, the newspaper, political materials and commercials, or conversations with friends, family, and co-workers about politics.

People have long debated the level of education needed for effective voting. In the 1850s, several states adopted tests of literacy or education that required voters to be literate in English before they could vote. An educational requirement, though quite controversial, was seen by many at the time as having positive attributes:

> It would reduce the 'ignorance' of the electorate and weed out sizeable numbers of poor immigrant voters . . . moreover, it would do so in a way that was ideologically more palatable than taxpaying restrictions or waiting periods for the foreign-born. Literacy tests did not overly discriminate against particular classes or ethnic groups, and literacy itself was a remediable shortcoming.[4]

Political scientists also have examined the role that education plays in voting and political participation, trying to determine whether less-educated voters have the information they need to understand the issues on which they vote. Starting with some of the earliest studies of voter behavior, scholars found that better-educated voters typically have a better grasp of the issues involved in an election, a clearer sense of their own ideology, and a greater desire to participate in elections even when their vote is unlikely to influence the outcome.[5] The better-educated voters are seen as being better able to understand the complexity of the issues put before them.

Because the Internet can put a world of information at voters' fingertips, it could be a critical new tool for creating informed voters. However, more recent research has shown that even small informational cues can allow voters to make informed choices without having to know everything there is to know about an issue. An important study in this regard was conducted by Arthur Lupia, who examined the ability of California voters to make informed choices on complicated ballot initiatives regarding insurance.[6] Lupia found that some voters had a vast amount of knowledge about the insurance initiatives but that most voters were not well informed about the vagaries of the initiatives. However, if the generally uninformed voters had just one additional piece of information—the position of the insurance industry on the ballot initiatives—based on that information alone they could infer the potential impact of the initiatives and cast the same vote as if they had taken the time and energy to become highly informed about these initiatives. This one informational cue packed a powerful punch. This example illustrates that small bits of information can help to inform voters and allow them to make informed voting choices.

Similar informational cues can be garnered from other sources in elections, such as candidate and policy position endorsements by various groups. Knowing that a union, a well-known media figure, or an interest group like the NAACP has endorsed a particular candidate or policy position can provide a wealth of information to a voter. Even if voters have never heard of the candidate or the issue, they are likely to have heard of the NAACP and can base their own position on their view of the NAACP. Such endorsements have been found to have an important effect on election outcomes.[7]

Furthermore, even less politically relevant cues can help voters determine whom to support in an election. Samuel Popkin relates two anecdotes from presidential campaigns: Gerald Ford's attendance at a campaign rally during the 1976 primary in San Antonio, Texas, where he bit into a tamale without first removing the corn husk, and George McGovern's attempt during the 1972 primary to court the Jewish vote in New York, where he ordered a kosher hot dog and a glass of milk at a Queens hot dog stand. Popkin argues that nonpolitical cues like these provide a great deal of information to voters:

> Would a Mexican-American voter who saw President Ford bite into an unshucked tamale be wrong to conclude that the president had little experience with Mexican-American culture, little feel for it? Would a Jewish voter who saw George McGovern order a kosher hot dog and a glass of milk, and plan to talk politics in synagogue on a Friday night, be wrong to conclude that the good senator knew little about Jews and Jewish concerns?[8]

Popkin answers these two questions in the affirmative: voters can and do make these sorts of inferences. The Internet can be invaluable to voters, providing them with a simple mechanism for getting such cues about how to vote for specific candidates or issues. Voters today can take advantage of the services provided by interest groups, political parties, and the media to have this information sent to them by e-mail. Consider three different scenarios.

—A voter who views herself as independent but likes George Bush and often votes Republican can go to the website of the Republican National Committee and sign up to be a GOP Team Leader. As a member, she will get e-mails informing her about Republican candidates and the party's stand on issues.

—A second voter, who views the environment as being the single most important issue facing the United States, can go to the Sierra Club's website and become a member of the Conservation Action Network. As a member, he will receive e-mail about environmental issues. He also can join other Sierra Club e-mail lists and learn about candidates and issues on which the Sierra Club has taken a position.

—A voter living in the Maryland suburbs of Washington, D.C., who wants information from a more newsworthy source can subscribe to the *Washington Post* online and receive daily e-mails with information about politics, including Maryland politics, that includes the paper's candidate and initiative endorsements for an election.

Each of these cases illustrates how the Internet can be used by voters to get information with minimal effort. If voters know what issues are important to them and what groups they trust to provide them with information, they can take the minor step of registering to receive informational e-mails from those groups. One can imagine an Internet voter with her ballot open in one window and the websites of various interest groups open as well, voting after looking at this information. An interest group might even offer software that would allow voters to cast a ballot for the group's preferred slate of candidates.

A great deal of research, beginning in the 1950s and continuing today, has documented that most Americans are poorly informed about politics and political issues.[9] Other research, some of which we have discussed above, shows that Americans deal with their imperfect information by using simple cues and information shortcuts to guide their political decisions. Moreover, the three scenarios above illustrate that the Internet can provide more information, more cheaply, and in an easier-to-use format than other sources. It can make Americans less inclined to use shortcuts in their political decisions and more inclined to seek out better information on the Internet, which would help them make more informed decisions. Intriguingly, some recent research indicates that voters who had Internet access and who used online election news sources were more likely to vote in the 1996 and 2000 presidential elections.[10]

Although the availability of political information on the Internet may seem like a great benefit for voters, having access to so much information may lead to significant and troubling problems. First, trying to process large quantities of information may lead to information overload, which could cause citizens either to totally tune out of the flow of political information or to selectively tune in to only certain sources.[11] If citizens respond to information overload by tuning out, obviously all of the possible benefits of the Internet to American democracy are lost. Even more troubling than information overload is the possibility that citizens will become selective information gatherers. Selective information gathering—using technologies like the Internet to select only information sources that are likely to present viewpoints consistent with voters' existing opinions—can lead to what Sunstein called "fragmentation" or to what Bruce Cain calls "segmentation of political information."[12] If used this way, the Internet does not expose people to new views, it only serves to reinforce their existing beliefs; in that case, the simple fact that the Internet makes so much information available is irrelevant.

Furthermore, with the cascade of political information available, essentially in real time, citizens have little opportunity or ability to check the quality of the information they receive. The problem of information "verification" was resolved in the pre-Internet era, when news organizations had long-standing norms and procedures for checking the veracity and validity of information they received before providing it to the public.[13] Real-time access to raw data makes it likely that false information, biased interpretations, and rumors will be distributed to thousands—or millions—of people in very short order, in what Sunstein called "cybercascades."[14] Virtually everyone who now uses the Internet has been affected by a cybercascade of some sort, typically e-mail "alerts" about computer viruses forwarded from person to person that often reach millions of Internet users but turn out to be completely false.

Because the Internet gives people the ability to tailor their information sources to suit their personal biases, it may in fact diminish the ability of voters to participate effectively in a democracy. The Internet allows voters to access more information, but it also permits them to select what kinds of information they receive to a much greater degree than do mass media like newspapers or television news shows. That the Internet allows for access to a huge amount of political information does not mean that the information will be accessed by all citizens—or even that it will be correct.

The Electronic Town Hall and Deliberative Democracy: Peril or Panacea?

But there are other visions of how information might flow in a democratic society when using the Internet as a medium for discourse. One vision is that of the electronic town hall, aptly described by *Wired* magazine:

> Good evening, citizens. The electronic town meeting is about to begin. Everyone take your seats and make sure your voter ID number is handy and your touch-tone phone or remote control device is by your side. Those of you tuning in via computer please click on the "start" icon on the top of your screen.
>
> Today's topic is gun control. We assume everyone has read the issue brochure sent to all of your electronic mailboxes one month ago. Our first speaker will be Robert Corbin, executive director of the National Rifle Association, followed by Sarah Brady, president of Handgun Control Incorporated. We will follow that up with a discussion among a panel of twelve randomly selected citizens and an impartial moderator. At the end of the meeting, we will ask you to vote on the proposed legislation.[15]

That, for some advocates of deliberative democracy, is the vision of the future of public policy, of how government should function.[16] This form of deliberative democracy is seen by its proponents as a mechanism for overcoming the problems with the political culture in the United States, where much of the public is disengaged from politics and alienated by politicians, disgusted with the money culture of politics, hostile to political institutions, and cynical about the motives of the news media. Deliberative democracy proponents assert that what is needed to overcome public cynicism is for citizens to become directly involved in the political process. In their view, the people should make important decisions about how the country is run, after careful consideration of all the options. The process is driven by informed public participation, through which all points of view and positions are carefully weighed against one another. Unlike the policy process in Washington and state capitals across the country, they say, deliberative democracy is not driven by highly paid lobbyists who peddle influence and government policy is not purchased by the highest bidder. In a deliberative democracy, the voice of the people—unfettered by professional politicians—is paramount.

The Internet can play an important role in promoting deliberative democracy. Every day on television—on news programs, sporting events, even MTV—people are asked to use the Internet to submit their views on the issues of the day. Unscientific polls are conducted on everything from what the United States' role in the world should be and whether Social Security should be privatized to whether a penalty call in a football game was correct and whether Pete Rose should be allowed in the Baseball Hall of Fame. Although some of these polls are trivial, they illustrate the potential power of the Internet as a tool for quickly aggregating information about preferences and providing feedback on pending decisions. This feedback mechanism could easily be expanded to facilitate electronic town halls. The Internet could serve both as an additional educational tool in an ETH—with participants able to link to websites that contain information regarding the pros and cons of various policy options—and as a voting tool.

Most people make a distinction between deliberative democracy and deliberative polling, the latter an idea championed by James Fishkin.[17] The primary difference between the two is that deliberative polling is not designed for direct decisionmaking by the citizenry, as is one form of deliberative democracy. Instead, deliberative polling is a tool for informing policymakers about the judgments of a small, statistically representative sample of the public at large after these individuals have reviewed an array of policy options and debated their merits. The results of deliberative polling are thought to mirror the position of the broad public on a given policy issue, allowing elected officials to represent their constituents more closely.

Proponents of deliberative democracy envision several different ways in which it can be implemented, but two scenarios are more common. The first scenario—iterative deliberative democracy (IDD)—brings together large numbers of citizens, either in person or through some technology, to discuss a specific policy problem and to develop a plan of action for addressing the problem; however, public officials still make the final decision. The second scenario—direct voting democracy (DVD)—builds on the populist tradition, which holds that the public should be able to legislate for itself directly, bypassing the legislative process. These two views of deliberative democracy are not harmonious. Advocates of the more iterative form of deliberative democracy often used at the local level find the direct voting form of deliberative democracy to be anathema. Consider how the Civic Practices Network, which advocates for the more iterative deliberative democracy, describes the initiative process:

Despite the intentions of the framers of the Constitution, a direct-majoritarian version of democracy has been in the ascendancy in the United States since the nineteenth century, and depletes our capacities for reasoned deliberation. In this version of democracy, those mechanisms that compel decisions to conform directly to existing majority opinion are seen as more democratic than those that filter decisions through representation. The ascendancy of opinion polls, talk show democracy, referendums, and primaries are manifestations of this. As a result, policy questions become oversimplified and stylized, and our capacity to solve increasingly complex public problems declines.[18]

The primary differences between these two views of deliberative democracy lie in the amount of actual deliberation that is involved in the process, the way in which information is used and manipulated in the process, and who makes the ultimate policy decision—individuals or their representatives. They also hold different prospects for the success or failure of Internet voting.

IDD in Action: Local Successes

Edward Weeks, a professor at the University of Oregon who directs the Deliberative Democracy Project, sees IDD as "the informed participation by citizens in the deliberative process of community decision making."[19] Public participation in the process must be both broad and representative. If participation is not representative, the public will likely perceive the entire exercise as dominated by special interests; if participation is not broad, the goal of civic engagement is thwarted. Participants must become knowledgeable about the problem at hand so that they can understand its causes and the various policy options for addressing it. In addition, the public should be able to deliberate publicly about the problem and the various options. Iterative deliberation encourages give and take among peers and encourages individuals to consider the viewpoints of others.[20]

Several examples of IDD have been put into action. The Civic Practices Network—a collaborative, nonpartisan project that promotes practical, community-based methods for public problem solving—notes that the Oregon Health Plan of 1990 was developed in large part through the methods of IDD. The plan was developed by two separate organizations. First, Oregon Health Decisions (OHD), a nonpartisan organization, conducted almost fifty community meetings to determine citizens' common values about health care. OHD later held community meetings and two statewide meetings to provide the public, state and local officials, and legislators with information about the deliberations. An appointed body, the Health Services Commission (HSC), used the work of the OHD as a roadmap to establish a treatment priorities list. The HSC also used a deliberative process: it met with expert panels, held a series of public open hearings, and conducted opinion surveys. The HSC's recommendations were adopted with bipartisan support in the legislature, in large part because the legislation, developed through this deliberative process, was seen as having broad public support.

Similar deliberative efforts have been made in local communities, such as Eugene, Oregon, and Sacramento, California. In these two cities, deliberations focused on balancing each city's demands for public services with available revenues. Each city council recognized that in order to achieve any politically viable, long-term solution to the city's budget problems, the public had to support its policies and feel as though its decision reflected their own views. Both cities hired the same consultant to manage the process of deliberative democracy and used a similar process, which began with a series of exploratory efforts to develop a sense of where the public stood on the city budget.[21] Polling was conducted, public meetings were held, and a questionnaire was published in the newspaper. The initial efforts provided policymakers with an understanding of how citizens viewed the budget problem—most citizens believed that it could be fixed by increasing the efficiency of operations—and allowed policymakers to use their views as a framework for subsequent deliberations.

The deliberative process began with a series of surveys that were sent to all households in each city asking citizens to review existing programs, existing taxes, and proposals for new spending and new taxes. Three surveys were used; most citizens received a simple survey, much like the Census Bureau's short form, and others received more detailed surveys. In Eugene, the response rate for the two simple surveys was approximately 71 percent; it was 53 percent for the detailed survey. In Sacramento, the response rate was lower, but the project there involved reaching a far more diverse population. From the surveys, policymakers could see residents' detailed preferences regarding spending and taxes. A series of public workshops also was held, in which almost 700 citizens engaged in small-group exercises that involved seven to nine people working with a

facilitator to develop budget proposals. The city council took the recommendations from the surveys and workshops and developed three
scenarios for balancing the city budget; the survey and public workshop
process then was repeated to determine which scenario had more public
support. Both city councils adopted the proposal supported by a majority of citizens.

One thing is clear from these examples of IDD—it is labor intensive. It
requires providing citizens with a wide range of information and determining their preferences through surveys, public meetings, and public
engagements on multiple occasions over time. Citizens came to a decision
literally through deliberation, through an iterative process in which they
reviewed more and more information to make careful distinctions about
the shape of a public policy. In the cases noted above, public involvement
allowed political leaders to make tough choices secure in the knowledge
that their decisions represented the views of their constituents.

Deliberative Democracy in Action: The 2000 Presidential Election

During the 2000 presidential election, a field test was conducted by the
Markle Foundation to determine how the Internet might work to enhance
deliberative democracy. Called Web White and Blue 2000, this project
produced a nonpartisan consortium of seventeen media organizations.[22]
Participating news organizations carried on their websites materials
related to Web White and Blue 2000, primarily links to online political
information, to political organizations, and to state electoral information.
Most important, from October 1 until election day on November 8,
2000, each site carried an ongoing debate among the campaigns of
George Bush, Al Gore, Pat Buchanan, Harry Browne, Howard Phillips,
and John Hagelin. The debate, which was called the Rolling Cyber
Debate, had two separate components: a Message of the Day from each
campaign and a response to a Question of the Day from some Internet
participant. The project also had an evaluation component, conducted by
Arthur Lupia.[23]

In some ways, Web White and Blue 2000 seemed like a stunning success. From the time it went online on June 28 through election day, the
website registered 7.5 million "page views" (the number of times a specific web page is viewed by an Internet user). One way to look at the
usage data is to note that approximately 111 million Americans voted in

the 2000 election; therefore as many as 6.8 percent of American voters might have viewed Web White and Blue 2000. However, page view data do not indicate whether each viewing is done by a different individual or by the same individual visiting the website repeatedly. Furthermore, there is no way to know whether the people who viewed the website were registered to vote—or, for that matter, even eligible to vote—in the United States. Visitors might have been under eighteen; they might not have been American citizens; they might not even have resided in the United States. So while 7.5 million page views seems quite significant, when the views might represent repeat visits or visits from people who do not vote or are not eligible to vote, the numbers seem much less striking.

During the last eight weeks of the campaign, the Rolling Cyber Debate—the main mechanism for promoting deliberative democracy through Web White and Blue 2000—had a total of 737,944 page views. Note first that this is only about 10 percent of the number of views for the website overall. While the Rolling Cyber Debate seems like a clever idea to encourage deliberative democracy on the Internet, it was not widely exploited by Internet users.

The evaluation of Web White and Blue 2000 contains useful data about the use of the Rolling Cyber Debate (RCD) and the Message of the Day and Question of the Day during the eight weeks the feature ran on the website. Some of these data are shown in figure 4-1; the data table at the bottom of the figure also gives the actual usage statistics for each week.

Interestingly, viewing of the Rolling Cyber Debate was greatest in the third week of October, when there were about 158,000 page views. The number of viewings falls off in the next two weeks and rises again right before election day. Lupia argues that the first peak probably occurred because the last of the three televised presidential debates was held during the same week or because one of the online debate topics during that period dealt with Internet and copyright issues, which may have drawn significant Internet traffic.

Figure 4-1 shows that viewings of the more deliberative aspects of the Rolling Cyber Debate—the Message of the Day and the Question of the Day—were orders of magnitude lower than those for the Rolling Cyber Debate overall. For example, during the peak in usage during the third week of October, there were 158,000 views of the RCD, but only about 27,000 views of the Message of the Day and about 50,000 views of the Question of the Day, or about 3,800 or 7,100 views a day respectively. That does not demonstrate a great deal of interest in either deliberative

Figure 4-1. *Web White and Blue 2000, Rolling Cyber Debate Page Views*

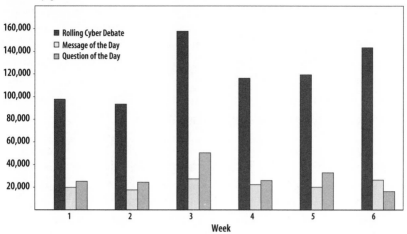

Number of page views

forum, even for Internet users who originally had taken the initiative to explore the Rolling Cyber Debate.

Furthermore, there is no evidence that this particular IDD project had an informative effect on visitors to the site nor that it made visitors more likely to participate in the 2000 presidential election. The evaluation report used three studies: a voluntary survey for visitors, an Internet survey focusing on people who had no prior knowledge of the Web White and Blue project, and experimental studies of University of California–San Diego undergraduates. As both the volunteer sample and the experimental sample are problematic for understanding the impact of this project, close attention must be paid to the Internet survey.[24]

The Internet survey was conducted by Knowledge Networks.[25] One of the first questions asked respondents, "Have you ever heard of webwhiteblue.org?" Only eleven of the 1,173 respondents said that they had heard of the website, less than 1 percent of the sample—another indication of the low level of overall impact that the project had on the 2000 election. (According to the evaluation report, this reported awareness was much lower than that of nine comparable Internet political news websites; for example, 80 percent of respondents were aware of CNN.com [figure 4-1].) The 1,162 respondents who were unaware of the Web White and Blue project were then sent to the website and asked questions about the information content of the site. The Internet survey respondents generally provided a positive evaluation of its information content, but when interviewed a week later, only 9 percent of them had revisited the site. The evaluation made no attempt to assess the actual impact of the website on political awareness or knowledge or on visitors' propensity to participate in the electoral process after visiting the website. Therefore it is very difficult to assess the real impact of Web White and Blue 2000, but we are somewhat pessimistic about this particular approach to encouraging IDD over the Internet.

The Initiative Process as Deliberative Democracy?

An alternative and radically different vision of deliberative democracy—direct voting democracy (DVD)—has been put forth by advocates such as the National Initiative for Democracy (NID). In their view, deliberative democracy means providing citizens with direct access to the policy process. Specifically, the NID supports a "democracy amendment" to the U.S. Constitution that would allow the public to "create and alter governments, constitutions, and laws, independent of existing governments." It would "establish legislative procedures through which the People can, in an orderly and deliberative manner, enact laws using ballot initiatives" and "create an independent government agency, the Electoral Trust, to administer those procedures on behalf of the People."[26]

Direct voting democracy is based on the notion that many government entities—especially legislatures—are inherently corrupt. The same assumption—that the political process is corrupt and that citizens need a more direct way to communicate their views—was shared by the early founders of the initiative process in many states, especially those west of the Rocky Mountains. In the late 1800s, populists and progressives began to press for the adoption of initiatives and referendums as a means of overcoming the money interests that they believed to control the state governments. Through the initiative process, the people could legislate for themselves, without having their desires thwarted by politicians. The claims of political corruption and calls for a more direct democracy heard at the turn of the twentieth century are echoed today by many people who see DVD as a critical source of popular power.

In his book on the initiative process, *Democracy Derailed*, David Broder notes that the progressive movement was able to achieve many important successes after the initiative process was put in place in many states across the country:

The years immediately following introduction of the initiative justified the reformers' faith in its power. Using the new tool, they levied the first serious taxes on railroads, utilities, and other big companies; regulated freight rates; introduced a presidential primary and direct election of senators; gave women the right to vote; and instituted the eight-hour [work] day and workers' compensation.[27]

Those initial successes were quite impressive. The public was able to circumvent state governments that were beholden to industry and directly regulate the businesses in their state. Tax burdens were made more equitable. The rights of workers were more clearly delineated and workplaces made safer. Moreover, the political process itself was improved, especially by enfranchising women.

All told, many believed that the new initiative process boded well for deliberative democracy, but the early enchantment with the process quickly soured. As Broder writes, "No sooner had the concept of popular sovereignty been implanted in the political system than clever politicians realized that the key to power now lay in the manipulation of public opinion."[28] In California, for example, special interest groups were able to get measures on the ballot advocating horse racing and gambling (Proposition 7 in 1912, Proposition 6 in 1926); prohibition (on the ballot in 1914, 1916, 1918, and 1922); licensing of dentists (Proposition 21 in 1918), chiropractors (Proposition 5 in 1920), and osteopaths (Proposition 20 in 1922); and regulation of the manufacture and sale of oleomargarine (Proposition 3 in 1926).[29] This range of ballot initiatives illustrates how quickly special interests learned that they could legislate through the ballot, instead of in the state capital.

Between 1912 and 2000, the initiative was used extensively in California, where 1,123 ballot initiatives were developed and prepared for signature. Of that total, 284—a mere 25 percent—actually received a sufficient number of signatures to qualify for the statewide ballot and only ninety-seven were approved, while 186 were rejected. California voters appear to be quite selective in their support for initatives—only 34 percent of qualified ballot measures in that eighty-eight-year period actually passed.[30]

These numbers, in the abstract, do not seem large enough to place an enormous burden on California's voters. After all, voting on 284 initiatives in the forty-four elections that were held during this period (every two years) required California voters to make decisions on only six or seven initiatives every twenty-four months. However, the situation looks more dire when one notes that those are just the measures that Californians voted on during *statewide* elections. Counties and municipalities can and do have their own initiatives on the ballot, multiplying the number of issues that Californians are asked to decide when they vote. For example, in the 1999–2000 period, there were twenty-eight statewide measures on the ballot, eighteen countywide measures, and 120 municipal measures— a total of 166 ballot measures.[31] On the March 2000 statewide primary ballot, there were twenty statewide ballot measures alone. Of the state measures, seventeen passed (61 percent), while twelve of the county measures passed (67 percent) and fifty-nine of the municipal measures passed (49 percent). Despite the historical averages, in this particular set of elections, Californians were willing to support these initiatives, especially state- and countywide ones. In any case, when county and local measures are added together, it becomes clearer that Californians are called on to make many decisions in exercising their right to deliberative democracy.

Unfortunately, in addition to the sheer volume of initiatives on each ballot in California, many initiatives are closely related, poorly written, and difficult to understand. Often there are two ballot initiatives in the same election on the same issue. A perfect example occurred in March 2000, when voters were asked to decide Propositions 30 and 31, two ballot measures dealing with litigation rights in regard to insurance companies. These two initiatives qualified for the ballot, but information about them was not sent to registered voters in the usual ballot information book; a special supplemental voter information guide, totaling sixteen pages of fine print, was distributed independently. Many experts who were called on to discuss the two initiatives professed difficulty in discerning the exact impact of either initiative and exactly how they differed. The summary description of Proposition 30 stated that "yes vote approves, no vote rejects legislation restoring right to sue another person's insurer for unfair claims settlement practices following judgment or award against other person; barring lawsuit if insurer agrees to arbitrate original claim against insured party." The description of Proposition 31 read "yes vote approves, a no vote rejects statutory amendments limiting right of injured party to sue another's insurer for unfair claims practices and exempting specified insurers under certain circumstances."[32] The text of the actual proposed law for both initiatives covered four pages. Perhaps reflecting the complexity of these two competing measures—or the $50 million spent by insurance companies opposing Proposition 30—California voters resoundingly rejected both, with 69 percent opposing Proposition 30 and 72 percent opposing Proposition 31.

Today, the initiative process is anything but democratic. Getting initiatives on the ballot and passed is no longer a populist effort; instead, it has become a vast political industry, run by professionals. There are professional signature gatherers, lawyers who specialize in writing ballot initiatives, pollsters to field-test different types of initiative language and then predict their likely success, ad men to develop pitches to be aired on television and radio to swing voters' views, and—most important—fundraisers who gather the millions of dollars necessary to pay for all of the signature gatherers, lawyers, pollsters, and ad men. By the late 1990s, the states that permitted the initiative process were flooded with money as political professionals battled it out. In 1997–98 more than $257 million was spent on statewide initiative campaigns and millions more were spent on local initiative efforts.[33] The initiative has become a powerful tool in the world of modern campaigns, and special interests now dominate the initiative process.

The same special interests that were tamed by the initiative process 100 years ago now find that their financial clout and organizational skills provide them with great advantages over the general public in crafting and selling initiatives. Today, the players behind initiatives often are large corporations, special interest groups, and wealthy individuals with a personal agenda.[34] In one case in California, gambling interests—California Indian tribes and Nevada gaming interests—battled it out over whether the tribes could have casinos. The fight cost $92 million, spent on campaigns for an issue that probably could have been dealt with more readily by the state legislature. Some academics have argued that voters can pick up important decisionmaking cues by observing campaign contributions and initiative endorsements.[35] While this might be true, especially for issues that are being contested by visible and well-endowed special interests, it is not always the case. Moreover, that voters are resorting to cues and shortcuts seems to undermine the basic idea of deliberative democracy. In addition, the either-or nature of the referendum process precludes meaningful deliberation.

But there is a final, and distressing, way in which the initiative process is not democratic. As discussed in an earlier chapter, the electorate is vastly different from the universe of Americans who are not registered to vote and who do not participate in the political process. For example, using 1998 survey data of California adults, Mark Baldassare documented that 68 percent of the registered voter population was white and 19 percent Hispanic and that 39 percent of the unregistered population was white and 45 percent Hispanic. Only 27 percent of the electorate was eighteen to thirty-four years of age, while 59 percent of the unregistered population was in that age bracket. Further, 42 percent of registered voters had incomes under $40,000 and 58 percent had incomes over $40,000; among unregistered voters, the reverse was true: 65 percent had incomes under $40,000 and 35 percent had incomes over that amount.[36] Clearly, the set of Californians who can and do participate in DVD is not representative of the larger population of the state.

Deliberative Democracy: The Possibilities and Perils of Internet Voting

The two visions of deliberative democracy presented above are radically different, and they have very different implications for Internet voting. Consider the initiative process first. In this case, all of the problems with large-scale Internet voting—especially the digital divide—come to the fore. This is especially the case because the initiative process is a majoritarian process, wherein a majority of voters can impose its will on a minority that has no power to defend itself. As Madison notes in *Federalist 10*, the Constitution employs a representative system of government in order to overcome the power of factionalism. The initiative process can strip away the protections provided by a system of representative democracy. When compounded by the issues associated with the digital divide—a divide that favors the wealthy and well-educated over minorities and those who are not as well off or as well educated—voting on initiatives over the Internet could create serious biases in the policy process.

Our analysis is common among political analysts. For example, Norman Ornstein sees the Internet as "[posing] a direct challenge to deliberative democracy and Congress as the framers designed them and as we know them." His concern is that cyberdemocracy will exacerbate inequality, with the world being divided between cyberinformation junkies—who are mostly white, wealthy, and well-educated—and everyone else. He argues moreover that legislative debate in Congress is well informed. Congress is full of staff who are knowledgeable about issues and who pass this information on to senators and representatives. Thus legislative debate is much more sophisticated than, for example, debate in California initiative campaigns.

Therefore there are serious concerns that the direct voting form of deliberative democracy will not protect the rights of minorities and other less-advantaged citizens. Bruce Cain recently wrote that "the pure direct democracy model (of Internet voting) bypasses the checks in the current system that were designed to protect minority viewpoints and produce more deliberative and stable collective choices."[37] Direct democracy typically has not protected the rights of minority and culturally diverse groups, in large part because it is not likely to produce changes in popular opinion. Because the process offers only two opposing positions—the voter is either for a proposal or against it—there is no meaningful deliberation or compromise. Instead, two very different views collide. Democracy thereby becomes strictly a means of aggregating preferences, with the majority always winning. There is no means for protecting the rights of a minority in direct voting democracy. James Madison, in *Federalist 10*, was harshly critical of the direct voting model of deliberative democracy, partly because of the lack of protections for minority rights, but also because what he called "pure democracy" was inherently unstable:

> A common passion or interest will, in almost every case, be felt by a majority of the whole; a communication and concert results from the form of government itself; and there is nothing to check the inducements to sacrifice the weaker party or an obnoxious individual. Hence it is that such democracies have ever been spectacles of turbulence and contention; have ever been found incompatible with personal security or the rights of property; and have in general been as short in their lives as they have been violent in their deaths.[38]

Social choice theorists, who study how individual choices are aggregated into group preferences, have in recent decades made the same argument Madison made 200 years ago. They point out that when individuals have to express their preferences across issues—for example, when members of Congress have to choose how much money should be spent on "guns" and how much on "butter"—such voting on multidimensional issues leads to policy and political instability. Social choice theorists who founded the "new institutionalism" school in social science have argued that "institutions"—legislatures, committee systems, political parties, and other methods of preference aggregation and selection—are the only way to avoid the instability inherent in frequent votes on multidimensional issues.[39] Thus the lesson taught by Madison and social choice theorists is that direct and frequent voting on policy issues is a bad idea because there are no intervening institutions to ensure that the preferences of individuals make for sound and coherent public policy.

Initiatives also are by nature divisive, all-or-nothing affairs that tend to polarize individuals, and the Internet has the potential to polarize Americans even further. In *Republic.com*, Cass Sunstein identifies his concern about the likely emergence of "The Daily Me."[40] Because the Internet can be customized to provide people with just the information that they want—thus filtering out alternative ideas and viewpoints that might help to broaden an individual's world view—it may lead people to narrow and harden their views. Specifically, Sunstein notes that when like-minded people engage in debate over a controversial issue, the group will tend to move to an extreme position because group members lack information on or interest in alternatives. Social scientists have known for some time that when an individual is exposed to a broad range of political viewpoints, he or she is better able to contrast alternatives, appreciate the views of others, and show tolerance.[41] Many scholars have argued that a democratic citizenry evolves when citizens make decisions after being exposed to conflicting viewpoints. One can imagine that the initiative form of deliberative democracy would serve only to further polarize the population, especially as the Internet becomes a more important source of information.

Although DVD clearly is problematic—and the problems are likely to be exacerbated by Internet voting—the possibilities of Internet voting for iterative deliberative democracy are much more positive. This version allows the multidimensional nature of a given policy issue to be effectively debated because of the iterative nature of the participatory process. In fact, one can easily envision how the efforts in Sacramento and Eugene could have been greatly enhanced by using the Internet. In each case, the public was asked to consider various options for handling city finances, and the Internet would have allowed citizens to interact with the budget more directly than they could in a pencil-and-paper exercise. Just as tax preparation software tallies up an individual's income and tax liability, the Internet could have been used to tally up the mix of city services that an individual wanted and weigh that against the mix of taxes that the person was willing to pay. People could also see more directly how changes in tax policy and service provisions would affect people like themselves. Because the process is iterative, individuals are not asked to make an all-or-nothing choice in one fell swoop but instead to choose from a series of options in several repeated exercises. Over time, people see and come to understand a wider array of options than is normally placed before them; therefore they can make a better choice.

IDD also is quite conducive to Internet voting because the security concerns are slightly lower than they would be in a normal election. Individuals are not making policy directly in this form of deliberative democracy; instead, they are serving as highly informed advisers to their traditionally elected governmental officials. This is a good environment for testing various aspects and forms of Internet voting. Different methods of voter verification, computer interfaces, and voting environments—for example, grocery stores as a site for voting kiosks—all could be evaluated. The use of the Internet to facilitate public involvement in the democratic process clearly is an area that is ripe for investigation and experimentation by entrepreneurial local governments across the country.

In conclusion, while it is important to examine different visions of how Internet voting might influence American political culture, clearly Internet voting can be implemented in the United States without any important conceptual changes in how or in how frequently citizens vote. Optimists like Dick Morris, who assert that the Internet will inevitably usher in a new era of direct democracy, are wrong. Internet voting need not necessarily be synonymous with direct democracy; in fact, using the Internet for initiative voting in places with a large digital divide could be quite problematic. In our opinion, the debate over iterative deliberative and direct voting democracy is an important one—but it should not be conflated with discussions of Internet voting. Whether Internet voting becomes a reality for American voters need not hinge on the outcome of the debate over direct democracy.

CHAPTER 5

Security and Internet Voting

Any discussion of Internet voting inevitably returns to one topic: security. All of the major reports on Internet voting—especially the National Workshop on Internet Voting and the California Internet VotingTask Force reports—have heralded its potential benefits.[1] However, these reports assert that regardless of how beneficial the Internet might be as a voting technology, the potential costs—specifically the security risks—outweigh the benefits. The risk of the system being hacked, targeted by terrorists or rogue nations, plagued by computer viruses, or hijacked by political groups intent on committing vote fraud are seen as challenges that at present are too difficult to overcome.

We do not deny that there are risks associated with using the Internet for voting. Any system that is as complex as the Internet, operating with as many different component parts—including different hardware, software, and interfaces—is going to face the possibility of failure. However, as Florida residents saw in both 2000 and 2002, no voting system is foolproof, including current voter registration, poll site voting, and absentee voting systems. Elections today are fraught with risks: voting machines that fail to work, ballots that are cast but not counted, polls that never open or open late, long lines, tabulation systems that have been tampered with or that simply have been programmed incorrectly, and allegations of vote fraud. Moreover, sadly, the September 11, 2001, terrorist attacks entirely disrupted a major citywide election in New York City. Given that current voting systems are not foolproof, there is no reason to think that Internet voting will be completely foolproof either. In most ways, the risks

associated with Internet voting are not much different from the risks associated with voting in other domains. The goal should be to have Internet
voting systems that are at least as effective as traditional voting systems,
especially in regard to their accessibility and security. However, there is in
fact reason to think that Internet voting will be better.

In this chapter, we examine the issue of security in elections, especially
as presented in the two major reports on Internet voting mentioned earlier. These form the basis for the broadly held view that Internet voting
should not be attempted at present. However, we place the issue of Internet security in the broader context of election administration and note
how many of the security problems debated in these reports already exist
with traditional voting methods. Our argument is two-fold: First, contemporary registration and voting systems are not foolproof, and therefore
the pertinent question about the security of Internet voting systems is not
whether they will be foolproof. Rather, the question is a relative one: in
what ways might Internet voting be more or less secure than contemporary voting systems? Second, once the relative risks associated with
Internet voting are identified, appropriate risk mitigation and management
strategies can be identified. We also discuss how other forces—including
market pressures and government pressures—will lead to improved Internet security in the near future.

The Online World: What Makes Internet Voting Security Different?

From a technological perspective, there is really nothing special about
Internet voting. There is a ballot, a mechanism for recording the votes, a
ballot box, and vote-tallying equipment. Many voters now use touch-
screen voting machines that present an electronic ballot through a
technology that is almost identical to that behind the personal computer.
The vote is recorded, and an electronic ballot box stores the ballot until
it is ready to be counted by electronic tallying equipment. Tabulation can
occur at the polling place after the polls are closed, or the ballots can be
transported to a central location electronically or by some other means
and tabulated there. Technologically speaking, most contemporary electronic voting systems are only a telephone or network connection removed
from being real Internet voting devices.

The main question about Internet voting is whether online ballot transmission is as secure as traditional transmission systems. Before answering
that question, we consider the question of Internet security more broadly.

One reason that computer security is such an important issue is popular perception. Many people have experienced computer failure. Their computer has crashed while they were working on something important, or it contracted a virus that rendered something they were working on useless. They have been kicked off a website or off the Internet entirely by their Internet service provider. They have read about people attacking the Department of Defense website and Microsoft's corporate network and about hackers stealing credit card numbers from online companies. They have, of course, also heard of widespread virus attacks like the Code Red worm. Even the websites of cybersecurity companies like RSA Security, Inc. have been hacked.[2] If the website of a cybersecurity company is not secure, what is?

In his book *Secrets and Lies*, cybersecurity expert Bruce Schneier notes that there is nothing unique about online hacking; people have been hacking ever since there were cool things to hack.[3] Before there were computers, people learned how to hack into telephone systems and make free calls. Bank robbers who break into bank vaults are hackers, getting around security systems to get what they want. Hackers are, in essence, people who figure out new ways of doing things and find weaknesses in existing technologies. There are good hackers and bad hackers. The good hackers are the ones who try to figure out how to write a better piece of software or design a better security system. The bad hackers are the ones who use their computer skills to commit crimes, from breaking into websites in order to deface them to stealing credit card numbers in order to commit fraud.

Schneier argues that what makes computer hacking different from other forms of hacking is that computer hacking takes less skill. There are two main reasons: First, because of the networked nature of the computer world, it is relatively easy to go online and find the tools necessary to engage in hacking. Hacker chat rooms, websites, and the like all contain tools that anyone can use to find flaws in websites and engage in misbehavior. "Script kiddies"—the pejorative term used to describe talentless hackers who just download hacking software and run it without any understanding of how it works or even of what they are doing—can use those tools to wreak havoc, much like a child left alone with a can of spray paint.

Second, the automated nature of computers allows even an unskilled hacker to break into websites. For example, imagine trying to break into a safe that has a combination of three numbers between one and forty. If a person tried to do it alone, by hand, turning the knob to every possible combination—there are 40 x 40 x 40 combinations, or 64,000 total combinations—it would take weeks. A computer, on the other hand, could determine the correct combination in seconds. Automation decreases the skill needed to attack a system because an attack can be attempted over and over until it succeeds. This type of activity is one that computers do quite well!

For example, on October 6, 2002, one of the authors (Alvarez) hooked up his laptop computer to the local area network at his office. He runs a commercially available software firewall that detects, blocks, and tracks inappropriate attempts to access his laptop. Automated computer hacking programs commonly run constant "probes" of computers hooked up to the Internet to see whether they can gain access to those computers through known holes in their security systems. From 9:00 a.m. in the morning until 2:00 p.m., the time this paragraph was being written, the author's firewall detected forty-three attempts to access his laptop from other Internet locations and blocked them; looking at past logs, it can be seen that the laptop receives about ten probes or other access attempts an hour, on a computer system that quite frankly is not very interesting.[4] Imagine how many probes are made on an hourly basis of a major Internet site—like amazon.com—where a successful hacker might gain access to important corporate information or consumer data like credit card numbers.

How Corporate Internet (In)Security Affects Internet Voting

Part of the reason why people think that the Internet is not secure is that they read reports on the insecurity of corporate websites, which have proven especially vulnerable to attack. The problem exists, in part, because historically many corporations have not taken cybersecurity threats seriously. Richard A. Clark, a former cybersecurity expert for President Bush, told corporate executives in April 2002, "You will be hacked. What's more, you deserve to be hacked."[5]

One reason for Clark's remarks is that he thinks that much of corporate America has failed to invest in cybersecurity. Although companies have made progress in adopting security measures—for example, using antivirus software and firewalls to prevent unauthorized access—several studies have argued that many U.S. corporations are not adequately prepared to combat cyberattacks. A 2002 survey conducted for the Business Software Alliance found that many corporate executives understand the overall high threat of Internet attacks in the United States but do not have a realistic view of the possibility of attack on their own corporation. In a survey of 602 information technology (IT) professionals, 62 percent said that in the last year the chance of U.S. firms suffering a major attack had increased, and 47 percent said that in the upcoming year businesses would have to respond to a major attack.[6] Although such perceptions might signal to company managers that they need to invest in better cybersecurity systems, that generally has not happened. In fact, most firms put more resources into preparing for Y2K than they put into security measures, even though hacking can shut down a company's operations and prove very costly to fix.[7]

Many firms have argued that it is difficult to invest in cybersecurity measures because of the current economic downturn. However, considering the costs that successful hacking can impose on a corporation, that is a very short-sighted view. In the first half of 2002, financial losses from cyberattacks—including all forms of attacks, from viruses and stolen laptops to denial of service and financial fraud—exceeded $445 million.[8] Corporations often fail to take into account the costs that they have to pay after the fact or to compare those costs with the costs of effective security measures. As a study by the Internet Security Alliance shows, fixing security problems often simply requires diligence and focus on the part of corporations.[9]

Corporate America faces an array of threats from predators such as foreign governments, foreign corporations, U.S. competitors, independent hackers, and disgruntled employees. Hackers acting opportunistically are responsible for the most common kinds of attacks on corporations, which typically are not premeditated; hackers just happen across a vulnerable website and attack it because they can. Because they have not invested in security, many corporations are easy to access and quite vulnerable to attack, and hackers take advantage of that. In February 2002, a twenty-one-year-old hacker was able to access more than seven servers linking the Internet to the private network of the *New York Times*, making supposedly private information on the network publicly available to anyone using the Internet. The hacker was able to tweak the password policies to broaden access to the names and Social Security numbers of employees, logs of customer orders, and contact information for the Metro and Business desks.[10] The attack was not perpetrated by a disgruntled employee or a competitor. It occurred simply because the company left itself open to such attacks.

There are, of course, many companies that have secure networks, but they are not written about because a secure corporate network that is not attacked is not newsworthy. The Riptech Corporation, which issues its *Internet Security Threat Report* about the problems encountered by corporations, found that 99 percent of attacks were not major security threats, although they often caused great inconvenience.[11] The report asserts that severe attacks can be prevented if firms take the necessary security precautions. Clearly, many corporations do take such precautions. The increase in online banking, bill paying, and tax filing, with no concomitant increase in complaints about system security, illustrates that the systems of many corporations are highly secure. Obviously, Riptech is touting these statistics in large measure to illustrate the strength of its monitoring capacity and its ability to combat and mitigate the damage from attacks on current and potential clients. Attacks over the Internet may be common, but proper security precautions can reduce the damage.

Security concerns affect not only corporations, but also their customers: 60 percent of online users are afraid to conduct business over the Internet because they feel that they will lose control of the use of their personal information if they do.[12] Most online payments are done by credit card, and fraud on the Internet is twelve times more likely than in regular stores;[13] recent data from Gartner Research indicate that just under 2 percent of total online sales in 2001 of $65 billion came from the fraudulent use of credit cards.[14] Many companies believe that threats to security are real but consider them manageable. However, the rise in online fraud and in consumer concerns suggests that some corporations do not take the threats as seriously as they should.

The General Nature of Internet Security

Garfinkel and Spafford, in a popular book on Internet security and commerce, argue that Internet security is a three-fold problem: securing central web servers and the data that reside on them; securing information as it travels between web servers and users; and securing the user's computer. They also point out that Internet security requires verification of identity (both user-to-server and server-to-user) and the retention of information about a transaction between a user and a web server for auditing and "nonrepudiation" purposes.[15]

Conducting any transaction on the Internet, from buying clothes to voting, presents a multitude of opportunities for tampering. A person with unauthorized access to a central web server can capture important information about a transaction and alter that information; the person also could access information in transit between user and server. Furthermore, software could be installed on a computer before a transaction to monitor or alter data being transmitted in either direction. Any important Internet transaction therefore requires close attention to security.

Given the huge stakes associated with commercial transactions on the Internet, a great deal of progress has been made in trying to mitigate the risks. The use of high-level encryption, with software firewalls on both user and web servers that monitor and block unauthorized access, makes it virtually impossible for information to be captured or altered in transit, and hardware firewalls and strong physical security systems make it difficult to gain unauthorized access, electronic or physical, to central web servers.

The important point to make here is that maintaining the security of an Internet voting system is quite similar and perhaps identical to maintaining the security of any other voting system. Anyone who has observed effective polling place operations on election day knows how much time and effort and how many resources are devoted to ensuring the security of ballots and voting machines by local election officials. In California, for example, before being sent to polling places, election materials are placed under seal under the monitoring of multiple individuals; when the polling places open, the seals are broken under the watchful eyes of polling place workers. At the end of the day, all election materials are accounted for, audited, and resealed for transportation to the election office. In many places, transportation is handled by public employees, often law enforcement personnel.[16] Once all election materials have been returned to the election office, they are unsealed and completely accounted for. Security is maintained further by the presence of election monitors (who may be associated with political parties, specific candidates, or interest groups), the media, and interested members of the public. In addition, voting machines, tabulation devices, and election data are kept in physically secure locations. Current practice thus seeks to maximize the security of voting systems and to reduce the possibility of intentional or unintentional tampering with the electoral process. We think that the same administrative controls can maximize the security of Internet voting systems and thereby minimize the risks of deliberate fraud or unintentional mistakes.

Specific Threats

Security experts have identified several types of threat to the security of Internet voting. In one of the more accessible papers on this topic, Avi Rubin outlines the basic security threats to voting over the Internet.[17] The first type of threat is a malicious payload threat. Consider two examples. First, software is readily available that allows a computer to be viewed and controlled remotely, and it has many nonmalicious applications. For example, a network administrator can adjust computers on a corporate network while operating from a remote location, making computer operations more efficient and effective. However, this software could also be used by a hacker to control the personal computer of an individual attempting to vote online. The hacker could control or record the keystrokes of a voter and cast her ballot for her—or a systems administrator could see how anyone using a computer on the network had voted—without anyone else's knowledge. Most people do not have software to detect remote operation software, and it typically operates in a manner that is not easily detected.

Second, a hacker could disrupt voting by using a virus to destroy computers. The Chernobyl virus, for example, is designed to sit benignly on a computer until a certain date, at which time it "explodes," destroying the computer on which it resides. Such a virus could be programmed to explode a week before an election, destroying an individual's computer before he or she is able to vote. Obviously, the individual could try to find another computer, but that makes the voting process more difficult.

Another potential threat to an Internet voting system is the possibility that the voting website will be subject to a denial-of-service attack. A denial-of-service attack occurs when a computer or series of computers sends a series of messages to a website. Websites, and the computer networks that support them, typically are designed to be friendly and to communicate with computers. However, too much communication can flood a network, and automation allows an attacker to send vast amounts of information. Such attacks became prominent in 2000, when a fifteen-year-old shut down several major websites—including those of Yahoo!, CNN, E*trade, and eBay—using this tool. He basically sent so many automated "hello" messages to the websites that they could not support the traffic.[18] As David Weatherall, the chief technology officer for Asta—a company that designs software for combating these attacks—noted, "The barriers for launching these attacks are falling even as the sophistication of these attacks are rising. You hear about script kiddies—teenagers who have been able to launch these programs because they simply download and run them."[19] These attacks cannot be stopped, even when launched by individuals who are not computer whizzes; it is possible only to mitigate their damage.

Another type of attack called spoofing is an attempt to fool an individual into believing that something that he or she is receiving online is legitimate when it is not. In the case of Internet voting, spoofing could result in a person voting at a website that is not the official voting website. Certain types of spoofing may be familiar. For example, if one keys in the name of a popular website with one character transposed or with the wrong domain name (for example, .com instead of .gov), often a website that is either wildly inappropriate or a parody of the original will appear. In the 2000 election, George W. Bush's campaign had to deal with a parody website, www.gwbush.com.

In the case of Internet voting, voters could be taken to a website that looked and functioned like the official election website but did not allow them to cast a real vote; voters would think that they had cast a ballot when they had not. Similarly, software could be installed on a computer to simulate online voting when in fact the computer was not even connected to the Internet. Spoofing also could be done through e-mail, by sending a voter a message that seemed like an official message from an election office but directed the voter to vote at a fraudulent website. Spoofing also has been used by hackers to get unwitting individuals to download Trojan horse software containing malicious code.

Spoofing raises a key problem for voters because the spoofing site could collect the voting authenticity information for all the people who used the site. The person or group hosting the website could then cast real ballots, using the stolen information, for its preferred candidate. This tactic is not unprecedented in the world of fraud. Criminals have placed in shopping centers phony ATM machines that do not dispense money but instead steal the account number and pin for every cardholder who attempts to use the system. The criminals then were able to create phony ATM cards and take money out of those individuals' accounts.[20]

Cybersecurity threats have existed for some time. However, after September 11, these threats are seen in a different light, and the issue of cyberterrorism has become quite prominent. Although hacking has always been a concern, today there is more concern it will be done by nation-states attempting to attack the United States. Cyberterrorism is a potential threat to the U.S. election process. A rogue state can decide an election or disrupt the conduct of an election, thereby undermining the democratic process. The threat of cyberterrorism is not hypothetical. The FBI has been tracking potential threats since September 11 and has found, for example, that individuals from Southeast Asia and the Middle East have been probing the computer systems of many of the nation's most critical infrastructure networks, such as power plants (including nuclear power plants), power grids, water and gas facilities, and emergency telephone systems.[21] The ability of terrorists to commit cyberterrorism is not limited by a lack of knowledge. They have the same access as others to online hacking tools, and as the September 11 attacks illustrate, many terrorists have attended universities and lived in the West. They understand the country's networks and are well versed in ways to exploit their vulnerabilities.

The U.S. Department of Defense has downplayed the threat of cyberattacks. Assistant Secretary of Defense John P. Stenbit has stated that al Qaeda does not like to use attacks that are "dependent on some sophisticated, tricky cyber thing to work." However, the National Security Agency (NSA) and the FBI both view the terrorist threat as significant. As Ron Ross from the NSA stated, "It is not science fiction. A cyber-attack can be launched with fairly limited resources." This threat has been shown to be real by simulations conducted by four Department of Energy national laboratories. Using off-the-shelf technology, the labs were able to mount successful test attacks against electricity grids across the country.[22]

These attacks also can be conducted anonymously. There are means to spoof the TCP/IP packet, the digital information that typically is used to identify the machine on which a cyberattack originated. It also is possible to "hop" from computer to computer and server to server online, making the process of tracing back to the host computer difficult. Even if the source computer can be tracked, the information can prove to be less than useful, as the kidnapping of Daniel Pearl proved. Pearl's kidnappers sent messages from Internet cafes where the computers were used by various people all day long and users proved difficult to track.[23] Terrorists could attack a system, and it would be difficult to know where the attack originated, who the attackers were, and whether a series of seemingly random attempts to breach the Internet voting system were in fact part of a calculated, coordinated effort to attack the system for nefarious purposes.

There are critics who argue that the government is overstating the threat of cyberterrorism.[24] At issue is whether the operational network that is the hacker's true target is actually connected to the Internet in a manner that allows the network to be manipulated and whether the network has the security features needed to keep hackers out. Many of the cyberattacks that people read about in the newspaper consist of annoyances; as James Lewis, director of technology policy at the Center for Strategic and International Studies noted, "When someone defaces a Web site, it's roughly equivalent to spray painting something rude on the outside of a building. It's really just electronic graffiti."[25]

Before concluding that all of these threats are too much to handle, one should remember that the common threats to any Internet voting system—malicious payloads, viruses, denial-of-service attacks, and spoofing—are known threats, with known solutions and mitigation strategies. There is no reason to think that Internet voting websites will be any different from commercial websites—they will come under attack, and they must be designed to eliminate or mitigate each threat. Well-designed networks mitigate the risk of attacks, and a well-designed Internet voting site should do the same.

Somewhat unusually, the critics of Internet voting do not seem to have done systematic research—there is none that we are aware of—to quantify the likelihood of attacks against Internet voting systems. The likelihood and difficulty of the attacks noted above are all quantifiable, especially across types of websites. An example comparable to Internet voting might be the security of financial networks, such as banks. If the destructive potential of security problems with Internet voting is as strong as some suggest, then attacks should be occurring on financial websites, which attackers have a financial incentive to strike. Studies should be done to determine the risk of each type of attack and the effectiveness of various mitigation strategies.

There has been a similar lack of discussion about what we call "dirty tricks campaigns"—ways in which individuals or groups might try to mount an attack on an Internet voting system to achieve some political goal. For example, some senior citizens in Philadephia's first city council district received an anonymous postcard, labeled Official Absentee Ballot Warning. Below that, the postcard stated that the city council incumbent Frank DiCicco (who just happened to be running for reelection) was backed by a "corrupt" political machine and that it was "illegal to vote by absentee ballot" except under some circumstances.[26] This is just one example of a "dirty tricks" campaign. These campaigns, which are commonly seen in elections throughout the United States, typically are mounted to suppress turnout or even to change people's opinions, usually in very close elections. Often they are deliberate misinformation campaigns—negative attacks on candidates or efforts to misinform a candidate's supporters about their right to vote. Such attacks might easily be mounted using the Internet, and they should be included in any discussion of potential security threats associated with Internet voting systems.

Elections as Systems

Cybersecurity expert Bruce Schneier has noted that systems have four key characteristics: they are complex; they typically come together to create a larger, more complex network of systems; they often function and are used in ways that the system designers did not intend; and they are prone to having bugs and failing.[27] These characteristics can apply both to an Internet voting system, which is a computerized system, and to traditional voting systems, which have computerized components but also include other systems—poll site systems, polling systems, vote counting systems, and canvassing systems. Both Internet voting and traditional election systems consist of multiple systems linked in a complex network, and both can be operated in ways that the designers did not intend, which can lead to system failure.

The goal for any system is that it operate with 100 percent reliability. In fact, the major criticism of Internet voting has been that the security or reliability of any Internet voting system cannot be as high as the security in a traditional voting system. But the concerns that have been raised about Internet voting exist today in regard to the existing voting system, and those concerns became evident to the average American—even to the average political scientist and politician—after the 2000 election debacle. That these problems are not unique was emphasized in 2002, when Florida had an almost complete replay of the 2000 election debacle in its primary elections.[28]

Comparing an Internet voting system and a traditional voting system shows that the traditional voting system—especially the traditional absentee voting system—suffers from as many potential threats as does Internet voting, threats that voters are willing to tolerate in part because they have never been as systematically exposed and explicated as have the threats to an Internet voting system.

Let's return to the threats identified by Avi Rubin. Consider, for example, denial-of-service attacks. A knowledgeable individual could initiate such an attack on a government Internet voting website, shutting down the election and denying voters the opportunity to cast their ballot. Such a shutdown might be instigated by a candidate who would benefit from low voter turnout or who wanted to take advantage of the fact that certain demographic groups of voters are likely to vote earlier in the day than are others.[29] Such an attack could bring the outcome of an election into question, with voters and candidates arguing with considerable merit that the election was tarnished and should be invalidated because all voters were not afforded access to the polls and the opportunity to cast a meaningful ballot in the election.[30]

However, consider what a denial-of-service attack would be in the context of Internet voting: a disruption of the ability of an individual to access an election website where he or she can vote. This type of complaint—that voters could not vote because they lacked realistic access to their poll site—is not a fanciful complaint made in some futuristic Internet election. It is a complaint that is heard today in almost any national election. In the 2000 election, there were reports in jurisdictions across the country that voters were denied easy access to the polls because of long lines, poll sites that did not open on time or closed before they were scheduled to close, polling places that ran out of ballots, absentee ballots that were delayed in the mail, and problems with voter registration.

In the March 5, 2002, primary election in California, the election in Los Angeles County went off almost without a hitch. In most of the county's roughly 5,000 precincts, everything was fine, but in 121 precincts, for a variety of reasons, polling places opened late. With approximately 900 registered voters per precinct in Los Angeles County, problems in even a relatively few precincts can affect more than 100,000 registered voters![31] In the 2002 Florida primary, the polls in many precincts did not open on time, machines did not work, and voters could not vote. In Broward County (809 precincts), at least twenty-four precincts opened late due to a lack of polling place workers or to technical problems, while in Miami-Dade County (754 precincts), at least sixty-eight precincts were not open two hours after polling should have begun at 7:00 a.m. and at least thirty-two still were not open at 10:50 a.m.[32] Voters in those precincts suffered a denial-of-service attack.

Other types of denial-of-service attacks occur in the current voting process in the United States, outside of polling places. In the 2002 general election, for example, a series of computer software snafus in King County, Washington (where Seattle is located), resulted in a huge denial-of-service attack on absentee voters. According to press reports and a review by the Washington secretary of state's office, the difficulties stemmed from problems in programming computer software; until the software was programmed correctly, ballots could not be printed and mailed.[33] For the November 5, 2002, election, absentee ballots were supposed to be available on October 16; however, it was not until October 22 that the first mailing of about 80,000 ballots occurred. Another 124,000 were mailed on October 25, and 216,000 more were mailed between October 26 and 29. An untold number of the more than 400,000 absentee ballots mailed to voters did not arrive in their mailboxes in sufficient time for voters to complete their ballot and return it. Voter turnout in King County was much lower in the 2002 election (53.2 percent) than in 2000 (74.7 percent) and 1998 (61.6 percent). The drop in turnout—combined with the apparent popularity of absentee voting in King County (in the 1998 and 1999 elections, of the ballots cast, 44 percent and 48 percent respectively were absentee ballots) and the absentee voting problems—indicates that the absentee balloting snafu might have had a dramatic impact on voter participation.[34] Again, this could constitute a denial-of-service attack of enormous proportions.

Next, consider the idea that, if a voter voted online, someone else could vote his or her ballot—or discover how he or she voted—by maliciously using special computer technology. Again, this threat to Internet voting already exists in the world of traditional absentee voting. Other than a signature, there is no way to be sure that the person who requested an absentee ballot is the person who completed the ballot, nor is it possible to verify that a voter completed the ballot without being coerced to vote or reimbursed for voting in certain ways. Critics also raise concerns about whether absentee voting is less accurate and less timely than in-person precinct voting, and they wonder whether it reduces the symbolic value of voting in person at a public polling place.[35]

We do not think that election fraud is rampant, especially absentee voting fraud, but it is clear that there are places throughout the United States where voting fraud has occurred and continues to occur. In a report on National Public Radio, Wade Goodwyn examined the types of vote fraud that occur in Dallas, Texas.[36] He found certain pockets in the city where absentee voting fraud had become an art. There, skilled political machines commited vote fraud by abusing a law allowing anyone over the age of sixty-five to vote as an absentee. Because Texas election law requires the names of all individuals who requested an absentee ballot to be made public along with the day that their ballot was mailed, these political machines have operatives waiting at the mailbox of absentee voters when their ballot arrives. These operatives provide "voting assistance" to voters, although voting assistance often involves taking the ballots from their mailbox and voting the ballot.

However, a recent empirical study of voting fraud in California found surprisingly few investigated cases of fraud.[37] Between 1994 and 2002, 1,581 voting fraud cases were opened by the California secretary of state's election fraud investigation unit; of these, seventy-nine were prosecuted and sixty resulted in convictions. During the same period, more than 77 million votes were cast in California statewide elections alone (this does not include the millions and millions of votes cast in local elections). Given those figures, California had one prosecuted case of voting fraud for every 975,000 votes cast in statewide elections and one conviction for roughly every 1.3 million votes cast! Furthermore, most of the voting fraud cases regarded allegations of voter registration irregularities; not a single case of absentee voter fraud was prosecuted during that period. There is every reason to be concerned about absentee voting fraud, but the empirical evidence indicates that it is relatively rare, even in states like California that have liberal absentee voting procedures.

Internet voting can provide a level of security sufficient to prevent people from intercepting a ballot not intended for them. By requiring voters to authenticate their identity electronically before they receive a ballot and after they vote their ballot, Internet voting can provide a higher level of security, ensuring that the correct voter both received and cast the ballot. This can be accomplished by using the same standard methods of encryption that are used in secure commercial transactions: voters can be required to use password-protected digital certificates to authenticate themselves; their ballot can be encrypted using 128-byte encryption technology; and if any attempt is made to read or alter the ballot, both the voter and election officials can detect the attempt. Of course, there is still the threat of voters being affected by Trojan horse software, but that is no different from the threat in the traditional absentee voting process that an absentee ballot will be intercepted and tampered with in some way.

Other critics of Internet voting have argued that there is a "black box" problem with voting online; voters have to trust that the system works as advertised since they cannot see their physical ballot.[38] These critics argue that voters who use the system will not be confident that the ballot they cast on their computer will actually be counted as cast by election officials.

Voters will fear that their vote will somehow vanish into the Internet ether or otherwise be lost or that it will be identified with them and thus not be anonymous. These critics also express concern that because there is no paper trail, an Internet voting system cannot be audited; if a problem was discovered with the ballots there would be no way to generate a recount.

Again, this is a problem that is not unique to Internet voting. Many people use voting technologies that have proven to be inaccurate in recording votes. For example, the Caltech/MIT Voting Technology Project found that a small but significant number of ballots cast on all existing voting technology platforms—punch cards, optical scan, direct recording equipment (DRE), and lever machines—are not counted.[39] Many voters who cast ballots in Florida during the 2000 presidential election were certain that they had used the voting equipment accurately but found that their ballot probably was excluded. These votes did not vanish into the Internet ether or into a computerized black box. Instead, they vanished into the existing netherworld surrounding the current poll site and absentee balloting process, which is ruled by paper punch-card and optical scan ballots. Voters who use lever equipment are in a worse position than online voters are. Lever machines, which are prevalent in the Northeast, count ballots using a mechanism designed at the turn of the twentieth century. Voters have no way of knowing whether the machine counted their vote at all. Equally as important, there is no way to audit voting on lever machines; these machines leave no paper trail, unlike electronic equipment, which leaves an electronic and digital imaging trail.

Mercuri also raises the issue of anonymity. Anyone who knows how absentee votes are counted across the nation probably would agree that the anonymity of Internet voters would be at least as protected as that of voters using the traditional absentee voting system, if not more so. Under the current system, the absentee voter's ballot comes in an envelope that contains all of the voter's identification information. The voter has to trust that the person checking absentee ballots against the voter rolls separates the voter information from the absentee ballot before examining the ballot; otherwise, it would be easy to see how a voter voted.[40] Similarly, there may be situations in which only a single individual votes by absentee ballot. Such votes, obviously, are not anonymous because they can easily be tied to a voter. And some states, like North Carolina, actually attach a unique number to all absentee ballots so that every absentee ballot in the state can be tied back to a voter. With an Internet voting system, the Internet ballots could be integrated into an existing system that could count all ballots, including the ballots voted over the Internet, at once, guaranteeing anonymity for the voter.

One last distinguishing characteristic of Internet voting pointed out by critics is the vastly increased scale on which fraud or tampering might be perpetrated. Critics allege that it is very hard to commit large-scale fraud or tampering in a contemporary election because that would require systematic coordination by hundreds or thousands of individuals, either across a number of polling places or at many different residential addresses. Most elections in the United States are not closely contested, but even those that are would require a shift of hundreds or thousands of votes to change the outcome. Under current practices, it would be very difficult, if not impossible, to coordinate the actions of enough individuals to change the outcome of an election fraudulently. However, these critics argue that with voting over the Internet, fraud could be automated. A hacker who cracked an Internet voting system would not have to worry about getting the help of hundreds or thousands of people to swing the outcome of the election. The hacker could do it alone, with just a few keystrokes and the click of a mouse.

There is no doubt that this is true, especially if a computer hacker was able to access the servers that received, stored, and tabulated all of the ballots cast on an Internet voting system. But again, we have to emphasize that this risk exists today in most election offices through the nation; except in the few small counties that still conduct paper ballot elections, most ballots are tabulated electronically, using computer technology that could be hacked and tampered with. The risk exists now that a hacker could insert a few lines of computer code into the software used to tabulate votes cast using punch cards, optical scanning devices, and electronic means. As long as the computers associated with voting or tabulation are, or at some point have been, connected to any network, they suffer from the same risk as an Internet voting system.

The likelihood of this type of attack is the real issue. On that point the critics of Internet voting are silent; as far as we are aware, not a single publicly available study has attempted to quantify the risks associated with different types of security threats to Internet voting systems. There is, from sources like the national Internet Fraud Complaint Center and the National Infrastructure Protection Center, a growing amount of quantitative information on the various types of online fraud and security risks.[41] Relatively little is known about the basic incidence of security risks and fraud associated with current election administration procedures and voting machines, however. Clearly these two sets of security risks, and how they might be enhanced or minimized in an Internet voting system, demand thorough and careful study and analysis.

Technical Solutions to the Internet Voting Security Problem

Many people think that Internet voting is inherently problematic; others think that just some basic encryption—the kind used to secure basic online transactions every day—can ensure that Internet voting is completely safe. In our opinion, neither view is correct. Every system faces threats that have to be minimized, and the threats to Internet voting are not so great that they cannot be surmounted. However, it is not possible to make voting work the way buying a book from amazon.com does. We are not technical experts; however, an examination of existing cybersecurity technologies shows that secure voting can occur online. Effective security for Internet voting requires integrating security measures that by themselves cannot make an Internet voting system secure. However, in tandem with other security tools, they can be part of an effective protocol that allows voters to use an Internet voting system with confidence that their vote will be counted. This protocol begins with the development of an effective physical security system for the server supporting the voting process. Then, through the use of identification and authentication procedures, secure connections between voter and server, and encryption, an effective Internet voting system can be created that is as secure, and likely more secure, than traditional absentee voting systems.[42]

Developing an effective Internet voting security system may require thinking "outside the box" about how U.S. elections are conducted. One of the most troubling security problems facing any Internet voting system is denial-of-service (DOS) attacks. Because any given U.S. election is held on a specific day, DOS attacks are one of the most significant security threats to Internet voting. However, the risk can be mitigated by ensuring that there is enough bandwidth to handle all of the extra packets that might hit an Internet voting site during a DOS attack and that the network is effectively monitored. Allowing Internet voting to occur over a fourteen- or twenty-one-day period before election day also would reduce the threat. Many jurisdictions already allow early voting and absentee voting—which is considered the closest analogy to Internet voting—over several weeks preceding an election. Allowing Internet voters to participate well before election day makes it much less likely that a DOS attack could "take out" an entire election; it also could make the process even that much more accessible to more voters.

Effective Physical and Logical Security

Ensuring physical security, especially for the servers housing election data, is a critical first step to creating a secure Internet voting system. There are two types of physical security concerns: the security of the host servers that process Internet voting data and the security of the user's computer. However, ensuring the physical security of a server goes beyond just making sure that there is a locked door controlling access to the host computer. A secure host site also protects against a range of catastrophic events, such as the physical severing of a digital connection to the host site, loss of service from a digital service provider, and destruction of the facility where the host data are stored.

Effective system monitoring at the host site also can serve to protect against some of the threats mentioned. State-of-the-art firewalls and monitoring systems can detect probes of the system and take appropriate action when warranted.[43] Monitoring can help to determine whether a DOS attack is occurring, allowing the host site to try to locate the source of the attack and isolate it. DOS attacks bring up a final characteristic of physical security: the host should have excess bandwidth that can be put to work when the network is threatened, as in a DOS attack. This increases the cost of an Internet voting system, but excess capacity provides insurance against DOS attacks, and if current trends in computer hardware costs continue, the marginal cost of adding more system capacity should not be very great.

Today, most large state and county election offices have some physical and computer security systems and knowledgeable information technology staff who can increase the security of their infrastructure to facilitate Internet voting.[44] However, for widespread use of Internet voting, standards must be established and guidelines developed to help state and local election administrators understand exactly how to secure their computer facilities.

The other physical security issue concerns the voter's computer. Securing the platform from which a vote is cast has long been considered essential to eliminating voting fraud. The idea has been that placing voting machines inside special public locations makes it difficult for various forms of fraud—for example, coercion and vote buying—to occur. Therein lies the basic concern that many observers have about liberalized absentee voting regulations; they eliminate this important device for maintaining clean elections. By extension, many observers are concerned about whether people should be allowed to vote from their home or office computer or some other electronic device unless the physical security of these computers or devices can be ensured.

This concern has led some to propose that any Internet system that is implemented include a procedure whereby voters essentially "reboot" their computer; install a new, "clean" operating system; vote; and then "reboot" again to reinstall their original operating system. Proponents argue that this will help ensure that users' computers are not infected with a virus or other malicious software that somehow affects their Internet vote.[45] Another idea is to build antivirus software, at least some minimum version that would check the voter's computer for the sorts of malicious code that might be used to target Internet voting, into the voting application itself (downloadable Java-applets, for example).

Security from Voter to Voting Box

Encryption often is seen as a panacea for Internet security problems, and it certainly is an important component of Internet voting security systems. One reason that encryption is important is that it assures voters that their vote cannot be read while it is stored in a digital format. However, there is more to the security of Internet voting than encryption. Security begins with an effective procedure for identifying and authenticating voters. With current by-mail and poll site voting procedures, voters identify and authenticate themselves through the most basic of methods—they swear on a form that they are who they say they are and that they are eligible to vote when they register. Then, with by-mail absentee voting, the voter is authenticated by comparing the signature on the signed envelope containing the ballot with the signature on the voter's registration form. Poll site authentication often is even less rigorous, not requiring any identification at all. In the end, the current system of voter identification and authentication is basically built on trust; generally speaking, unless there is reason for suspicion, people can register and vote without providing much identifying information and need not necessarily even appear in person.

With Internet voting, identification and authorization can be done in a multistep process. First, voters register, either in person or online, and obtain credentials that allow them to vote online. This is the process that was used in the 2000 Voting Over the Internet project run by the Federal Voting Assistance Program for eligible American citizens overseas. The system can be made more secure by adding password protection to the system, whereby voters must have a digital certificate to vote and also provide a user name, a password, and an answer to a challenge question in order to access the system.

Once a voter is authenticated, it is possible to secure the pathway between the voter and the voting server through standard techniques, such as use of secure socket layers (SSL) connections. The key to security here is for voters to be able to cast their votes secretly and to validate that their ballot has not been tampered with in transit. The first issue can be addressed with encryption. The voted ballot can be encrypted by using public key technology to ensure that even if the ballot is intercepted, no one can determine its contents. The second issue also can be dealt with by using public key technology. The ballot cast by the voter can be "signed" and sent to the election server, where it is signed and then sent back to the voter to be verified. If the ballot sent from the server does not match the one sent by the voter, the voter will know that there is a problem with the system and can abort the process and alert an election official about the problem so it can be further investigated. Another proposed solution calls for the voter's choices to be stored on some medium (paper or electronic) at the same time that the vote is electronically stored and for this medium to be given to election officials as an independent audit record. This latter solution is the modular voting architecture (nicknamed the FROG system) proposed by the Caltech/MIT Voting Technology Project (2001).[46]

It is possible to design and implement an Internet voting system with a high degree of security, but important trade-offs must be made. Although many security problems associated with the transmission of voting materials from voters to election officials can be solved by increasing the level of security, higher security can make it more difficult for some potential voters to access and use the system. We return to this point in chapter 7, when we discuss some recent attempts to implement real Internet voting systems in the 2000 election.

Pressures to Improve Cybersecurity and Security for Online Voting

The current political and business climate is likely to create pressure to improve cybersecurity. Post–September 11 concerns about cyberterrorism have increased the government's interest in protecting the nation's infrastructure, including the Internet. The war on terrorism and the creation of the Department of Homeland Security have done much to change the climate in government about cyberterrorism. In January 2003, the President's Critical Infrastructure Protection Board issued *The National Strategy to Secure Cyberspace*, a report that outlined the federal role in securing the Internet and made recommendations for actions to be taken by corporations, universities, state and local governments, and private individuals to secure their systems.[47] The report identified the need for greater responsiveness among corporations and citizens to ensure that their computers are secured from basic threats, such as viruses, and that they have firewalls to discourage attacks. More advanced recommendations were made regarding the need for effective system maintenance and monitoring by the government and the corporate community. One of the reasons why many cyberattacks are successful is that the entity attacked is not aware of basic flaws in its security and does not monitor the traffic on its network. Monitoring can identify many of the threats that currently exist online.

The government also will fund more research into cybersecurity. The Cyber Security Research and Development Act, which was enacted in November 2002, allocates $903 million over five years for basic research into a variety of computer security issues, including authentication, cryptography, intrusion detection, networking, privacy, network security architecture, risk quantification, wireless security, and emerging threats. The National Science Foundation (NSF) also will fund several centers for cutting-edge computer and network security research that will bring together scholars from a variety of disciplines and institutions to produce new Internet and network security techniques that can be widely disseminated, tested, and adopted.

In addition to supporting research, the cybersecurity act provides funds to increase the pool of experts in computer security. Grants will be awarded to colleges and universities to establish or improve computer and network security programs for undergraduate and graduate students and to promote collaboration among schools, government agencies, and the corporate community. Internship programs will be developed to give students practical experience in corporate security, and other programs will bring academics into corporate and government settings. The NSF also will fund a trainee program to encourage doctoral students to pursue dissertations in network security and to bring people doing security research into government and corporate settings so that their research has practical applications in the broader community. The program also will encourage new graduates to continue their research in academic settings after completing their dissertations.

There are likely to be growing pressures from the private sector as well. In a recent magazine article, Charles C. Mann wrote about how security may change in the future, pointing out that the growing threat of Internet attacks on corporations may create incentives for dramatically improving the security of computer software, hardware, and the Internet in general.[48] Specifically, Mann noted that the potential for corporate losses from cyberattacks will likely lead Wall Street analysts to begin seriously evaluating corporate security; corporations that have lax security or that use products known to have security holes could find their stock downgraded. The insurance industry likewise could dramatically raise the premiums for companies that do not follow appropriate Internet security procedures. The financial implications of such actions and the threat of negative publicity will force corporations to improve their security.

Similar pressures could be placed on the makers of home computers and computer software. For example, the government or private groups could rate computers for "cybersafety" by using the same data that would be used by Wall Street and the insurance industry. A computer might receive a failing score if it uses an operating system with known security flaws or if it does not come with virus protection software and a free year of online virus software upgrades. Computer manufacturers could be required to note the computer's rating in all advertising and on the package it comes in. To avoid having to place a "failed" sticker on all of their products, computer and software manufacturers would make security a higher priority. Some computer security experts have begun to call for measures to hold software companies accountable for producing and selling software products that are easily exploited by viral and other malicious electronic attacks.[49]

Of course, pressure would trickle down to hardware manufacturers as well. Imagine, for instance, that Wall Street announced that it would downgrade the stock of any corporation that used specific products from certain technology companies because of the associated security risks. Two outcomes would be likely. First, the threat would force hardware manufacturers to take security more seriously. Products would be more thoroughly tested before being brought to market, and products would be monitored more carefully in the field. Second, there would be more entrants into the market, putting additional pressure on manufacturers to innovate and invest in the research and development of more secure products. Such pressures are leading to industry efforts to develop new approaches to computer security. For example, the Trusted Computing Group, founded by industry heavyweights Advanced Micro Devices, Hewlett-Packard, IBM, Intel, and Microsoft, is working on the development of industry standards for hardware-based computer security.[50]

We believe that in addition to the private and public sector pressures noted above, the need for Internet voting itself should drive state and federal agencies to push the research and technology envelope by supporting additional study and development of basic computer and network security technology. Earlier we criticized the National Science Foundation for not initiating and funding Internet voting research and development programs as called for in the IPI Internet voting workshop report. Other agencies involved in technology and communications, like the Defense Advanced Research Projects Agency (DARPA), the National Institute of Standards and Technology (NIST), and the Federal Communications Commission (FCC), could get involved in these efforts as well. Agencies that assist in the conduct of elections, like the Federal Election Commission (FEC), and any new national election agencies that are formed in the immediate future as a result of new federal election reform legislation also should get involved in funding research and development for Internet security systems.

Security Concerns and Internet Voting: Two Sides of the Coin

For many critics, the primary source of concern about Internet voting comes from two highly touted reports: *A Report on the Feasibility of Internet Voting*, which was produced by the California Internet Voting Task Force, and *Report of the National Workshop on Internet Voting: Issues and Research Agenda*, which was sponsored by the National Science Foundation and produced by the Internet Policy Institute. The text of the second and third paragraphs of the executive summary of the California report italicized below, with italics added, is perhaps the most widely quoted of either report:

> The implementation of Internet voting would allow increased access to the voting process for millions of potential voters who do not regularly participate in our elections. *However, technological threats to*

the security, integrity and secrecy of Internet ballots are significant. The possibility of "Virus" and "Trojan Horse" software attacks on home and office computers used for voting is very real and, although they are preventable, could result in a number of problems ranging from a denial of service to the submission of electronically altered ballots.

Despite these challenges, it is technologically possible to utilize the Internet to develop an additional method of voting that would be at least as secure from vote-tampering as the current absentee ballot process in California. *At this time, it would not be legally, practically or fiscally feasible to develop a comprehensive remote Internet voting system that would completely replace the current paper process used for voter registration, voting, and the collection of initiative, referendum and recall petition signatures.*

Reading the italicized portions, it is easy to understand the qualms that people have about Internet voting. Such a system is portrayed as being subject to serious and specific threats. Computer viruses—which anyone with a computer has encountered—might attack a computer or the system itself. Hackers could attack a voter's computer and even alter the ballot without the voter's knowledge. And the whole system might come crashing down on itself in a denial-of-service attack, which would ensure that no ballots reached the central voting system. Such security problems lead up to the claim that for many is the final nail in the coffin: "At this time, it would not be legally, practically or fiscally feasible to develop a comprehensive remote Internet voting system that would completely replace the current paper process used for voter registration, voting, and the collection of initiative, referendum and recall petition signatures."

Now go back and read the portions of the text that are not italicized. These sections strongly suggest that, as we argue, Internet voting could be beneficial to the citizenry, feasible, and conducted securely. The benefits of Internet voting are touted at the very beginning of the report's executive summary. As we discussed in chapter 3, a sizable percentage of the population does not vote, and many of these individuals do not vote because doing so is inconvenient. Internet voting can allow them to cast ballots easily because they can vote on any computer that can be connected to the Internet. Also, note that these experts point out that although the possibility of attacks is real, it also is preventable. It is impossible to create a perfectly secure voting system; the current system of paper ballots is not completely secure, and neither would an Internet voting system be. However, tools exist today to overcome the security challenges posed by Internet voting—something that opponents of Internet voting often fail to note.

This excerpt of the executive summary closes with a sentence noting that a comprehensive Internet voting system that would completely replace the current paper process is not feasible. We agree wholeheartedly with that statement, and we do not propose completely replacing the current system with Internet voting tomorrow. We believe that Internet voting can be successfully implemented now for specific populations of voters—such as military, overseas, and disabled voters—to supplement, not supplant, the existing election system.

CHAPTER **6**

Analogies

Imagine this: Instead of voting on a single election day at poll sites across the state, citizens cast ballots from the comfort of their home, office, or local coffee shop or even while they are away on business. In fact, there is no fixed election day to speak of; registered voters are given access to their ballots a month before the election and can cast them at their convenience up to the close of what is "election day" everywhere else in the United States. From the perspective of election administrators, managing this system is different from managing a traditional election system but also in many ways easier. No longer must they find and reserve poll sites—maybe only one in a small jurisdiction, but 5,000 in the nation's largest—for election day. No longer must they recruit, train, and pay poll workers.[1] No longer is there one day on which all things—poll sites, poll workers, equipment, ballots, voter rolls, and of course, the voters themselves—have to come together flawlessly. Instead, the new system allows citizens to vote at their leisure during a multiweek voting period. The election administrator, having given all voters access to the ballots at the beginning of the election period, waits to count the ballots.

For many, this sounds like the world of Internet voting, which can give voters access to their online ballot at the beginning of the voting period and allow them to cast their online ballot any time until the polls close. However, the preceding is not a futuristic description of Internet voting; it is a broad description of how voting has been done recently in the state of Oregon, which uses universal vote-by-mail balloting for its elections. It also describes voting for roughly one-third of the participating electorate in states like California that have liberal absentee voting procedures that permit anyone to obtain and cast an absentee ballot, without a special reason.

In Oregon, there are no polling places, no rush to vote on election day, no effort to recruit poll workers or select poll sites. Voters are sent ballots in the weeks leading up to the election, along with a detailed voter information packet that includes information about the ballot, the races, and the proper way to vote. Then, between the time they get the ballot and election day, voters cast their ballots however they want, whenever they want, wherever they want. There is no pressure to fit the democratic process into a twelve-hour window on a single day in libraries, schools, firehouses, and garages across the state.

Most states do not use voting by mail as the only means of voting. However, as table 6-1 shows, in twenty-two states a voter can get an absentee ballot without giving any special reason. In many states, such as California, any voter can ask to be listed as a permanent absentee voter; being so listed qualifies the voter to receive an absentee ballot without having to request one for each election. In addition, thirteen states—fourteen including Oregon—have early voting, which allows voters to go to certain centralized polling places, typically in government buildings, and vote before election day using the same equipment they would use at the polls. Both liberal vote-by-mail procedures and early voting are designed to make voting easier and more accessible to those who find it difficult to get to a polling place on a certain day and to thereby increase voter turnout.

Today, many election administrators are clamoring for expanded early and absentee voting to address the growing population that they have to serve. In Maryland, for example, election administrators view "no-fault" by-mail absentee voting and early voting as a means of facilitating voting and increasing turnout while decreasing the long lines that form on election day.[2] Additional poll sites can be difficult to acquire, and voting by mail provides an opportunity to put a poll site in every home in the state. Similarly, Internet voting could turn every computer attached to the Internet into a polling site.

Critics and supporters alike often compare Internet voting and absentee voting. Here we examine both absentee and early-voting programs to learn what they can teach about Internet voting. We are especially interested in how these programs have affected turnout among various parts of the voting population. Because of Oregon's move to universal voting by mail, its system is the focus of our discussion; however, we consider other

Table 6-1. *Early Voting and Liberalized Absentee Voting Provisions, by State*

State	Early voting, 2000	Percentage of votes cast in person before election day, 1996	Liberalized absentee voting, 2000	Percentage of votes cast by absentee ballot, 1996	Total percentage of votes cast before election day,1996
Alabama		0		3	3
Alaska		4	Y	5	9
Arizona	Y	2	Y	22	24
Arkansas		9	Y	5	14
California	Y	0	Y	19	19
Colorado		11	Y	10	20
Connecticut		0		7	7
Delaware		0		6	6
District of Columbia		1		3	4
Florida		1		7	7
Georgia		1		2	3
Hawaii	Y	1	Y	11	12
Idaho	Y	1	Y	6	7
Illinois		1		4	4
Indiana		1		5	6
Iowa	Y	3	Y	9	11
Kansas		5	Y	11	15
Kentucky		1		5	6
Louisiana		1		2	3
Maine		1	Y	5	5
Maryland		1		3	3
Massachusetts		1	Y	3	4
Michigan		1	a	14	14
Minnesota		1		6	7
Mississippi		1		2	3
Missouri		1		3	3
Montana		1	Y	8	9
Nebraska		0	Y	6	6
Nevada	Y	5	b	6	11
New Hampshire		1		6	7
New Jersey		0		3	3
New Mexico	Y	10	Y	6	15
New York		0		3	3
North Carolina	Y	1	Y	3	4
North Dakota		1		5	6
Ohio		2	a	7	9
Oklahoma	Y	2	Y	3	5

Table 6-1. *Early Voting and Liberalized Absentee Voting Provisions, by State, continued*

State	Early voting, 2000	Percentage of votes cast in person before election day, 1996	Liberalized absentee voting, 2000	Percentage of votes cast by absentee ballot, 1996	Total percentage of votes cast before election day, 1996
Oregon	Vote by mail	0	Vote by mail	46	46
Pennsylvania		0		4	4
Rhode Island		0		3	3
South Carolina		0		2	2
South Dakota		3		6	8
Tennessee	Y	19		2	21
Texas	Y	23		4	26
Utah		1	Y	3	4
Vermont		1	Y	7	7
Virginia	Y	1		3	5
Washington		0	Y	37	37
West Virginia		1		2	3
Wisconsin	Y	0	Y	3	3
Wyoming		1	Y	12	13
United States	15 states	3	23 states	8	10

Source: Committee for the Study of the American Electorate, "Two Pro-Participation Reforms Actually Harm Voter Turnout," January 9, 2001 (Washington); J. Eric Oliver, "The Effects of Eligibility Restrictions and Party Activity on Absentee Voting and Overall Turnout," *American Journal of Political Science*, vol. 40 (May 1996), pp. 501–02; Bureau of the Census, 1996 Current Population Survey Voter Supplement, by courtesy of Raymond E. Wolfinger. Table originally was constructed by John Mark Hansen for the National Commission on Federal Election Reform.

a. Oliver classifies Michigan and Ohio as states with "expanded" eligibility for absentee voting.

b. This omission is in error in the original source.

examples of universal vote-by-mail elections and absentee voting from other jurisdictions. There is much to learn from absentee voting, much of which flies in the face of conventional wisdom. However, we argue that there is nothing in our findings to show that Internet voting is in some way hindered by comparison with absentee voting. Neither method is a panacea. However, in today's mobile society, there is a clear niche for voting methods that allow voters to vote over multiple days from multiple locations.

Absentee and Early Voting: The Broader Trends

Although Oregon is a pioneer in the use of absentee voting, it is not the only state that has found it to be useful. In fact, absentee voting has been around in various forms since before the United States was an independent nation. Massachusetts introduced absentee voting in 1635 to allow people who lived on the state's western frontier to vote in elections by proxy.[3] However, until recently, absentee voting laws were narrowly tailored to accommodate voters in only the most pressing situations, such as absence due to military service. The modern impetus for absentee voting laws was the Civil War. Some Civil War military units were allowed to return home during lulls in the fighting (for example, units from Indiana). Other states (for example, Illinois) allowed military personnel to mark a ballot, seal it in an envelope, and mail it to a person in their home state who would cast the ballot at a polling place on election day, in what was essentially a vote by proxy.[4] Each state determined the way in which military personnel outside the state could participate in elections. They developed multiple mechanisms for military absentee voting that resulted in a hodgepodge of rules and regulations. The nonmilitary voter was left out of the loop; only Vermont and Kansas passed limited procedures for civilian absentee voting.[5]

Several states adopted absentee voting laws between the Civil War and World War I. During the Spanish American War, Delaware, Nevada, New Jersey, New York, and Rhode Island all adopted laws enfranchising soldiers engaged in military service away from home; by the time the nation entered World War I, many states had done so.[6] However, the laws became moot in 1918, when high-level Army officials announced that voting would interfere with military operations in Europe and other foreign locations and that military personnel on foreign soil would not be allowed to vote. B. A. Martin summarized the impact of the confused situation on the military vote in 1918: "It is evident, however, that with the difficulties involved, such as the problem of establishing state election commissions in each military camp and the general absentee-ballot red tape of voting through the mail, a very small percentage of the servicemen voted in the 1918 congressional elections."[7] In addition, Virginia adopted a law in 1916 that explicitly permitted absentee by-mail voting by residents who were temporarily in a foreign country, the first instance of nonmilitary overseas absentee voting that we found in the historical record.[8]

The situation for military personnel became even more complicated during World War II, especially in the federal elections of 1942 and 1944. Millions of American military personnel were located all across the world, unlike in previous military mobilizations, which were fought in a much more geographically limited theater of operations. In addition, military units consisted of personnel from many different states, making it virtually impossible for states to establish temporary polling locations in military camps. Also, by the 1940s all but three states (Delaware, Kentucky, and New Mexico) had absentee voting provisions, and all but another three (Arkansas, Texas, and Vermont) required voter registration.

Although most states had absentee voting laws, the specific procedures and regulations varied greatly. For example, there were important differences in the number of days between when absentee ballot applications were received and when the ballot had to be back in the hands of election officials to be counted. Vermont required that ballots be returned in twelve days, Connecticut allowed for ninety, and twenty-seven other states provided voters with a minimum of thirty days to return their ballot.[9] In September 1942, Congress passed Public Law 712, which allowed any citizen eligible to vote in his or her state of residence who was serving in any branch of the armed forces in a time of war to vote in federal elections. These voters would not be required to register; instead they could simply complete a postcard application (developed by each state in accordance with its own registration and absentee voting laws) and return it by mail to their state. Once the state election officials received the postcard application, they would return a special "war ballot" containing all federal and state races in which the citizen was eligible to vote.[10] Of course, members of the armed forces also could choose to vote by using the general absentee voting procedures for their state of residence instead of voting the war ballot.

Although only twenty states adopted the federal ballot, this expansion of federal involvement in military absentee voting led thirty-eight states to significantly change their existing laws or to pass new legislation simplifying voting procedures for absent military personnel.[11] Only 111,773 federal war ballots were cast in the twenty states that adopted it, but evidence indicates that the federal expansion led states to liberalize absentee voting procedures in ways that increased the participation of overseas military personnel. It has been estimated that approximately 48 percent of all eligible armed forces personnel voted in the 1944 presidential election, casting roughly 4.4 million ballots.[12]

Absentee and Early Voting Today

Absentee voting became a national phenomenon after World War II, but many different rules still governed the process. New York state today has roughly the same strict restrictions on absentee voting seen in many other

Table 6-2. *Variations in Absentee Voting Laws among States*

States with traditional restrictions on absentee voting eligibility		
Alabama	Louisiana	North Dakota
Arkansas	Maryland	Pennsylvania
Connecticut	Massachusetts	Rhode Island
Delaware	Minnesota	South Carolina
Florida	Mississippi	South Dakota
Georgia	Missouri	Tennessee
Idaho	Nebraska	Utah
Illinois	New Hampshire	Virginia
Indiana	New Jersey	West Virginia
Kansas	New York	Wisconsin
Kentucky	North Carolina	
States with expanded absentee voting eligibility		
Alaska	Maine	New Mexico
Colorado	Michigan	Ohio
District of Columbia		
States with universal liberal absentee voting eligibility		
Arizona	Montana	Texas
California	Nevada	Washington
Hawaii	Oklahoma	Wyoming
Iowa	Oregon	

Source: J. Eric Oliver, "The Effects of Eligibility Restrictions and Party Activity on Absentee Voting and Overall Turnout," *American Journal of Political Science,* vol. 40, no. 2 (1996), pp. 501–02.

states decades ago: voters can cast an absentee ballot only if they are going to be out of the jurisdiction on election day or if they are disabled; in order to receive an absentee ballot, they have to give what the election administrators consider a valid reason. Other states have more moderate restrictions on eligibility. For example, in Ohio, voters must give a reason for voting as an absentee, but the list of acceptable reasons is quite long. Finally, states like California allow voters to cast an absentee ballot without giving any reason. Residents in these "no-fault" absentee voting states can sometimes register as permanent absentee voters; before every election, they are sent an absentee ballot without having to request one. Table 6-2 lists the eligibility standards for absentee voting by state, with states defined as having strict, expanded, or universal absentee voting.

With these reforms, use of absentee voting exploded in many states. In 1972 less than 3.5 percent of all ballots cast across the nation were absentee ballots; twenty-two years later, more than 7 percent of all voters voted as absentees.[13] In states with no-fault absentee voting, the results were even more striking. For example, in California, absentee voting went from 4.4 percent of votes cast in 1978 to 26 percent in the 2002 primary.[14] More and more voters want to vote in the privacy of their own home. This often is especially true in general elections in states like California, where ballots are very long and cluttered with numerous ballot measures.[15]

There are demographic differences between absentee and poll site voters. Absentee voters are more likely to be well-educated, higher-income suburbanites, and they also are likely to be senior citizens or students. Absentee voting is more prevalent in states that have strong political parties and election laws designed to support the parties—for example, by requiring individuals to state a party preference when they register to vote and by holding closed primaries. In these party-friendly states, the political parties can identify their members easily and often use the absentee voting process to mobilize their absentee voters. In states with both liberal absentee voting laws and strong parties, citizens are 2.2 percent more likely to vote, which is a significant increase in a close election.[16] Absentee voting does have the potential to increase turnout, which many consider an important goal in a democracy.

An additional benefit of absentee voting is that voters may cast a ballot with fewer errors. A recent study of voting in Los Angeles County found that absentee voters were less likely to undervote or overvote than poll site voters. It also is important to remember that voters who vote as absentees in Los Angeles County use the same punch-card ballots that are used by voters at the poll site, but they cannot use the punch-card voting machine, which is designed to line up the ballot for the voter. Nevertheless, as table 6-3 shows, absentee voters are able to vote more effectively than voters at the polls.[17]

Another major change in the election process over the past two decades has been the rise of early voting at official poll sites in the weeks prior to an election. Early voting currently is used in at least eight states; it is especially prevalent in Texas, which began using it in 1988. One of the key benefits of early voting is that it allows voters to cast their ballots at a poll site at their own convenience. Those who have studied the absentee voting process in the United States look favorably on early voting, because unlike voting by mail, early voting is conducted at an official polling place, among observers and election officials, providing a more secure, coercion-free, and private voting environment.[18] As does absentee voting,

Table 6-3. *Polling Place Compared with Absentee Overvotes and Undervotes*
Percent

Election	Polling place overvote	Absentee overvote	Polling place undervote	Absentee undervote
President	2.43	0.22	9.99	2.35
Senate	2.84	1.46	22.61	5.87
District attorney	0.47	0.06	25.94	12.73
Assessor	4.33	0.65	86.54	24.91
Measure A	0.53	0.07	62.94	15.38
Measure 32	0.53	0.08	49.24	14.21
Measure 33	0.52	0.06	61.30	16.97
Measure 34	0.81	0.08	58.30	16.40
Measure 35	1.09	0.12	55.04	16.38
Measure 36	1.18	0.08	41.98	12.58
Measure 37	0.87	0.09	66.30	18.61
Measure 38	0.80	0.09	27.50	8.05
Measure 39	0.85	0.11	41.50	11.41

Source: These data are taken directly from D. E. "Betsy" Sinclair and R. Michael Alvarez, "Who Overvotes, Who Undervotes, Using Punch-cards? Evidence from Los Angeles County," 2002, unpublished manuscript, California Institute of Technology, table 5.

early voting frees voters from having to fulfill their civic duty within a twelve-hour window on a Tuesday.

Early voting makes voting easier, and it does not create partisan or major demographic divides. Robert Stein found that in Texas voting patterns of early voters and traditional Election Day poll site voters tend to be similar. Early voters were just as likely as election day voters to be Democrats or Republicans and just as likely to vote for either party's candidate for governor or U.S. senator. Early voters tend to have stronger partisan identification and to be better informed, which is not surprising, since strong partisans are much more likely to make their choices early. Early voting also is more likely to be used by the elderly, which is not surprising, and lower-income voters, which is somewhat surprising as lower-income citizens are generally considered to be low-propensity voters.[19]

The combined effect of absentee and early voting has been to expand voting opportunities. However, there is some question about whether expanding options leads to higher turnout. Curtis Gans, with the Center for the Study of the American Electorate, has argued that early voting and universal absentee voting have not increased turnout and in fact may decrease it.[20] However, the actual data show that while early voting and universal absentee voting may not strongly boost turnout, they do not depress it either. Also, others have found that liberalizing absentee voting procedures can increase voter turnout.[21]

Concerns about privacy and fraud are two reasons why critics have expressed reservations about liberalizing absentee voting procedures. With voting by mail, there is no guarantee that voters can mark and seal their ballot in private, without coercion or pressure. A traditional polling place allows voters to stand in a voting booth or behind a curtain, alone, after verifying their identity for a polling place worker. In addition, state laws are quite strict about the partisan and political activities allowed in the vicinity of a polling place. Concerns about the privacy of mailed ballots are especially acute for voters in certain environments, such as nursing homes or other care facilities. Privacy concerns also have been raised regarding overseas ballots, especially since some military personnel have been allowed to fax their ballots to election officials.

The unsecured transmission of ballots to voters and back to the election office through the regular mail gives rise to fraud concerns. Moreover, the only way the election office can verify the identity of the voter is to compare the signature on the ballot envelope with the signature on file. With precinct voting and early voting, the voter is required to appear in person.

Privacy and fraud are indeed issues of concern. If citizens are unable to vote in private—or if liberalizing vote-by-mail systems allows for widespread fraud—election outcomes will be cast into doubt and controversy and the basic legitimacy of the electoral process will be questioned. However, the available evidence (from recent elections in Oregon) shows little support for claims of widespread coercion and lack of privacy. Specific instances of absentee voting fraud have occurred: in a widely publicized case in Miami in 1997, significant fraud was alleged in the absentee voting process and the courts eventually decided not to count any absentee ballots in determining the election outcome.[22] Unfortunately, there is no good way to know exactly how much absentee voting fraud actually occurs, other than through the scattered allegations that arise. A recent study of California found little evidence of significant absentee voting fraud: between 1994 and 2002, fourteen cases of absentee voting fraud were opened by the secretary of state's election fraud investigation unit— seven cases of fraudulent absentee voting, four cases involving violations of absentee voting requirements, and three cases focused on absentee ballot applications that were not returned. Surprisingly, only one case involving absentee voting fraud was referred to a county district attorney for further investigation, and not a single case of absentee voting fraud was prosecuted in that nine-year period.[23] Earlier studies, including a long-overlooked 1948 book by George Frederick Miller on absentee voting, found very little evidence for absentee voting fraud.[24]

Liberalized voting by mail and early voting programs also have been criticized as having other, even harder to document effects on the democratic process. For example, many are concerned about the effect on civic values of so many citizens avoiding the polling place on election day; these critics talk about the ceremonial and symbolic aspects of election day voting and their value in fostering a sense of citizenship. However, there is no research indicating that compared with precinct voters, absentee voters are less civic minded or that civic values in Oregon or California are any worse than in states like New York, which has restrictive absentee voting laws. Moreover, critics tend to ignore the impact that long lines and other polling place problems may have on a citizen's civic values!

Another related critique is that early voters do not cast informed votes. For example, scholar Norman Ornstein wrote in 2001 that early voters "voted from a smaller base of knowledge than the rest of us had; it was the equivalent of deciding the winner of a basketball game at the end of the third quarter."[25] True enough, early voters miss out on the last week or so of the campaigns. But there is a wealth of research showing that much of the campaign rhetoric is less than informative, and many voters can cast informed ballots without paying close attention to the negativity of the candidates' final campaign salvo. Furthermore, there is no research that we are aware of that indicates that absentee voters are less informed than precinct voters. In fact, research from Oregon points in the opposite direction; it finds little difference between absentee voters and the public at large. There also is evidence that absentee voters are less likely than precinct voters to over- and undervote on punch-card ballots. Last, at least in two recent vote-by-mail (VBM) elections in Oregon, most ballots were cast in the final days of the campaign: in the 2000 general election, 45 percent of the VBM ballots were received by election officials in the final two days of the election; and in the 2002 general election, 48 percent were received by election officials in the final two days.[26]

Whatever the claims of the critics, the trends are clear: voters like early and absentee voting, as can be seen in the data presented in table 6-1. In the 1996 presidential election, 10 percent of all votes across the nation were cast before election day; in states with broad early and absentee voting, the figure was much higher. In Washington state, 37 percent of all votes were cast before election day, while in Arizona 25 percent and in California 20 percent of all votes were cast early. In Oregon, almost 100 percent of the votes were cast before election day.

The Oregon Experiment

Oregon has had an innovative system of election administration for some time. It is one of the few states to have a comprehensive voter education program, through which voters receive an election pamphlet before every election.[27] It also was the first state to engage in universal vote-by-mail trials. In 1981 Oregon enacted a law that allowed VBM pilot programs to be conducted in local elections; after six years, the law was modified to allow VBM to be used in all special and local elections.[28] Local governments quickly adopted VBM for local elections because of the savings they reaped by not having to select poll sites and hire poll workers. The adoption of VBM by local governments allowed the state to examine the successes and failures of the VBM system and to compare its merits with those of the traditional system.

Oregon continued to use VBM for local elections through the early 1990s, and the system was very popular with Oregonians; by 1994 almost one-quarter of voters were casting absentee ballots. The legislature attempted to authorize use of VBM for all elections in 1995, but the governor vetoed the legislation, calling for additional study before the law was adopted. The opportunity for a major study of VBM soon arose; in 1995 U.S. Senator Robert Packwood resigned from the Senate. The governor decided that the party nominees should be chosen through primary elections, with the two nominees facing off in a general election. The Oregon secretary of state took advantage of the fact that the primary and general elections were "special" elections to order that they be conducted by mail. Primary election ballots were sent to the approximately 1.8 million registered voters between November 15 and 17 and were required to be in the hands of election officials by December 5, 1995. The process was repeated in the general election in January; ballots were mailed out between January 10 and 12, 1996, and had to be cast by January 30. Voters could either mail the ballot in or drop it off at designated sites, such as the county courthouse. In the primary election, approximately 58 percent of eligible voters cast a VBM ballot; in the general election, the turnout rate was 66 percent, which is close to typical for a congressional election in Oregon.

Table 6-4. *Oregon's Vote-by-Mail Postelection Survey, 1996*

Question	Percent (*N*)
When you voted, were you alone or was another person in the same room with you?	
Alone	74.4 (642)
Other present	25.6 (221)
If another person was present, who else was there?	
Spouse or partner	81.4 (180)
Child	7.7 (17)
Friends/roommates	4.1 (9)
Other	6.8 (15)
If another person was present, because another person was there, did you feel under pressure to vote a certain way?	
Yes	1.4 (3)
No	98.6 (217)
If another person was present, would you have voted the same or differently if you had been alone when you voted?	
Same	99.5 (219)
Differently	0.5 (1)
If another person was present, did you mark your ballot yourself, or did someone do it for you?	
Self	96.8 (214)
Someone else	3.2 (7)
Did you sign your ballot yourself, or did someone do it for you?	
Self	99.8 (884)
Someone else	0.2 (2)
Were you at home when you marked your ballot?	
Yes	96.3 (853)
No	3.7 (33)
If not at home, where were you when you marked your ballot?	
Work	60.6 (20)
Friend's house	15.2 (5)
Ballot drop-off site	12.1 (4)
Other	13.1 (4)
Did you mail your ballot back or drop it off, or did someone else mail or drop it off for you?	
Mailed by self	78.3 (588)
Dropped off by self	10.3 (77)
Someone else	11.5 (86)
Were there any difficulties returning your ballot?	
Yes	1.4 (12)
No	98.5 (873)
If yes, what were these?	
Drop box location unclear	33.3 (4)

Table 6-4. *Oregon's Vote-by-Mail Postelection Survey, 1996, continued*

Question	Percent (*N*)
Forgot to sign it	25 (3)
Other/don't know	41.7 (5)
On what date or day was your ballot returned?	
A few days after receiving it	51.8 (459)
Five to fifteen days after receiving it	36.8 (326)
A few days before Election Day	8.9 (79)
Don't remember	2.5 (22)
Do you have any difficulties that make it hard for you to get to a polling place?	
Yes	15.3 (188)
No	84.6 (1036)
If yes, what are these difficulties?	
Car-related issues	23.4 (44)
Job constraints	21.3 (40)
Disability or poor health	18.1 (34)
Child-related issues	10.1 (19)
Age-related issues	5.3 (10)
Weather-related issues	4.3 (8)
Other	17.5 (33)

Source: Priscilla Southwell and Justin Burchett, "Survey of Vote-by-Mail Senate Election in the State of Oregon," *PS: Political Science and Politics*, vol. 91, no. 1 (March 1997), pp. 53–57.

Because the Oregon special elections marked the first use of VBM for major statewide elections, there are several sources of survey data that indicate what voters thought of the experience. Tables 6-4 and 6-5 show the results of a survey conducted jointly by the Survey Research Center at Oregon State University and the Center for Political Studies at the University of Michigan. The results illustrate the striking ease of the VBM process. Almost all voters voted alone, at home. For those who did vote with others present, there is no evidence that they felt any sort of pressure to vote a certain way because a family member or friend was around. The survey shows that coercion, which is often brought up as a threat by those who oppose absentee voting, was not present in the VBM process. Fewer than 2 percent of voters encountered any difficulties in returning their ballot, in part because almost 90 percent of voters recalled casting their ballot within two weeks of receiving it; more than half recalled voting in the first week.

Table 6-5. *Characteristics of Respondents to Oregon's Vote-by-Mail Postelection Survey, 1996*

Percent, except as indicated

Characteristic	Traditional voter	Vote-by-mail voter	Registered nonvoter
Race (percent nonwhite)	5.5	9.9	10.3
Single-parent household	2.1	4.2	8.7
Mean age	52.1	46.7	42.3
Male	39.6	43	41.3
Female	60.4	57	58.7
Mean number of children under eighteen	.57	.72	.91
Length of residence (moved within last two years)	21.2	29.3	36
Party registration			
Democrat	48.2	44.5	43.3
Republican	41.8	37.2	28.4
Independent	8.5	16.2	20.9
Other	1.4	2.1	7.5
Employment status			
Working	61	69.1	72.9
Keeping house	6.3	5.9	4.9
Going to school	.7	2.5	3.5
Retired	29.6	19.2	12.5
Unemployed	1.5	2.1	4.9
Other	1	1.4	1.4
Attention to political events in Oregon			
A great deal	45.2	34.2	21.5
Some	45.6	49.8	44.3
A little	8.3	13.2	25.5
None	.9	2.9	8.7
Know name of governor (percent correct)	34.7	30.4	6.7

Source: Priscilla Southwell and Justin Burchett, "Survey of Vote-by-Mail Senate Election in the State of Oregon," *PS: Political Science and Politics*, vol. 91, no. 1 (March 1997), pp. 53–57.

There also is evidence from the survey that a small but significant number of potential voters—approximately 15 percent—historically have had difficulty getting to the polls because of physical disabilities, lack of transportation, or job time constraints. The VBM process allowed such citizens to easily overcome their problems. Table 6-5 presents demographic data from the postelection survey showing that the VBM population was different from traditional election voters in many significant ways. In 1995 the VBM population contained a significantly higher percentage of non-white and single-parent voters. VBM also possibly enfranchised voters who found voting difficult because they had moved or because they worked; the percentages of VBM voters in both categories were higher than in traditional elections. The typical VBM voter tended to be about five years younger and to have more children than the typical traditional voter. Finally, the 1995 VBM voter seemed to include more casual voters; fewer VBM voters said that they followed elections closely and could name the governor when asked.

What this one survey cannot reveal, however, is what the impact of VBM would be on the electorate over time. There is a conventional view that maintains that every election has a core group of voters who participate and that the core voters are joined in varying degrees by more marginal, casual voters. Turnout is driven by mobilizing casual voters and retaining habitual voters. This means that a transition to VBM in a state like Oregon can increase voter participation over time if it makes it easier for both habitual and casual voters to vote. If it leads primarily to increased participation by habitual voters, then participation by others should increase only slightly.

In an innovative study, three scholars tracked the voting histories of 846 voters to determine the impact of VBM. They found that VBM had two very important effects.[29] On one hand, it helped to retain habitual voters; once a citizen participated using VBM, he or she was likely to continue voting in subsequent elections. Some of these voters historically voted in only one election, on average, before they dropped out of the electorate. With VBM, they continued to vote. Because VBM captured and held voters, it has the potential to increase turnout.

However, VBM does not tend to pull new voters—registered voters who traditionally have not voted—into the electorate. Recent reforms in the voter registration process—most recently with passage of the National Voter Registration Act (Motor Voter), which allows voters to register at most government offices, such as the department of motor vehicles—have increased the population of registered voters. Unfortunately, increases in the number of registered voters have not translated into increases in voting. VBM would seem to be perfect for the traditional registered nonvoter; voting cannot get much easier than filling out a ballot delivered to one's door. However, even with its ease of use, VBM does not pull persistent nonvoters into the population of voters; if they do not use VBM when initially introduced to it—the first time a ballot arrives at their door—they will persist in ignoring future ballots. Of course, all registered nonvoters are not equally likely to avoid the temptation to vote. Not surprisingly, voters with higher socioeconomic status are more likely to move into the electorate, even if they abstained from VBM initially, than are potential voters of lower socioeconomic status. Thus for VBM to overcome potential disparities in participation, it is critical that voters be brought into the voting population the first time they are exposed to it. Otherwise, VBM has the potential to reinforce the participation gaps we noted in chapter 3.[30]

There also is clear evidence that those who use VBM like it. After the two special elections, the Oregon legislature was unable to agree on a bill to allow VBM for all primary and general elections; Republican legislators feared that the system benefitted Democratic voters. However, Oregon is an initiative state. The issue of whether to allow VBM for all elections was put on the ballot in November 1998 and resolved in favor of the measure, which garnered a lopsided 69 percent of the vote.

Although VBM is popular, one issue that has become quite important since the 2000 presidential election is whether the technology used for absentee voting is effective. Currently, VBM requires voters to use either punch-card or optical scan balloting. Both technologies have inherent error rates: voters can either fail to vote (intentionally or unintentionally) or vote twice when using them. At a poll site, these problems can be mitigated by the use of poll site scanners that inform a voter if his or her ballot contains an over- or undervote. However, with absentee voting, there are no mechanisms to identify errors on the ballot.

How significant a problem is under- and overvoting in Oregon? That question can be readily answered with data from the office of the Oregon secretary of state, which released a report that identified the ballot error rate in every county in every general election since 1992.[31] The data represent the average error rate across all statewide races. They show that historical residual vote rates in Oregon are high for both punch-card and optical scan balloting technologies compared with rates seen in other states.[32] The use of punch-card voting typically has resulted in an error rate above 7 percent, and the error rate with optical scan systems has been at or above 5 percent for the decade, approaching 4 percent only in 2000. However, when looking at presidential elections, the data are more promising. For example, Jackson County had an error rate of approximately 2 percent using punch cards, and its error rate declined to less than 1 percent (0.92 percent) when the county switched from punch cards to optical scan voting. As we note later, this finding of relatively low error rates with absentee voting in high-profile elections is not unusual. Equally important, the trend data related to the error rate do not show a clear change in errors after absentee voting was introduced. There is not a sharp change in errors in 1996; in fact, with optical scan technology, the error rate has declined steadily in every presidential election since 1992.[33]

Our conclusion about the use of VBM in Oregon is that it has had a positive impact on the state's electoral process. Voters in Oregon appear to like VBM, and it increases their opportunities to vote. There is no evidence that the widespread use of VBM in Oregon has led to any significant problems. In some ways, VBM actually results in a higher degree of security because the envelope for each absentee ballot must be signed and the signature compared with the one on file to identify the voter. Last, published research on the use of VBM in Oregon indicates that it has had a positive effect on voter participation. A recent study by Priscilla Southwell and Justin Burchett, in which they examined forty-eight statewide primary and general elections between 1960 and 1996 while controlling for various factors that might influence voter turnout, found that "after controlling for the nature of the race, all-mail elections increased registered voter turnout by 10% over the expected turnout in a traditional polling place election."[34]

VBM in the United Kingdom

The United States is not the only nation experimenting with VBM. Recently, the British parliament created the Electoral Commission, which is charged with encouraging participation and increasing registration and voting levels.[35] The commission has been encouraging local election administrators to conduct experiments and try innovations that could improve voter turnout. Table 6-6 shows the criteria that the commission uses to evaluate pilot programs and some evaluations, which go beyond determining whether a program increased turnout to examine how voters viewed the pilot, whether it resulted in cost savings, and whether it increased the potential for vote fraud. When an evaluation is complete, the commission issues a report that is distributed to all election officials; if the pilot is a success, the report can serve as a best practices document for future pilots.

The commission has evaluated pilot VBM experiments, which the British refer to as "all-postal elections," that were conducted in elections

Table 6-6. *U.K. Electoral Commission Evaluation Criteria*

Mandatory criteria

The scheme's success or otherwise in facilitating voting or the counting of votes or in encouraging voting or enabling voters to make informed choices at the elections

Whether the turnout of voters was higher than it would have been if the scheme had not applied

Whether voters found the procedures provided for their assistance by the scheme easy to use

Whether the procedures provided for by the scheme led to any increase in personation or other electoral offenses or in any other malpractice in connection with elections

Whether those procedures led to any increase in expenditure or to any savings by the authority

The extent to which the pilot facilitated or otherwise encouraged participation among particular communities, including young people, ethnic minority groups, and people with disabilities

Overall levels of user awareness and comprehension of the voting method being tested, including an assessment of the effectiveness of any literature or other materials used in the promotion of the pilot

Additional optional criteria

The attitudes and opinions of key stakeholders, including voters, with a view to determining overall levels of confidence in the voting method being tested

Whether the pilot resulted in measurable improvements or had any adverse impact with respect to the provision of more efficient and effective service delivery to voters

Whether the pilot resulted in measurable improvements to or had any adverse impact on the existing system of electoral administration

Whether the pilot represented good "value for money"

Source: The Electoral Commission, "Modernising Elections: A Strategic Evaluation of the 2002 Electoral Pilot Schemes" (Boundary Committee for England, August 2002), p. 12 (www.electoralcommission.gov.uk/elections/may2002.cfm [October 1, 2003]).

in both 2002 and 2003. One such pilot was conducted in a district council election for West Wiltshire, a stable upper-middle-class bedroom community outside London where most residents commute to London to work. The VBM election was for a local office; 257 residents were eligible to vote. Voters had two weeks to cast their ballot and, as in Oregon, they could return the ballot either by mail or by dropping it off at a designated collection point. The local government conducted a voter education effort before the election to inform all potential voters that the election would be conducted by mail. It also attempted to conduct a survey of both voters and nonvoters to determine their views on the new election procedure, but given the limited amount of time between the decision to use VBM and the election, they were unable to get a meaningful response rate.

The commission's evaluation of the VBM pilot has been quite positive. Turnout in the special election was 56 percent, almost three times higher than in recent by-elections and almost 70 percent higher than in the most recent general local election. More than half of all voters cast their ballots in the first three days after receiving it; only six of 150 ballots were rejected. The election also was very cost effective: it cost only £300 ($462), including the surveys and voter education effort. Historical data show that the typical special election would have cost £450 ($692); VBM resulted in a savings of £150 ($230) for the locality. This success with VBM led the Electoral Commission to recommend that it be used in all local elections. As the commission noted,

> Our evaluation of the all-postal pilot schemes suggests that this approach is effective in boosting participation rates in local elections—to an extent that was largely underestimated when the pilots process began, and which appears to be sustainable. . . . We recommend that there should be a statutory presumption that all local elections be run as all-postal ballots unless there are compelling reasons why an all-postal ballot would be inappropriate.[36]

The commission did raise two points of concern about the VBM experiment: First, they noted that VBM does not necessarily improve access for voters who are blind or who have impaired coordination. However, in this experiment, there were no complaints regarding that issue. In fact, the VBM was beneficial for people with physical mobility problems because the traditional poll site was not very accessible for the infirm or people in wheelchairs. The voting precinct—which the British refer to as a parish— also made arrangements for special voting services to be available to the blind should they have been requested. Second, the commission noted that fraud was not a problem in the election, but that it would be important to keep close watch in any future VBM pilots to ensure that fraud did not occur.

In 2002 and 2003 there were many other VBM experiments in the United Kingdom; almost all of these experiments have been a success. Their results are similar to those in the West Wiltshire election: VBM increased turnout, cost less, and did not result in an increase in vote fraud. The costs of sending ballots out by mail and educating voters about VBM are much lower than the costs associated with actually running an election at poll sites, which involves paying poll workers, purchasing equipment, and developing materials for poll workers.

What We Can Learn from Absentee Voting, Early Voting, and Voting by Mail

For decades, people have touted various election reforms—early voting, absentee voting, new voting equipment, new ways of voting—as being a panacea that would increase turnout and make elections work better. And for every person touting a solution there has been someone else explaining why the proposed solution would not work. However, only by implementing reforms and testing the results can one learn whether a proposed reform works as it is alleged to work.

In the case of VBM, the state of Oregon was able to collect a decade's worth of data on how effective it was before it was used in a statewide special election. Officials were able to assure themselves that the reform was likely to be effective and accepted by the voters. Likewise, the United Kingdom has now embarked on a program of pilot testing vote-by-mail and Internet voting programs in special elections across the nation in order to determine whether they are effective. What the current data show is that, as in Oregon, VBM lowers the cost of elections while either increasing turnout or maintaining historical turnout levels. There is no evidence of any significant problems in Oregon—no allegations of widespread fraud or coercion, no evidence that Oregonians lack civic values, and no sign that voting in these elections is less informed. Cases like Oregon offer a model for how to think about the transition from current voting systems to an Internet voting system.

The critical facet of the Oregon experience is that the process of moving to VBM was gradual. Internet voting should be implemented in a similar fashion. Efforts should start small, with pilot projects that target specific audiences. These pilots should collect important data from project participants and from nonparticipant "control" voters in order to assess the outcome of each project. It then will be possible to "scale up" to full-fledged Internet voting in the future.

More generally, two other key lessons can be learned from expanding both early voting and VBM across the nation. First, voters are seeking to participate in ways that do not involve voting at a polling place on election day. There is a clear need for the greater access that early voting and VBM provide, and voters are clamoring for it. True, voters in certain parts of the country are more vocal about their desire for alternatives to traditional polling place voting, but after the experiences in Oregon and other states over the past decades, the need and interest are obvious.

Second, the supposed downside to greater access is always fraud. We have noticed that since 2000 many debates about election reform have dealt with the access/fraud issue in what social scientists call zero-sum terms. Many recent election reform debates, especially at the federal level over the Help America Vote Act, which President Bush signed into law in late 2002, literally assume that there is a direct and necessary trade-off between access and fraud: if voting is made more accessible, voter fraud increases.

That supposed trade-off is at the heart of the debate about liberalizing absentee voting—and it also is at the heart of the debate about Internet voting. However, another important lesson from the Oregon experience with VBM—and from the experiences of other states, like California, with liberalizing absentee voting regulations—is that there is not necessarily a trade-off. Greater access can be had without fraud, both with VBM and Internet voting. Officials just need to follow the Oregon and U.K. models to develop a serious and sustained strategy for implementing Internet voting throughout the United States.

CHAPTER 7

Trials of Internet Voting

The 2000 presidential election was important, among other reasons, because it exposed so many of the flaws in the U.S. electoral process. However, the election and the campaign were important in another, little-known regard. Internet voting systems were used for the first time in real elections, with real voters casting real ballots over real remote Internet connections. The three significant trials of Internet voting were a straw poll of Republican voters in January; the Arizona Democratic primary in March; and the Voting Over the Internet (VOI) project of the Federal Voting Assistance Program (FVAP) in the presidential election. These trials provide an important touchstone for our arguments on how to develop and deploy Internet voting for all Americans in future elections.

Although the 2000 trials demonstrated the basic feasibility of Internet voting, their primary lesson is that truly understanding how Internet voting affects the electoral process requires thoughtful, scientific, and experimental examination. Unfortunately, none of the trials were conducted in a way that allowed for scientific study; that is why we call them trials, not experiments. In this chapter, we review the trials—and tribulations—of Internet voting in 2000 in the United States. We then briefly consider Internet voting trials in other nations and propose new experiments in upcoming U.S. elections.

Alaska: A Cold Introduction for Internet Voting

In a number of ways, Alaska is a perfect environment for Internet voting. The state covers a vast geographic area, and many voters live in places that because of bad weather are difficult to access for weeks or months at a time. Furthermore, it has the highest computer ownership and Internet access rates of any state.[1] For Alaskans, Internet voting could make the electoral process much more accessible.

The Alaska Republican party looked to Internet voting to improve access in its January 24, 2000, statewide straw poll of Republican party members. In the middle of the Alaskan winter, voters in some parts of the state can find it literally impossible to get to polling places and even absentee voting by mail can be quite difficult. The straw poll, conducted by VoteHere.net, was confined to voters in the most remote and inaccessible areas of the state: legislative districts 36, 37, and 38, which lie in a region roughly bordered by Canada on the east, the Bering Sea to the north, and the Yukon River to the west. Members and staff of the state's congressional delegation in Washington, D.C., also were eligible to vote in the online election.

Alaska typically is not a player in the national presidential primaries, and the state Republican party hoped to sharpen its profile in national politics by using the Internet for its straw poll. Alaska is one of only a handful of states that have never held a presidential primary; instead, the Republicans rely on a caucus-like system for allocating delegates to the national convention. In the past few presidential elections, the Republican party has held its caucus in late January, in conjunction with a statewide straw poll, in an attempt to play a greater role in the Republican nomination process.

With both voters in the remote regions of Alaska and the congressional delegation included, approximately 3,500 people were eligible to vote in the online Republican straw poll. Each one received digital identification and a form; to participate in the election through the Internet, a voter needed only to complete the form and return it to the party. Of the 3,500 potential online voters, only fifty-six returned the form. Of the fifty-six eligible voters, only thirty-five—1 percent of eligible Internet voters— actually cast a ballot in this online trial.

In the paper ballot straw poll held throughout the rest of the state, 4,295 ballots were cast. The total turnout for the straw poll was 4,330, so the Internet vote was less than 1 percent of the total. Interestingly, voters who cast paper ballots were closely divided in their support between George W. Bush, who received 1,548 of the paper votes cast, and Steve Forbes, who received 1,562. On the basis of the paper ballots alone, Forbes would have been declared the winner of the straw poll. However, online participants voted decisively for Bush: twenty-three of the thirty-five Internet votes cast (66 percent) were for Bush, six votes (17 percent) were for McCain (who received only 406 paper votes, 9 percent of the total paper votes), and four votes (11 percent) were for Forbes. When the paper and Internet votes were tabulated, George W. Bush emerged as the overall winner of the Alaska straw poll by a five-vote margin over Steve Forbes (1,571 total votes for Bush, 1,566 for Forbes).

In a sense, the Internet vote was decisive in the Alaska Republican straw poll, and the poll therefore might have been an interesting Internet voting trial. However, the trial turnout, only 1 percent of the voters contacted, was pathetic. The low turnout was blamed after the election on a poor effort by the state Republican party to advertise both the straw poll and the Internet voting option to eligible voters. A spokesperson for Vote-Here.net said after the election that "people either had not received the mailing or they threw them away thinking they were junk mail."[2] Others, especially supporters of Steve Forbes, argued that the state Republican party deliberately worked to depress turnout in the straw poll because of concern that a big Forbes victory so early in the election season would jeopardize Bush's campaign. Following the straw poll, Forbes stated on C-SPAN that "the establishment had to scramble and do sort of the electronic equivalent of bringing late precincts to win the thing. And what they did was count e-commerce, electronic voting from apparently congressional staffers outside of the state to try to tie the thing up."[3]

What lessons can be learned from the Alaska Internet voting trial? The most obvious lesson—if the postelection analysis offered by VoteHere.net officials for the poor Internet turnout is correct—is that voters will not use Internet voting just because it is an option. Given the novelty of Internet voting, its availability and benefits must to be made much more clear to voters. Otherwise, the Alaska trial sheds little light on the important issues regarding Internet voting. With only thirty-five of more than 4,000 voters voting by the Internet, it is impossible to make any definitive statements about how well the process worked.

Even basic questions—Did it work well technically? Did it improve access to the electoral process? Did voters find Internet voting easier or harder than paper ballot voting?— cannot be answered because there was no scientific plan for a meaningful evaluation of the Alaska straw poll. More than 3,500 people were invited to participate, but no attempt was made to randomly select a control group of people who would not be allowed to vote over the Internet. Instead, voters themselves were allowed to determine whether to participate in the Internet voting trial, producing what social scientists call selection bias—simply put, people who choose to participate might be fundamentally different from those who do not. Unless a great deal of data about participants are collected and the process by which people opt into the Internet voting trial is well understood and incorporated in the evaluation of the Internet voting experience, no strong conclusions about the trial can be made. The same problems plagued each of the important trials of Internet voting in the 2000 election.

Arizona: A Lukewarm Reception in the Desert

The Arizona Internet voting trial differed in both large and small ways from the Alaska trial. The Alaska trial was a straw poll for the Republican party; the Arizona trial was part of a binding Democratic primary election. Arizona offered every registered Democratic voter the option of casting an Internet ballot; only limited participation was allowed in Alaska. As a result, Internet participation was roughly 1,000 times greater in Arizona. The two states also are very different—politically, socially, and economically. Arizona has a much lower rate of households with computers (59.4 percent compared with Alaska's 68.7 percent) and Internet access (51.9 percent compared with Alaska's 64.1 percent).[4] Arizona's population is, on average, older and less educated than Alaska's; residents' incomes also are lower, and they are less likely to speak English at home. Arizona has a sizable population of Native Americans (5 percent of the population), but it is not as large as Alaska's (15.6 percent); however, more than 25 percent of Arizona's population is Hispanic, in contrast to 4.1 percent in Alaska. Finally, Arizona's population is much less rural (12.5 percent) than Alaska's (33 percent).[5]

The Arizona Internet voting trial for the Democratic presidential primary was unique in a number of ways. First, Arizona has a very short history of presidential primaries. Arizona's first use of a presidential primary occurred in 1996, when Arizona Republican senator John McCain established a Republican primary to enhance the prospects of Senator Phil Gramm's (R-Tex.) presidential candidacy. The Democratic party also wanted to conduct a presidential primary in 1996, but it was prohibited from doing so by national party rules barring any state from holding such an early primary.[6] The Democrats were instead forced to conduct a preference vote at a limited number of polling places throughout the state.

Second, the Arizona primary was held on March 11, 2000, too late in the electoral calendar to matter for the Democratic nomination. It occurred the week after "Super Tuesday"—when primaries and caucuses were held in sixteen states, including California and New York—and just before a series of southern state primaries, including those in Florida, Tennessee, and Texas. After Super Tuesday, it was clear that Al Gore had wrapped up the nomination; his opponent, Bill Bradley, all but conceded Gore's victory. The lack of competitiveness and interest in the race most likely had a negative effect on voter turnout.

Third, Democratic voters in Arizona could cast their votes in a variety of ways. Most important for our purposes, they could cast their vote over the Internet from any remote connection or by voting at an Internet-connected kiosk located in polling places. Of course, they could also vote by traditional means, either at a polling place or by mailing an absentee ballot. Given that each Democratic voter could vote in so many different ways, the Arizona trial had the potential to answer a variety of questions about Internet voting, such as those raised in the discussion on Alaska's trial.[7]

In the Arizona trial, all registered Democratic voters—40.46 percent of all registered Arizona voters, or 843,323 people—received a personal identification number (PIN) in the mail sometime in February or early March and a form to request a traditional paper absentee ballot.[8] The PINs were generated by election.com, the company conducting the election for the Arizona Democratic party. Beginning after midnight on Tuesday, March 7, 2000, through midnight on Friday, March 10, 2000, voters could log on to two different websites, one run by the Arizona Democratic party and the other by election.com, to cast their vote. At both websites voters had to accept the rules of the election, enter their PIN, and answer two personal questions for verification purposes. The PIN and the personal information then were cross-referenced against the voter registration database. After voters were authenticated, they were allowed to vote for their preferred candidate. After selecting a candidate, voters were asked to confirm their choice, and on confirmation they received electronic verification that their vote had been cast. After the close of the Internet voting period, 124 polling places throughout the state opened for business. In-person or kiosk Internet voting occurred on Saturday, March 11, throughout Arizona. The PINs issued by election.com were used to prevent double voting.

What actually happened in Arizona? Table 7-1 shows the votes cast by voting method for each of the fifteen counties in Arizona, as well as some relevant state statistics. Despite the fact that the Democratic nomination

Table 7-1. *Percentage of Votes Cast in 2000 Arizona Democratic Primary, by Method*

County	Internet	Mail	Electronic Polling	Paper Polling	Votes cast (N)
Apache	27.0	26.8	28.2	18.0	799
Cochise	42.2	33.2	6.0	18.6	2,090
Coconino	49.9	25.8	11.4	13.0	1,374
Gila	32.2	35.6	5.6	26.6	1,353
Graham	28.8	27.7	8.4	35.2	466
Greenlee	36.4	36.4	1.7	25.6	121
La Paz	26.8	58.0	0.5	14.7	224
Maricopa	43.0	40.6	4.0	12.4	51,827
Mohave	39.3	10.1	7.7	42.9	1,803
Navajo	28.6	32.7	7.3	31.4	1,160
Pima	42.0	33.0	2.8	22.2	16,518
Pinal	34.2	39.0	2.0	24.8	2,840
Santa Cruz	27.4	34.9	5.3	32.5	591
Yavapai	37.0	40.1	5.8	17.1	3,596
Yuma	33.1	51.8	3.4	11.8	1,694
State (N)	35,768	32,748	4,174	14,217	86,907
State percent	41.6	37.7	4.8	16.4	

Source: See Arizona Democratic Party, Paper Ballots vs. Internet Votes, and Arizona Department of Commerce, *Arizona Demographics: Population by County*, in R. Michael Alvarez and Jonathan Nagler, "The Likely Consequences of Internet Voting for Political Representation," *Loyola of Los Angeles Law Review*, vol. 34, no. 3 (2001), pp. 1115–53.

Note: Paper polling means voters cast ballots at a poll site using a paper ballot. Electronic polling means that voters cast ballots at a poll site using electronic voting machines.

already was decided before the Arizona primary, 86,907 Democrats cast ballots. Almost half of the ballots cast were cast over the Internet, with 35,768 ballots cast from remote connections (41.6 percent) and 4,174 ballots cast at Internet voting stations in polling places (4.8 percent). Most of the remaining votes, 37.7 percent, were cast in the traditional vote-by-mail process; only 16.4 percent were cast in polling places using traditional paper ballots.

There was a great deal of variation across Arizona's counties in the form of voting used. Almost half of Coconino County's 1,374 Democratic primary voters used the Internet voting process, and more than 40 percent of votes in Cochise, Maricopa, and Pima Counties were cast over the Internet. By contrast, in Apache, La Paz, Navajo, and Santa Cruz counties, just over 25 percent of the votes were cast over the Internet; each of these counties had much higher rates of voting by mail and traditional polling place voting. Although many votes were cast over the Internet, the use of Internet voting was not uniform across the state.

In addition to pointing out that almost half of the ballots in this primary were cast either over the Internet or from electronic machines in polling places, enthusiastic supporters of the Arizona Democratic party's Internet voting trial also claimed that the trial saw great gains in voter participation. Frederic Solop, a political scientist at Northern Arizona University who studied this election, claimed that

> [h]istorically, turnout in Arizona's Democratic presidential primary has been small. The rate of turnout, however, grew 723 percent between 1996 and 2000. In terms of the absolute number of people voting, turnout in the 2000 election was 579 percent larger than turnout in the 1996 election.[9]

This is an interesting claim, considering that in 1996 there was no real Democratic presidential primary in Arizona! Instead, in 1996 the Democratic Party held a nonbinding presidential preference election in which only 12,884 voters participated, casting 12,303 votes for President Bill Clinton, who was running for a second term.[10] In the 2000 election, the private company running the Internet trial for the state Democratic party had strong incentives to publicize the election widely and succeeded in attracting a great deal of state and national media attention. Clearly, the 1996 presidential primary is a problematic baseline from which to evaluate the potential effects of the Internet voting trial on voter participation in 2000.

In table 7-2, we present a more appropriate baseline, which compares voter turnout in the 2000 Democratic presidential primary for each Arizona county with the average turnout in three previous state-run Democratic primaries in 1994, 1996, and 1998 involving candidates for state and local partisan races, as well as some ballot measures. By averaging turnout in these three statewide primaries, we obtained a reliable estimate of the general propensity of Democratic voters in each Arizona county to vote in primary elections.[11]

Comparing voter turnout in the 2000 Democratic Internet primary with previous statewide Democratic Party primaries produces a stark contrast. While proponents of the 2000 Internet primary enjoyed making sweeping statements about tremendous (and unrealistic) increases in Democratic voter turnout in a primary election, in reality the turnout in March 2000 was extremely low. Only 10.6 percent of Arizona Democrats

Table 7-2. *Percentage of Voters Voting in Arizona Democratic Primary, 2000, Compared with 1994–98 Average*[a]

County	2000 turnout	1994–98 average
Apache	3.0	31.2
Cochise	8.6	33.2
Coconino	5.6	18.6
Gila	8.7	40.1
Graham	5.0	38.9
Greenlee	2.9	50.1
La Paz	6.1	25.1
Maricopa	13.3	18.2
Mohave	7.4	24.2
Navajo	4.5	27.8
Pima	9.4	24.0
Pinal	7.4	33.8
Santa Cruz	6.1	38.5
Yavapai	14.1	22.8
Yuma	7.1	26.3
State	10.6	23.9

Source: See Rhodes Cook, *United States Presidential Primary Elections 1968-1996: A Handbook of Election Statistics* (Washington: CQ Press, 2000).

a. The Arizona Democratic Party before 2000 did not conduct a true statewide presidential primary, so it is impossible to make comparisons to earlier Democratic presidential primaries. The statewide primaries involve state and local partisan primaries, as well as various ballot measures, which provide many stimuli to attract voters to the polls. On the other hand, presidential races are very salient and often are accompanied by much media attention, fueling voter interest and participation. In the end, the previous statewide primary turnout data provide a solid indication of the general propensity of Arizona voters to participate in primary elections.

participated in this election, despite the novelty of the Internet voting option, despite the campaign by election.com and the state Democratic Party to get voters involved, and despite the great deal of media attention given to the election. By contrast, about 24 percent of Arizona's Democratic electorate participated in statewide primaries held in the 1990s.

Furthermore, there was a great deal of difference in the turnout rates across counties. Turnout in Maricopa and Yavapai counties was somewhat higher than the statewide average: 13.3 percent and 14.1 percent of registered Democrats in those two counties voted in the 2000 presidential primary. In other counties, most especially Greenlee and Apache, few registered Democratic voters participated in the election—only 2.9 percent in Greenlee and 2.8 percent in Apache. Furthermore, there is an inverse relationship between general Democratic voter turnout in earlier statewide

Figure 7-1. *County Turnout in 2000 Arizona Democratic Primary by Race*

Percent turnout

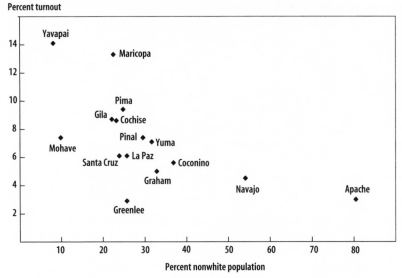

Percent nonwhite population

primaries and in the 2000 Internet primary. Counties like Greenlee had generally high Democratic voter turnout in the earlier primaries but low turnout in the 2000 primary. Counties that had generally low Democratic voter turnout in statewide primaries (like Maricopa) had high Internet primary turnout. Just as there was variation in the use of the Internet to vote in this election, there was variation in basic voter interest and participation.

What can we make of this? Unfortunately, with only fifteen counties to examine, we cannot engage in a very elaborate statistical analysis. Instead, we look at one important characteristic of Arizona counties and how it might correlate with turnout and Internet voting rates in this election—racial composition, specifically the percent of nonwhites. We focus on racial composition for two reasons. First, race is one of the most important digital divides. As discussed earlier, nonwhite Americans are much less likely to use the Internet than white Americans. Second, race is a critical legal hurdle for Internet voting trials because of the Voting Rights Act (VRA). The VRA states clearly that voting systems that make it more difficult for nonwhites to participate in the political process are illegal.[12]

In figure 7-1 we graph the nonwhite population of each Arizona county by Democratic voter turnout in the 2000 presidential primary. The pattern here is stunning: counties with small nonwhite populations had the highest turnout rates, and counties with large nonwhite populations had the lowest turnout rates. The strong negative relationship between these two variables is clear from the figure; it also is absolutely apparent from the estimated correlation between the two variables, which is a strong -0.62. The figure and correlational analysis provide strong evidence that race played an important role in determining the relative turnout rates across Arizona counties in the 2000 presidential primary.

Race also is an important part of the explanation for the relative turnout rates between the 2000 presidential primary and the previous statewide Democratic primaries in Arizona. Alvarez and Nagler undertook an elaborate statistical analysis and estimated that, on average across Arizona counties, white Democratic voter turnout fell by just over 7 percent from the 1998 statewide Democratic primary to the 2000 presidential primary.[13] However, nonwhite Democratic voter turnout fell by more than 36 percent between the two elections. According to these estimations, nonwhite Democratic voter turnout fell five times more than white Democratic voter turnout, a stunning finding. From our simple graphical analysis in figure 7-1 and the more complicated statistical analysis of Alvarez and Nagler, it is clear that race played a strong role in determining voter turnout in the 2000 Democratic presidential primary in Arizona.

Figure 7-2 presents a similar analysis, but here we graph the use of the remote Internet voting option in each county by the percent of nonwhites. Again, the pattern is clear, though not as strong as in figure 7-1: counties with small nonwhite populations made more use of the Internet voting method in the 2000 presidential primary and counties with large nonwhite populations used it less. The basic bivariate correlation between these two variables is -0.38, about half the size of the correlation in figure 7-1 but sizable nonetheless.

Alvarez and Nagler dug more deeply into the same data presented in figure 7-1 to perform a multivariate regression analysis, which allowed them to study the impact of a county's racial composition on the use of the Internet voting method while controlling for the effects of other variables including gender, age, unemployment, and urbanization. Of those variables, they found that only gender did not have a statistically significant effect. Counties with more elderly people, more nonwhites, more unemployed people, and a more rural population all showed significantly less use of Internet voting.[14] Of the statistically significant variables, age and unemployment had the strongest effects on the use of Internet voting, while urbanization and race had much weaker effects.

Figure 7-2. *County Internet Voting in 2000 Arizona Democratic Primary by Race*

Percent internet voting

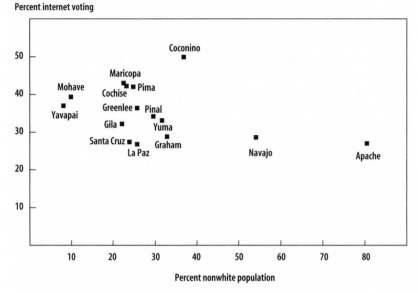

Percent nonwhite population

A host of technical problems also plagued the 2000 Arizona Internet primary. Phillips and von Spakovsky noted that voters reported not receiving their PIN in the mail, losing their PIN, and being unable to obtain a new PIN from the Democratic Party. Many voters apparently had problems with their Internet browsers, including incompatibilities between the voting system and certain computer systems (especially Macintosh computers) and some older Internet browsers. Voters having these problems also found it difficult to obtain technical support.[15] Other minor technical problems arose, including problems with computers that would not accept "cookies," ballots that did not appear on computer screens, confusing directions on how to vote, and problems with verifying the voter's personal information. Solop states that "four percent of registered Democrats tried to vote over the Internet but were unsuccessful and never cast a ballot," but that estimate is difficult to corroborate. The number of Arizona Democrats who had problems that prevented them from voting on the Internet might have been significantly greater.[16] Because the Arizona preference primary was a private election, not state run, no significant postelection report on the conduct of the Internet voting trial has been made public.

What can be learned from the Arizona trial? Again, surprisingly little. Few data about the trial have been released except for the county-by-county statistics reported above that came from the state Democratic party. Furthermore, there is no information on the full extent of technical problems, the number of voters having technical problems, or any security problems that might have arisen.

We do know from this Internet voting trial, like the Alaska trial, that the fact that Internet voting is available does not necessarily translate into increased voter participation. Despite overblown claims to the contrary, voter participation in the 2000 primary was embarrassingly low—lower than in previous Democratic statewide primaries and, according to some estimates, much lower for nonwhites than whites. Of course, a number of factors make this situation unique: it was a private election that occurred after the Democratic nomination was a done deal, and because presidential primaries were a new thing in Arizona, it was difficult to gauge underlying voter interest. We also have evidence that the digital divide might have been an issue in this election: nonwhites appear to have been much less willing or able to use the Internet voting option than the usual voting options. However, without a solid evaluation, these issues are impossible to address.

Voting Over the Internet: Overseas Citizens Try Internet Voting

At any point in time—including election season—millions of voting-age Americans are overseas. Many also are away from their voting residence during the election season because they are a member of the armed services or a dependent of a service member. These Americans are covered by the Uniformed and Overseas Citizens Absentee Voting Act (UOCAVA) of 1973, which guarantees them certain voting rights, especially absentee voting rights, and to assist state and local governments in implementing the act's requirements, Congress established the Federal Voting Assistance Program (FVAP).[17] FVAP is administered by the Department of Defense, which has responsibility for implementing UOCAVA voting procedures.

Under UOCAVA, citizens have what seems to be a simple and streamlined process for registering and voting. They only have to obtain, complete, and send a Federal Post Card Application (FPCA)—which serves as both an absentee voter registration application and a request for an absentee ballot—to the appropriate county election office. Once the county election office receives and processes the FPCA, it sends an absentee ballot to the voter. The voter then votes and sends the ballot back to the county election office.

However, as was well-documented in the wake of the 2000 presidential election, this seemingly simple and streamlined process poses many problems.[18] First, given the federal nature of American elections, there are no national regulations regarding absentee registration and voting, so UOCAVA citizens must inform themselves about specific requirements and regulations in their locality and follow them exactly in order to register and successfully cast a ballot. Consider these examples of the lack of uniformity: some states require that certain affidavits be signed and even witnessed for absentee registration; the deadlines for registration vary widely across states; and different regulations govern exactly when an overseas absentee ballot has to be received by a county election office to be considered a valid ballot.

Second, as noted by the Government Accounting Office (GAO), "County officials said that problems in processing absentee voting applications arise primarily because voters do not fill in the forms correctly."[19] In a postelection survey of county election officials in 1996, FVAP found that

—66 percent of the FPCAs that were invalidated were invalidated because of a missing or inadequate home address

—25 percent were invalidated because of an inadequate or illegible mailing address

—18 percent were invalidated because of illegible handwriting

—13 percent were invalidated because the forms were incomplete

—11 percent had no signature

—4 percent had no witness signature or address.

Clearly, UOCAVA voters encounter significant difficulties completing the FPCA, and those difficulties create an important barrier to their participation in the electoral process.

Third and most important, "mail transit time"—the time it takes voting materials to get from point A to point B—creates a major problem. While this may sound trivial to those used to receiving domestic first-class mail within a few days, many Americans overseas have to wait weeks for mail to work its way through the U.S. postal system and then through the postal system of the nation in which they reside. For uniformed service personnel, mail service can be very spotty, especially for those on active duty in remote and inaccessible locations—for example, on nuclear submarines.

The FVAP has been aware of the mail transit time problem for many election cycles, and it has initiated several programs to try to alleviate the problem, including making it possible for UOCAVA citizens to use fax machines and even e-mail to receive and submit absentee voting materials.

Internet registration and voting seems like an ideal solution to the problems facing UOCAVA voters, an observation that did not escape the FVAP. Accordingly, in the late 1990s, it launched the Voting Over the Internet (VOI) project, which was billed as a feasibility study. The FVAP wanted to determine whether a secure Internet registration and voting system could be constructed for use by real voters to cast binding votes in the 2000 general election. To answer that question, the FVAP solicited the participation of four states—Florida, South Carolina, Texas, and Utah—and the counties within them. The project involved developing registration and voting software for the system and making hardware purchases for all participating election jurisdictions. All told, the VOI project cost $6.2 million dollars.[20]

The VOI system ensured a very high degree of security. UOCAVA participants were sent a CD-ROM with the software necessary to register and vote, including a version of Netscape Navigator with 128-bit encryption and browser plug-ins to operate the VOI system. Voters could use only the strong-encryption version of Netscape Navigator; they had to use a computer that ran Microsoft Windows 95/98 (VOI did not support the MacIntosh platform); and their computer had to be connected to the Internet. Voters also had to have a Department of Defense–issued digital certificate, since the FVAP used the department's medium assurance public key infrastructure (DoD PKI) for voter authentication. That decision was made early in the system development process because it was thought that the DoD PKI program would have issued digital certificates to many if not most DoD personnel by 2000. To get a DoD PKI, an individual had to apply in person, using official DoD identification, and then download the digital certificate to a floppy disk within a short time period. Unfortunately, the DoD PKI rollout was slow, and the FVAP had to scramble to issue digital certificates to voters so that they could use the system.[21] In addition, many voters did not download their digital certificate to a floppy within the time allotted and the certificate expired, or they simply forgot their password and could not access their certificate. Of the 157 digital certificates issued, seventy-five had to be replaced.[22]

To log on to the VOI system to register and vote, voters began by logging in to a central server that authenticated their digital certificate and allowed them to vote. When a voter was authenticated, an electronic version of the FPCA came up on the computer screen. The citizen could then complete an FPCA online for the specific state and county in which he or she was registering to vote. The voter then submitted the completed form as an encrypted object directly to the appropriate local election office. At any time, the citizen could electronically determine the status of his or her registration request. Notice that this system was designed not only to resolve the mail transit time problem but also to assist voters by providing an FPCA for their election jurisdiction and by requiring the provision of all necessary information.

Once a citizen's registration and absentee ballot request was approved by the local election office, the citizen could initiate a voting session. This required logging in to the central server, where the voter's digital certificate was verified. The server next requested that the local election office return an electronic ballot to be delivered to the voter's workstation. The voter then completed the ballot and submitted it as an encrypted object to the local election office. If the ballot was received by the local election office, the voter received an electronic return receipt.

How successful was the VOI project? The VOI assessment report reached a muted conclusion.

A principal finding was that within a small-scale, tightly controlled demonstration, the risks introduced by the technology could be sufficiently mitigated to maintain the integrity of the process for remote registration and voting. It also stated that this approach could significantly promote the enfranchisement of UOCAVA voters—in particular, military service members.[23] Neither the VOI Pilot Project Assessment Report nor a peer review evaluation of the VOI system in which we participated gave any indication of significant technical problems during the project that prevented citizens from voting, nor was there any evidence of the system suffering security violations. This pilot project did fulfill its primary objective—to document the basic technical feasibility of Internet voting for UOCAVA citizens.

However, while the technical objectives seem to have been met, the voter participation rate for the VOI project was extremely low. Beginning in July 1999, the FVAP worked to obtain volunteer participants for the VOI project, primarily from the uniformed services, advertising VOI through various means, including the active recruitment efforts of Voting Action Officers (VAO) in each branch of the armed forces. Even with these efforts, the initial response rate was low, and the FVAP extended the

Table 7-3. *VOI Participation*

Location	Registrants	Voters
Okaloosa County, Florida	38	38
Orange County, Florida	17	14
Weber County, Utah	14	14
South Carolina	21	17
Dallas County, Texas	1	1
Total	91	84

Source: Taken from Federal Voting Assistance Program, *Voting over the Internet Pilot Project Assessment Report* (Department of Defense, June 2001), pp. 1–14.

deadline for program participation for as long as possible in an attempt to get additional participants. Furthermore, special efforts were needed to get participants in Weber County, Utah, and Dallas County, Texas, where volunteers were few in number.[24] In the end, 127 eligible volunteers were identified in the participating jurisdictions, of whom 104 were uniformed service members, nineteen were military dependents, and four were civilians. Table 7-3 gives the breakdown of the number of UOCAVA citizens in the participating jurisdictions, including the number of voters who registered and then voted.

Of the 127 eligible volunteers in the VOI project, ninety-one registered using the VOI system and eighty-four voted. The VOI voters were located in twenty-eight different states and territories and in twelve different countries across Europe, the Middle East, and the Far East. Okaloosa County, Florida, had the largest number of VOI voters (thirty-eight); seventeen voters were in the state of South Carolina; and fourteen voters each were in Orange County, Florida, and Weber County, Utah. There was only one VOI voter in Dallas County, Texas.

These participation statistics proved to be the most disappointing aspect of the VOI project. Media accounts of the project focused on the fact that only eighty-four people voted using this system at a cost of $6.2 million, which works out to about $74,000 per vote. The Caltech/MIT Voting Technology Project found that counties typically spend approximately $3.50 per voter and that the purchase of a new touch-screen or ATM-style voting system costs about $25 per voter at most.[25] In comparison, the VOI project was somewhat expensive!

Unfortunately, the very low voter participation rate also makes it impossible to evaluate the effectiveness of an Internet voting system for

UOCAVA voters. Such a small sample is statistically meaningless, especially when the voters are distributed across a number of fundamentally different election jurisdictions. Furthermore, the VOI participants (both the voters and the election jurisdictions that were involved in the project) all were volunteers, as were the participants in the Alaska and Arizona Internet voting projects.

Why is this a problem? The VOI participants, in the parlance of social science, are "self-selected." There is every reason to believe that the VOI participants—voters and jurisdictions—were in various ways different from non-VOI participants. One obvious and important way in which VOI voters differed from the larger UOCAVA population is that they had Internet access. Furthermore, they somehow became aware of the VOI program, were sufficiently motivated to seek information about it, and volunteered to participate. Neither the VOI voters nor the jurisdictions were randomly selected; therefore we cannot extrapolate from their voting experience to model its possible impact on UOCAVA citizens or election jurisdictions in general.

The extremely small sample, combined with the self-selection problem, makes it difficult to make meaningful scientific statements about the VOI project. However, some of the data reported by participants in the VOI project provide interesting insights into possible issues in implementing Internet voting. For example, the VOI project had a help desk that was open twenty-four hours a day, seven days a week. The help desk recorded seventy-one calls, the overwhelming majority of which (close to 100 percent) were resolved. Data from the help desk call logs, shown in table 7-4, document some of the problems encountered by VOI participants.[26]

Most of the problems (34 percent) that VOI participants reported related to the DoD PKI digital certificate. Participants lost their PKI floppy disks, could not download the certificates, or forgot their password and therefore could not use their certificate. The second-most-common problem involved errors accessing the VOI website (25 percent); participants either could not access the website or received error messages while using it. The website access errors usually were attributed to typographical errors when users typed in the URL; not clicking on the appropriate buttons on the website; error messages that arose on the website; and incorrect spelling of participants' names on the access control list. The third-most-significant problem involved difficulties installing the Netscape Navigator software (24 percent of reported problems). There were seventy-one technical assistance calls for ninety-one voter registrations

Table 7-4. *Percentage of VOI Help-Desk Calls by Problem Type*

Problem	Percentage of help-desk calls
DoD PKI digital certificate usage	34
Access errors on VOI website	25
Installation of Netscape software	24
Local election official unavailable	8
Citizen shifting IP address	7
Other	7

Source: From VOI evaluation data provided to the authors by the Federal Voting Assistance Program.

and eighty-four voters, which is an extremely high rate—almost one call per vote cast.

The data in the help desk logs were confirmed in exit interviews conducted with VOI participants after they had registered to vote. When asked whether they understood the instructions for obtaining a DoD digital certificate, 17 percent said that they did not, 68 percent said that they did, and 15 percent did not respond. However, 30 percent said that they had difficulty connecting with the digital certificate registration center, while 56 percent said that they had no trouble and 14 percent did not respond. Twenty-two percent said that it took between ten and twenty minutes to complete the certificate download process; 21 percent said that it took more than twenty minutes. Almost half of the respondents to the postregistration survey (43 percent) had to wait more than ten minutes just to download their digital certificate. These statistics, while not necessarily scientifically valid, illustrate that VOI participants had trouble with the DoD PKI digital certificates.

The 2000 VOI project demonstrated that the technology could work; there were no reports of security breaches, no serious technical glitches, and no significant problems that led to loss of votes. However, this pilot project—despite the fact that it cost a great deal of money—did not lead to any scientific understanding of how Internet voting affected the UOCAVA voting experience, whether it made the electoral system more accessible for UOCAVA voters, or what its effect was on the county and state election officials who had to implement it. Again, there was surprisingly little solid data with which to assess the efficacy of Internet voting, although we do commend the FVAP for issuing a thorough report about the VOI trial that contains a great deal of evaluative information.

What Have We Learned from These Trials?

We have learned little from the three experiences with Internet voting in the 2000 presidential campaign and election. Both the Alaska and VOI trials yielded too few voters to make any scientifically valid conclusions. The Arizona experience, while involving many more Internet voters, produced little publicly available data for subsequent study—a criticism of the Alaska primary as well. Looking at the limited data available from the Arizona trial, we find disturbing evidence of very low voter turnout, especially among nonwhite voters, who also were less likely to use the Internet voting option. In addition, in the Arizona and VOI trials, we either heard (Arizona) or saw (VOI) information indicating that Internet voters encountered technical problems that required substantial support to resolve or that might have kept them from voting.[27]

A much more disturbing problem with these Internet voting trials is that not a single one was designed to test the impact of Internet voting in a scientifically meaningful way. We see two other problems with the design of the trials. First, none appears to have been designed with specific hypotheses in mind; the only goal seemed to be to build a functioning system. Many important questions can be raised about the impact of Internet balloting on voters—from whether it can increase voter participation (especially for certain segments of the electorate) to whether it influences voters' perceptions of the importance of their vote or affects other civic values—but none of these questions were asked or answered in 2000. Second, these trials have largely ignored the broader impact of Internet voting on others involved in the electoral process. For example, what impact does Internet voting have on the strategies used by candidates seeking election? How does it influence election administration practices in counties throughout the country? Is it cost effective or affordable as a way to vote? Again, in 2000 none of these questions were asked or answered.

Although the three Internet trials that were conducted for the 2000 election are most relevant to understanding how Internet voting might develop in the United States, there is interest in Internet voting in other nations. Both the United Kingdom and the European Union have recognized the potential of Internet voting and are examining ways to test various Internet voting technologies. Some tests already have been conducted, and other tests are being planned. These trials differ from those in the United States in three ways. First, there is less of a local flavor to elections overseas, where national governments play a greater role in managing elections and promoting new technologies than in the United States. Second, the electoral process in most other nations is much simpler. Many nations have universal or compulsory voter registration, and ballots generally are less complicated and contain far fewer races than in the United States. Third, the European trials have been much smaller in scope than the U.S. trials, giving them the advantage of being easier to control and potentially easier to evaluate.

Two organizations are carrying out trials in Europe. First, the European Commission is sponsoring CyberVote, a €3.2 million project designed to demonstrate the effectiveness of Internet voting. This technology is intended to be much more innovative than the existing technology for online voting in the United States. CyberVote will test the effectiveness of Internet voting on what is referred to as fixed connections (land lines like telephone lines or cable) and mobile connections (including wireless devices like cellular telephones and hand-held computers or personal digital assistants). The goal is to create a fully verifiable, absolutely private, and highly versatile system that operates on an array of platforms. Because of the variations in election laws across the European Union (EU), the project also will examine the various legal impediments to implementing Internet voting in EU nations and make recommendations for how the laws can be modified to allow for Internet voting in the future.

Beyond testing the efficacy of the technology, the evaluation of Cyber-Vote will examine three important measures of the success of Internet voting. First, does the system increase voter participation? In seeking an answer to that question, the evaluation will look at the impact of Internet voting on subpopulations, especially people whose mobility is limited (including people with disabilities and the elderly), people traveling on election day, and expatriates. Second, is the system cost effective? The evaluators want to determine whether the system would reduce administrative costs, as it might if elections can be held without printing as many paper ballots and hiring as many polling place workers. Third, do voters like the voting technology? Is the CyberVote interface user friendly on all three platforms—hard connections, mobile telephone connections, and wireless hand-held PC connections?

CyberVote has conducted Internet voting trials in three jurisdictions.[28] First, the city of Issy-les-Moulineaux ran a trial on December 11, 2002, in an election of the district council. All voting was done over the Internet, with voters voting remotely either from home or from work or at Internet kiosks at local polling stations. The results of the trial, which was intended to test the effectiveness of the technology and to determine how the Internet could be used in a second trial, illustrate the benefits of conducting small-scale trials. The system worked perfectly well at polling sites and home locations, where voters had little difficulty. However, the trial showed that the system was not effective when voters tried to vote from work sites that had certain firewall specifications on their networks. The trial allows the CyberVote system to be modified to address this problem.

A second trial was conducted January 27–31, 2003, in the Kista area of Stockholm, Sweden, to examine how Internet voting could be used to support local government decisionmaking, in the participatory form of deliberative democracy discussed in the previous chapter. This trial was unique in that it targeted only citizens fifty-five years of age and older. Because of the demographics of the community, which has a large number of immigrants, many of whom do not speak Swedish, the trial examined the difficulties in recruiting and implementing Internet voting among special populations. Most voters voted at kiosks, since most had never seen a computer, let alone owned one. The trial illustrated that sucessful Internet voting is possible with such a population, but that voter education and intensive recruitment was necessary to make the initiative a success.

A third trial was held January 13–15, 2003, in Bremen, Germany, at the Bremen University for Public Administration, where Internet voting was used for university elections. This trial tested three aspects of Internet voting. First, it allowed CyberVote to examine online voter registration. Second, it tested the use of digital signatures and smart cards as an authentication method. Third, it tested a system in which many elections often are combined on one ballot. This is not as common in Europe as in the United States, but it is common in Germany, which like the United States has a federal system of government made up of various states. Therefore, testing the system in a multirace university election simulates the multirace aspects of typical German government elections. The test showed that smartcards, along with strong encryption, allowed for a secure election. As for the voting itself, there were few problems, although voter turnout was low with both Internet and paper balloting.

Note how different the EU trials are from the trials that have been held in the United States. While the Arizona and Alaska trials were held in U.S. presidential primaries and the FVAP trial was held in the 2000 general election, the EU trials are testing Internet voting in very small-scale elections. The goal here is to examine Internet voting in various countries, using various voting platforms (from PCs with a land-line Internet connection to wireless PDAs), various populations of voters (including well-educated university students, recent immigrants, and older citizens), and various purposes (from voting in municipal and regional elections to encouraging deliberative democracy). These projects were small, well-contained efforts to evaluate the effectiveness of Internet voting and to plan for expanding on any successes and mitigating any problems.

Online voting also is being considered in the United Kingdom, Germany, and Australia and is being pilot tested in Switzerland. These nations all are working deliberatively to examine the issues associated with Internet voting. In Germany, a phased approach is planned, much like the one that we are advocating, with Internet voting to be tested first in local elections—possibly as soon as 2006—with the goal of having an online national election in 2010.[29] In Switzerland, where voters vote on a variety of referendums throughout the year, Internet voting was pilot tested in Geneva in January 2003 without incident. In the country's first legally binding Internet election, 323 voters cast ballots over the Internet and 370 voted by mail; only forty-eight went to the polls. The Swiss also hired a team of "white-hat" hackers to try to break into their security system over a three-week period—the system was online to voters only for two days—but the hackers failed.[30]

In the United Kingdom, the Electoral Commission and the Office of the e-Envoy have hired a research team at De Montford University to conduct a series of studies of Internet voting. The studies will analyze the legal framework to identify barriers to Internet voting; survey the public about its attitudes; examine the perceptions of different stakeholders; analyze the full range of technologies that can be used for Internet voting; analyze the experiences of other nations and the private sector; and determine the capacity of local governments and election officials to support Internet voting, including pilot projects. The goal is to ensure that the public supports any Internet voting efforts, that they are secure and private, and that local governments can administer them. The United Kingdom held a series of trials in 2002 and 2003 that allowed the Electoral Commission to study Internet voting in smaller, controlled settings before attempting a broader trial. Another key factor in the Internet voting effort in the United Kingdom is that it does have a clear goal, which is to increase voter turnout. Voter participation in U.K. elections has been declining, and it is hoped that making voting easier through Internet voting will combat the problem.

In 2002, real remote electronic or Internet voting was conducted for five races: Liverpool City Council, Sheffield City Council, St. Albans City and District, Crewe and Nantwich Borough Council, and Swindon Borough Council; in each of these locations other voting methods also were allowed, like telephone voting, text-message voting, or touch-screen voting. Interestingly, the Electoral Commission's report on the 2002 projects found no strong evidence that the availability of the Internet voting option led to significant increases in voter turnout. But it also found that "[t]hose who voted appeared to find the procedures relatively easy to use; and even among those who did not vote there was also positive feedback about the convenience of the methods available."[31]

In the United States, the FVAP is conducting another Internet voting project in the 2004 election called the Secure Electronic Registration and Voting Experiment (SERVE). It is an ambitious project, with planned participation of at least thirteen states and a stated goal of facilitating registration and voting over the Internet of perhaps 100,000 citizens overseas. We, the authors, are the primary contractors in designing and implementing this evaluation, and we are applying a study design that will allow us to evaluate the impact of Internet voting on voters and election officials alike in order to answer some of the broader questions posed earlier. Everyone knows that an Internet voting system can be built; we will focus on learning more about how such systems affect the way that people vote and the way that elections are administered. We see the SERVE project as an important stepping stone to the broader deployment of Internet voting in the near future in the United States, a point we will return to in the next chapter.

Because the three 2000 Internet voting trials in the United States failed to follow basic experimental design principles, an important opportunity to provide data that would be scientifically meaningful was completely lost. And without scientifically meaningful data, it is really difficult to assess what impact Internet voting had in these three trials and to make policy recommendations about the future of Internet voting. We hope that the European trials and the SERVE project will provide much stronger research designs, better data, and enlightening analysis of the impact of Internet voting on elections.

CHAPTER **8**

What Can Be Done to Make Internet Voting a Reality?

Our argument to this point can be quickly summarized:

—The idea of bringing real, remote Internet voting to the American public is not a pipe dream of computer geeks, think-tank scholars, academics in ivory towers, or Silicon Valley dot-com wannabes looking for a quick buck.

—Internet voting should solve many of the pressing problems with U.S. elections and may actually stimulate the interest and participation of some groups.

—The major stumbling blocks in the path of Internet voting are the digital divide and security concerns. These are problems that have solutions.

In this chapter we address the final point of our argument by discussing the solutions needed to make Internet voting a reality for all Americans within the next decade.

Solution 1: We Need Real Experiments!

When we discussed the three 2000 Internet voting projects in chapter 7, we were careful to call them trials, not experiments. Unfortunately, in the popular mind, the Alaska, Arizona, and FVAP projects were experiments, even though they were far from being what scientists think of as experiments.

All scientific experiments—whether conducted by high school chemistry students or by biologists trying to determine the basic functions of human genes—follow the same basic principles.[1] The subjects of the experiment—whether people, cells, or something else—are divided into two groups, the control group and the treatment group. Usually subjects are assigned at random to one of the two groups because random assignment helps to ensure that the outcome of the experiment is due to the experiment and not to systematic differences between the control and treatment groups. As suggested by the terms, the control group does not receive the treatment but the treatment group does. With Internet voting, the control group would vote through the traditional process and the experimental group would vote using the Internet. The researchers, by measuring something about the subjects in both treatment and control groups before and after administration of the treatment, could then be confident that as long as the experiment was done correctly, whatever changes they observed in the treatment group that did not appear in the controls were due to the treatment.[2]

The three 2000 trials of Internet voting did not follow the basics of experimental design. They neither randomly assigned individuals into treatment and control groups nor engaged in strong before-and-after-treatment data collection so that the effects of the Internet voting process on voters, election officials, and the political system could be documented with clarity and precision. Not surprisingly, these trials never produced much in the way of usable data for researchers (like us) after they were completed. Only the FVAP project produced a report that contained useful information. Given that these projects failed to follow the basic principles of experimental design, they really do not have much to say, positive or negative, about the impact of Internet voting.

Future attempts to test Internet voting need to follow those principles. The only way that the impact of Internet voting on the electoral process will ever be assessed is through careful experimentation. Unless careful experimentation is conducted, opponents of Internet voting will always be able to argue that the results of any Internet voting project are meaningless—and, unfortunately, they will be correct.

More important, we believe that a real experimental process needs to be developed by the new federal election organization—the Election Administration Commission (EAC)—created by the 2002 Help America Vote Act. The populations of citizens who have the greatest difficulty voting under the current system should be identified, and Internet voting systems should be developed and offered to them for use in elections from 2004 to 2008. The FVAP's current SERVE project, slated for the 2004 election cycle, is a case in point: American citizens overseas, whether they are working in U.S. embassies or elsewhere, serving in the armed forces, or studying, clearly need a better way to register and vote than the current mail-based system. Other populations should be targeted, either by federal or state agencies, especially those who find it difficult or impossible to get to the polls on election day and who have access to the Internet. For example, states could make Internet voting available to all eligible college students who are away from home. Once the populations are identified, control and treatment groups can be formed, before-and-after-treatment data collection strategies can be developed, and the effectiveness of Internet voting can then be assessed.

Solution 2: Give States Grants for Internet Voting Experiments

The federal government should initiate a program under the guidance of the new EAC that would give states grants to conduct Internet voting experiments. This strategy mirrors what is being done currently in the United Kingdom, where the national government is helping to fund local experiments in election reform, including Internet voting. The British also have developed national standards for evaluating these experiments, helping to ensure that the data from each test are comparable.

To qualify, a state would have to provide a clear, research-based plan for making the transition from their current voting systems to a real Internet voting system. The plan must be built on a strong experimental design, all data collected must be disseminated to the public, the study must be done in ways that involve the interested public, and all stages of the project must preserve the basic integrity of the electoral process.

That may sound like a tall order, and it is. But it can be delivered. We can easily envision a sound state transition plan, one that carefully outlines the transition and starts small but has big ambitions. For example, a state could propose to use real Internet voting in real elections—municipal, school board, or county elections. These small-scale projects could be set up to follow the principles of scientific experimentation, to have strong before-and-after measurement strategies in place, and to randomly assign voters to the treatment group (Internet voting system) or control group (current voting system). A state plan could have other wrinkles, too—for example, the state could compare kiosk and remote Internet voting.

Then, on the basis of the state's experimental studies of local elections, a transition strategy could be developed. Taking what it learned from the local experiments, the state could plan to "scale up" the experiments: to move to larger-scale experiments, perhaps statewide elections in which entire counties are allowed to vote on the Internet and others are not. The state would need to establish clear benchmarks for system performance during the transition, with the eventual goal of fully implementing a statewide Internet voting system within a set period.

In our minds, an approach like this, in which states are allowed to experiment with Internet voting, would be ideal. First, states would not be forced by the federal government into a set Internet voting agenda. While some states would jump at the chance to begin a transition to Internet voting, others probably would prefer to wait until the bugs were ironed out. Second, a decentralized experimental approach would not disrupt the basic mode of election administration in existence today, which is characterized by strong state and local control. Third, each state would be its own Internet voting laboratory, meaning that as many as fifty different Internet voting experiments could be conducted in coming years. Admittedly, some will perform better than others, but that is to be expected. Taking multiple approaches to implementation would be the only way to learn about the pros and cons of each. States could develop their own approach, use radically different software and hardware configurations, and experiment in vastly different contexts.

Solution 3: Phase In Internet Voting

Clearly, part of our mantra in Solution 2 is to "start small and scale up." We think that this is an important principle that we need to explain. Internet voting must be thought of as a development process, a transition, from how elections are run now to how they will be run in the future. Going from where the country is today—when many citizens are still forced to vote on antiquated voting systems like lever and punch-card machines—to real Internet voting cannot and should not happen overnight.

Our analogy, and we are serious when we use it, is the process that was used to land Neil Armstrong and Buzz Aldrin on the moon in 1969. NASA did not try to shoot astronauts to the moon immediately. Instead, NASA started small. It launched unmanned rockets into space. Before Alan Shepard made his suborbital flight in space and John Glenn orbited the earth, Ham the chimpanzee made a suborbital flight in space and Enos the chimpanzee orbited the earth. Once NASA had figured out how to get animals into space without killing them, it moved on to the Mercury and Gemini projects, with suborbital flights, orbital flights, and two-man crews in orbit. Then NASA transitioned to the Apollo project, which involved a series of incremental steps: getting boosters to work, putting astronauts in orbit, allowing astronauts to experiment with orbital procedures like docking and undocking the lunar-landing module, sending missions around the moon, landing men on the moon, and then landing men with cool toys like the lunar rover on the moon's surface. NASA identified goals, set benchmarks, started small, and achieved its goal of getting Americans on the moon before the end of 1969.

NASA followed this approach because it wanted to be cautious. It was embarking on an experiment the likes of which had never been conducted in human history, and it knew that the costs of failure were enormous. The prestige and stature of the nation were at risk. It was not just a question of American pride; a nation that could place men on the moon clearly could also lob intercontinental ballistic missiles to the other side of the world. And it should not be forgotten that the astronauts sat at the top of a tower of explosives; the death of too many American astronauts would have had a chilling effect on the moon effort.

The NASA example also underscores the need to remain vigilant and continue experimenting long after a program or technology has become mature. The recent space shuttle Columbia disaster and the 1986 Challenger disaster both were largely the result of a failure on the part of NASA to maintain an organizational culture that continued to experiment and to question how things were being done. Fortunately, the world of election administration—and Internet voting in particular—are among the most scrutinized public policies, with candidates, election attorneys, interest groups, and the media all carefully watching over all aspects of the process. These groups will serve an important role in ensuring that experiments with Internet voting are carefully conducted and that the lessons learned from these experiments are not construed too broadly.

The transition from how elections are run today to full-blown Internet voting should be incremental and cautious. First, fundamental steps still need to be taken to study Internet security and resolve the digital divide, problems that require research and resolution. Second, we are concerned about the same types of gross system malfunctions that troubled NASA engineers. If the country rushes headlong into Internet voting and major glitches arise, it could set the development of Internet voting back for years, maybe even permanently. We expect that some of the small-scale pilot projects that we propose to study Internet voting will fail and that things will go wrong. But there is much to be learned from failed experiments, and the risk of failure should not stop efforts to develop a strategy for implementing Internet voting. However, the developers must work to minimize the risks during any experimental pilot projects and to maintain redundant systems so that the basic legitimacy of the democratic process is not compromised. Third, there is a lot at risk, just as in the cold war. The 2000 election revealed a dark underside of American democracy that exposed the nation to ridicule across the world—and that arguably shook the faith of many Americans in their political system. The country needs to continue to work to fix those problems, but it must ensure that its efforts to fix the existing problems do not lead to other, possibly greater, problems in the future.

Today, many states and counties are spending millions of dollars in a rush to get rid of their old voting equipment and buy the new touch-screen technology, often spending thousands of dollars per touch-screen unit. We think that in many cases they are moving too quickly and not spending enough time and effort to conduct a rational and realistic transition from their old system to a new one. As discussed earlier, problems were seen in Florida's 2002 primary elections involving many counties that had jumped from their old voting system to new touch-screen units without any real transition. More problems were witnessed in the 2002 elections in other counties throughout the nation.

The rapid, nonphased introduction of these high-tech machines into the voting process is problematic for two important reasons. First, it inevitably leads to glitches, mistakes, and errors that mar the public's perception of the benefits of using newer technologies for voting. Most of these problems could be avoided by allowing for a careful transition period in which local election officials and voters adjust to the new voting systems over time. Second, and more important, it is unfortunate because the transition to touch-screen voting systems really should be part of a transition to Internet voting. Election administrators seem to believe that these new high-tech voting machines are the solution to the problems with their old voting systems, and in many cases they may be solutions to some problems. But, after all, they are just computers, and with some reconfiguration many of them could be turned into Internet-ready voting stations, for poll site Internet voting, for example. So, we urge caution regarding the current rush to purchase and use these new voting systems; we think that their implementation should be phased in gradually.

Again, as voting on these systems is being conducted on computer systems, the change should be seen as an opportunity to learn more about how voters respond to the new technology, how it affects the efforts of local election officials, and what effect it has on the electoral process. Information collected about the transition to touch-screen machines can provide invaluable insight into issues that also are likely to be associated with the transition from touch-screen voting to Internet voting.

In any case, Internet voting will not—and should not—happen overnight. For decades, many citizens have used punch cards, lever machines, and even paper ballots to cast their votes; many of these citizens now are being asked to use computers. That transition should take place over the span of the next ten years. Such gradual implementation will allow for further research and development, help to iron out the bugs without enormous risks, and minimize any negative impact that the transition to Internet voting might have on the U.S. political process and society.

Solution 4: Use the Internet to Promote Deliberative Democracy

One way to make Internet voting acceptable to governments and voters alike is to make voting and civic participation more a part of everyday life. E-government is a worldwide phenomenon; governments everywhere already are doing more to become part of the wired world, for example, by allowing citizens to pay taxes, renew licenses, file documents, and gather information about their governments using the Internet. Demand is growing for these types of citizen-to-government and business-to-government interactions, which reduce transaction costs and make government more efficient and effective.

Deliberative democracy initiatives that use the Internet also can improve communication between the public and governments and make governments more effective, and the federal government and private foundations should provide funding to cities and counties to develop such initiatives. These initiatives could use the Internet infrastructure that now exists in libraries, schools, and homes, combined with Internet kiosks in public places such as malls and grocery stores. City and county governments could then use the Internet to provide the public with information about key community issues and use public input to determine how those issues should be addressed.

The current attempts of cities and counties across the nation to solve their budget shortfalls are a case in point. This issue often is presented to voters in zero-sum terms—raise taxes or cut spending—and it is hard for them to make a decision about what should be done. For example, voters may not want to pay higher taxes, but they also may not want services at their children's schools to be cut. Deliberative democracy initiatives would allow voters to study relevant information on the web and then make choices—in essence, vote for specific policies. Government officials then could take voters' informed responses into account as they make their decisions.

Deliberative democracy activities also would be beneficial because they would allow local election officials to examine various issues that arise with Internet voting. For example, different security procedures could be tested in an ongoing deliberative democracy initiative. Various voter interfaces and voter mobilization efforts also could be tested. All told, the use of deliberative democracy would be helpful to governments, which would gain valuable information about the policy stance of voters; to election officials, who would gain valuable insight into the ways that voters interact with voting technology; and to voters, who would be able to inform the government of their views in a meaningful way.

Solution 5: More Research on Internet Voting Security

Ensuring system security is one of the most significant hurdles in implementing Internet voting today, and the opportunities for breaching the system are a source of constant criticism. The federal government should play a major role in coming years in basic research and development efforts to produce new and improved Internet security systems. The recently passed Cyber Security Research and Development Act will provide $903 million over five years to university and industry research programs through a competitive grant process run by the National Science Foundation and the National Institute of Standards and Technology. Under the provisions of the act, research is to be pursued in the areas of authentication, cryptography and secure communications, intrusion detection, computer and network reliability, privacy and confidentiality, network security architecture, emerging threats and vulnerability assessments, wireless security, and enhancement of law enforcement efforts. Through this expansion of effort, the federal government can continue to be a major catalyst for basic research and development of Internet security solutions now and after 2007, when appropriations under the act end.

Four important areas will continue to need significant research. First, studies are needed to document legitimate security threats to Internet voting systems and to assess the relative likelihood of their occurrence with different types of Internet voting architecture. For example, a quantitative determination needs to be made for specific types of Internet voting systems of the likelihood that a denial-of-service attack would impede the ability of voters to access the servers. The relative risks of interference in the electronic transmission of ballots with different methods of ballot transmission also could be assessed. Instead of wasting time on heated rhetoric and uninformed debate, researchers should gather solid information about the relative importance of different threats for different types of Internet voting architecture. Furthermore, studies of election and voting fraud in current voting systems and comparisons of known threats in those systems with estimated risks for Internet voting systems are crucial. Research on security risks for current and future voting systems is a critical area for social science and information technology scholars.

The second area involves the development of methods to combat the various threats to Internet voting, most especially denial-of-service attacks and viruses. These efforts should encourage innovative efforts to enhance Internet voting security, such as those based on distributed computer networks. One particularly exciting new research area is the Infrastructure for Resilient Internet Systems (IRIS) project, currently being funded by a $12 million National Science Foundation grant to MIT, the University of California at Berkeley, New York University's International Computer Science Institute, and Rice University.

IRIS seeks to change the basic architecture of the Internet from the common client-server relationship (wherein one or a small number of centralized servers run a particular website) to a "distributed hash table"(DHT) technology that allows applications to be run across a more widely distributed network of computers. Under the current conventional Internet architecture, a request for information travels to a known computer; thus an Internet voting system would involve some servers storing balloting information and data at a known location that could be targeted in a denial-of-service attack. A DHT approach to an Internet voting system would break this conventional design. Information requests could be sent without anyone necessarily knowing the location of the server providing the requested data (ballots, for example).[3]

Cybersecurity also will benefit from the increased attention this problem will receive because of its importance to the war on terrorism. In a move of critical importance, the Department of Homeland Security (DHS) has recently taken the lead in addressing problems associated with cybersecurity. Its National Cyber Security Division (NCSD) is charged with three distinct tasks: identifying the risks facing America's cyber assets and helping reduce those risks in coordination with the private sector; overseeing the consolidated Cyber Security Tracking, Analysis, and Response Center (CSTARC), which will detect and respond to Internet events, track potential vulnerabilities of and threats to cyberspace, and coordinate cybersecurity and incident response with federal, state, local, private sector, and international partners; and creating, in coordination with other appropriate agencies, cybersecurity awareness and education programs and partnerships with consumers, businesses, governments, academia, and international communities.[4]

The NCSD is a central implementation of *The National Strategy to Secure Cyberspace*, a report released by the Bush administration in February 2003.[5] Critics have argued that the report, which emphasized public-private cooperation, does not contain effective regulatory incentives to improve cybersecurity. However, proponents have pointed out that both Microsoft and Cisco Systems created companywide security initiatives after their executives met with federal officials. A report released last year by the Computer Science and Telecommunications Board of the National Research Council recommended mandatory reporting by businesses of hacking incidents that might endanger critical infrastructure.[6] Such measures would be similar to the Security and Exchange Commission's requirement for mandatory disclosure of Y2K preparation. At present, the DHS has not pursued the mandatory reporting option, but it is likely that the way in which cyberattacks are handled will change in the future. The DHS is currently planning to continue its effort to promote business partnerships; the new division will not regulate corporations but instead act as a bully pulpit for creating a culture of cybersecurity.

Cybersecurity also will likely benefit from a large increase in federal funding. Key members of Congress, such as Representative Christopher Cox (R-Calif.), who chairs the House Select Committee on Homeland Security, have expressed concern that there needs to be a marked increase in funding for critical infrastructure protection, a category that includes cybersecurity. Over the next several years, it is likely that funding for protection of the cybersecurity infrastructure will increase as funding for homeland security increases.

Third, research on methodologies for secure voter authentication also is necessary. The current technology relies on some form of digital certificate, which the voter obtains through an independent entity that verifies the voter's identity. The voter then uses the digital certificate, often with an accompanying password, providing a strong form of authentication; however, it is not foolproof. This procedure and the current vote-by-mail system have the same sort of problem: a voter can obtain a ballot but someone else can vote the ballot. Just as an absentee ballot will be honored as long as the signatures match sufficiently, as long as a digital certificate and password combination is valid, an electronic ballot will be counted no matter who submits it.

Clearly, additional research is needed into mechanisms to tighten security at this stage of the Internet voting process. Tools must be designed to tie a digital certificate to a single eligible voter and only that voter, perhaps by using some form of biometrics or similar future technology. Only by encouraging and funding research and development is the country likely to find technological solutions to the problem in the near future.

Furthermore, research should be done to enhance the security of any electronic devices that can be used for Internet voting, especially wireless devices like cellular phones and personal digital assistants. Although we have conceptualized Internet voting as being conducted by voters on personal computers and workstations, as the digital revolution continues, people increasingly will rely on smaller and more portable electronic devices. Use of Wi-Fi technology already is exploding in Asia, and Intel and other high-tech companies are making Wi-Fi standard on their mobile products. More and more locations in the United States are becoming Wi-Fi accessible as well, with the number of wireless-enabled sites quadrupling to 4,000 nationwide in 2002. The amount of network traffic and number of subscribers also are increasing dramatically.[7] As long as the Internet connection from these devices is secure, there is no reason why they cannot be used for voting. The EU CyberVote project is currently examining whether Internet voting can be supported on wireless devices, and the United States may be able to learn much from those tests.

Fourth, careful studies of different types of architecture for Internet registration and voting are essential. Comparative analysis of different approaches to the implementation of Internet voting systems can answer a myriad of questions. Are some types of architecture more accessible? Does a system make the job of election administration simpler or more complicated? Are some types of architecture more cost effective than others? Are some more secure than others? How can Internet voting systems be built that allow for independent recording of the voter's intentions, and how do systems that allow for multiple and independent recording of voter intentions affect security and accessibility? Questions like these can best be answered by comparing different types of voting system architecture, either by direct comparison of different Internet systems or by comparison of Internet and current non-Internet voting systems.

A caveat is in order. Although we are recommending that the federal government make a serious effort to promote development of Internet security applications, Internet voting should not be made so secure that it becomes accessible to just a small number of voters. New developments in Internet voting security should be as transparent as possible. They should not require complicated procedures, lots of new software, or the use of expensive hardware. One of the major reasons for implementing Internet voting is to enhance voter access, and systems developers must not forget that strong security procedures can disenfranchise voters.

Such research and development efforts, while aimed at producing reliable security systems for Internet voting, are likely to have numerous commercial applications. In the long run, building more secure computer systems and portable and wireless devices should have a significant payoff; they may even pay for themselves. Stronger Internet security systems will be used by both the government and the private sector, and developing them should be seen as a public investment in making the Internet a better medium of communication for everyone. Furthermore, increasing government-funded basic science research and development efforts in the United States may make economic and educational sense: currently the United States ranks last among the G-8 nations in terms of research and development performed in the academic sector as a percentage of total research and development. By this measure, the United States, at 12 percent, was last, dramatically outstripped by the United Kingdom (20 percent), Canada (24 percent), and Italy (25 percent).[8]

Solution 6: Resolve the Legal Issues Involved in Making Internet Voting a Reality

Existing state legislation is another important barrier to Internet voting, and in many states it will have to be changed. For example, the use of technologies like digital signatures (and their successor technologies) for voter authentication will have to be authorized. The changes to state election codes needed to allow remote Internet voting should be researched and identified now.

Moreover, making Internet voting a reality will require altering a mindset that dates back to the 1600s, when voting on a single day and in person was necessary. No longer will elections occur on a single day; they will take place over a period of time—two, three, or even four weeks. This change may substantially reduce the likelihood of successful denial-of-service attacks on Internet voting systems; more generally, a longer voting period would make voting easier for more people.

Another important conceptual change that is needed is to break the association between the geographic location of the voter and the act of voting. Currently, voters typically are required to vote at a specific poll site determined by their residential address, but as no-fault absentee voting and early voting continue to take hold across the United States, that is changing. However, remote Internet voting will be truly any time, any place voting. And again, it is likely to require changes to the election codes of many states.

Regulations associated with the certification and testing of voting systems are a final aspect of state election codes that might need examination. There are federal standards for voting systems, but they are voluntary, and many states have adopted their own. The federal standards program, initiated in 1984 and conducted by the Federal Election Commission, produced a new set of standards in 2002 that, although they updated the existing standards and testing process, do not appear to cover remote Internet voting systems.[9] Given that few Internet voting systems are currently available in the marketplace, that may be understandable, but for remote Internet voting to become a reality in the near future, either the Federal Election Commission or the EAC should begin to study the issue and develop standards. The recent revision of the federal standards took three years of hard work by many individuals and groups, and there is no reason to believe that the production of useful and flexible Internet voting standards would be any quicker or easier.

In addition, states need to make legal and procedural changes in order to test and certify Internet voting systems. In many states, the current certification process can take a very long time—months if not years. The development of Internet voting systems is likely to be a rapid, dynamic process that may outstrip the ability of many states to test and certify new systems quickly and adequately. States should consider changing their election laws to allow for more flexibility. They may especially benefit from turning to other agencies with significant experience with testing new technologies, such as the National Institute of Standards and Technology.

States should also work to provide more openness and public involvement in the testing and certification of electronic voting systems, in particular, Internet-based systems. As computer software continues to become more vital to voting systems, states need to develop clear regulations and procedures for how the public can have the ability to examine and scrutinize the inner workings of all electronic voting systems. In particular, we believe the Caltech/MIT Voting Technology Project is correct to recommend that states should require that important components of voting system software be open source: "the source code for all vote recording and vote counting processes must be open source. The source code for the user interface can and should be proprietary, so that vendors can develop their products" (page 46). Openness and transparency are critical to ensuring that the public has confidence in the integrity of the electoral process.

State election laws will require substantial change in many different areas for Internet voting to become a reality. A state-by-state survey of current election codes is needed in the very near future so that aspects of each state code that would block implementation of Internet voting can be identified and revisions proposed. The EAC, which the Help America Vote Act directs to conduct research on election administration issues, would be well positioned to direct this study, which would lay the legal and procedural groundwork for any implementation of Internet voting, especially within the next decade.

Solution 7: Eliminate the Digital Divide

The current digital divide is the most significant barrier to Internet voting in the near term. A considerable number of Americans still do not have ready access to the Internet, and better-educated, higher-income, younger, and white Americans are more likely to have access than are less-educated, lower-income, older, and nonwhite Americans. If Internet voting were instituted in the 2004 presidential election, for example, there is no question that some Americans would have easier access and would be better able to participate than others. That would be unfair to those without ready Internet access, and it would probably violate the Voting Rights Act.

What can be done to eliminate the digital divide? On one hand, the trend is clear—with every passing day, more and more Americans are gaining access to the Internet, and slowly the racial, economic, educational, and age gaps between those with and those without access are diminishing. The cost of computers is declining rapidly, and the number of Americans who can afford an Internet-ready computer is increasing.[10] To date, computer sellers and Internet access providers have tended to largely ignore minority and lower-income communities in their advertising and marketing strategies. As the market for computers and the Internet services in higher-income households becomes saturated, however, these companies will have to market their products better to new consumer groups, and there is some evidence that they already have begun to do so.[11] And the digital divide's age gap will by necessity diminish over time, due to population replacement effects. Younger Americans have long been exposed to computers and the Internet, and they will continue to use them as they grow older.[12]

Time must pass before the vast bulk of the American population adopts any new technology. The adoption trends for computers and the Internet are similar to those for televisions and VCRs.[13] These trends will diminish the digital divide at some point in the next decade without any government intervention, and Internet use in American households will be essentially universal. Furthermore, Americans will continue to have better, faster, and cheaper (possibly free) Internet access in workplaces, schools, and public places. Internet kiosks are now appearing in locations like airports, and Internet cafes are a common sight in many U.S. cities. So while we acknowledge that a digital divide exists today, it is shrinking, and in time the market will put computers in the hands of more people, even low-income and minority consumers. The price of a computer has declined markedly over the past two decades and will continue to decline in the future. The digital divide will disappear at some point in the near term; the question is whether it will disappear rapidly enough.[14]

We believe that increasingly Americans will want to conduct their business with the government, including voting, over the Internet, especially younger Americans who are used to using the Internet in other aspects of their lives. If a twenty-something banks online and shops online and pays taxes online, he or she will want to vote online. Moreover, the problems with voting systems that appeared throughout the United States in 2000 and 2002 are likely to continue to plague future elections; they might even get worse. If pressure builds for Internet voting but the digital divide still exists, what positive steps can the government take to provide Internet access for everyone?

In his January 20, 2000, State of the Union Address, President Clinton proposed a series of initiatives to close the digital divide. He mentioned in particular proposals in the budget to make sure that all new teachers have computer skills, to develop technology centers for adults in 1,000 low-income communities across the nation, and to provide new tax incentives for computer companies to donate computers to schools and libraries. In sum, his package called for roughly $2.3 billion to help eliminate the digital divide within the next decade.[15] Unfortunately, most of Clinton's ambitious proposals were "dead on arrival" in Congress, and even this proposal did not go far enough to deal with the digital divide, even within the next decade.

The policy model we propose follows the basic historical approach used by the federal government to ensure that all Americans have access to electronic means of communication. In 1934, the Federal Communications Commission (FCC) was created; its purpose, as amended, is "to make available, so far as possible, to all the people of the United States, without discrimination on the basis of race, color, religion, national origin, or sex, a rapid, efficient, Nationwide, and world-wide wire and radio communication service with adequate facilities at reasonable charges."[16] The creation of the FCC launched a new regulatory era that over time led to the nearly universal use in the United States of telephones, radios, and television and newer means of communication like cable television and wireless devices. In 1996, the Telecommunications Act greatly revised the original 1934 act, especially in establishing the principle of competitive competition in all markets for communications.

The 1996 Telecommunications Act, oddly enough, failed to make any significant effort to deal with the Internet as an aspect of U.S. communications policy. A very important component of the 1996 act was a revision and expansion of "universal service" programs, initiatives designed to expand telecommunications access to rural residents, schools, and libraries and to low-income Americans. For low-income citizens, there are two programs: LinkUp America, which provides up to $30.00 in subsidies for telephone installation charges, and the Lifeline Assistance Program, which provides as much as $7.85 a month in discounts for telephone service to qualified individuals. These programs are financed through contributions that come from companies supplying interstate telecommunications services.

However, Internet service is subsidized only through the universal service programs to schools and libraries, which leaves out rural and poor Americans. A recent study by Austan Goolsbee and Jonathan Guryan found that in California public schools this FCC program accelerated the spread of Internet access dramatically: there were 66 percent more Internet classrooms than there might have been without the program.[17] Nevertheless, the FCC needs to play a more direct and proactive role in addressing the digital divide and ensuring that universal access is a reality, especially by providing subsidized services to the poor and to individuals in rural areas. As telephone, cable television, and Internet technologies converge, the FCC needs to ensure that its policies create a level playing field for all individuals and technologies and that traditional subsidies for one technology carry over to new technologies.

According to the most recent data available from the U.S. Census Bureau, approximately 46.3 million households in the United States do not have computers and 52.6 million do not have Internet access; about 88 percent of households with computers have Internet access.[18] Clearly, the easiest way to eliminate the digital divide is to get computers into the remaining households. Although this will happen inevitably due to market forces, what can the government do to speed up the process?

During the 2002 holiday shopping season, a brand new Dell Dimension 2300 desktop computer—complete with a 1.8 Celeron processor, a fifteen-inch monitor, a modem, software, and a six-month AOL membership—could be purchased for less than $500. In many ways this is much more computer than an average household may ever need for basic Internet access and routine tasks such doing homework and preparing income-tax forms. But the cost is a good estimate of what it might take to get an adequate computer with Internet access into a household. It would take $23 billion dollars over the next decade to get one computer into every American household that currently does not have one, or $2.3 billion dollars per year (which would put 4.6 million computers into households each year). Of course, not all of the households that do not own computers are so impoverished that they cannot afford to purchase one, and some individuals simply do not want to own a computer.

Typically, the government uses two means of helping households to acquire things. Either it subsidizes the purchase of the item, or it creates a tax incentive for purchasing the item. For example, low-income households often receive rent subsidies for housing, while Americans who purchase real property can deduct the mortgage interest from their taxes. The mortgage interest deduction has proven to be exceptionally effective in making the United States a nation of homeowners, and housing subsidies have ensured that many low-income families live in adequate housing. Computer and Internet purchases could be promoted by similar means. Either the government could assist low-income households in purchasing computers through a direct subsidy, or it could allow Americans to deduct the cost of a computer from their taxes (low-income households that owe little or no taxes would receive a tax credit from the government to cover the purchase).

How much would this subsidy total? Assume that 50 percent of households that do not own computers need some government assistance to buy one. That means that 23 million households need a computer, which would cost approximately $11.5 billion total, or $1.15 billion a year for ten years. If instead of buying each household a computer outright, the federal government paid half of the price of the computer, that would reduce the government's annual outlay to $575 million a year for ten years.

There are many ways that this digital divide reduction program could be financed, regardless of whether it is offered as a tax credit or a direct subsidy. For example, it could be financed entirely or partly by fees from FCC spectrum auctions—competitive bidding events for FCC communications licenses, including those for cellular service and the television spectrum—which the government believes will bring in revenues of at least $25 billion between 2003 and 2008.[19] The elimination of even a few pork barrel projects—for example, just a handful of the estimated $5 billion in pork barrel spending identified by Senator John McCain in the defense appropriations bill for 2003—would easily cover the costs.[20] A small federal tax on Internet purchases or transactions— a tax that would fall most heavily on higher-income households—also would cover the cost.

But there are other strategies that should be pursued to eliminate the digital divide quickly. For example, all public school classrooms in the nation should have not only a computer but also Internet access. Surprisingly, Mississippi is the only state that has come anywhere near the goal of having all public school classrooms connected to the Internet, and only because Mississippi's governor established a deadline to achieve that goal by the end of 2002. Mississippi has approximately 30,000 classrooms, and as it turned out, wiring them for Internet access was not the most important hurdle—it was finding enough computers. To obtain enough Internet-ready computers, Mississippi embarked on a novel approach—it got the components and had groups of students build the computers, creating an opportunity to teach them basic computer science and electrical engineering and to give them some vocational skills as well.[21] Other innovative policies are needed to ensure Internet access for every classroom in the remaining forty-nine states.

Efforts also are being made in many lower-income communities to promote community computing activities. These efforts—which typically are supported by schools, nonprofit organizations, and government organizations such as housing authorities—attempt to promote computer access for low-income households to show them how technology can help them achieve their personal and community goals. Such programs are becoming easier to offer with the continuing decrease in the cost of computers and the low cost of connectivity to the Internet. While the programs do not ensure that every individual is able to have a computer at home, community computing can play an important interim role in ensuring that all Americans have access to the online world.[22]

Internet Voting In the Next Decade: A Rough Roadmap

In a nutshell, Internet voting in the United States can be feasible by the end of the decade. Not only will it be feasible, it should be a superior way for Americans to participate in the political process. In this chapter, we have presented a series of policy recommendations and plans aimed at getting the country to the point that all Americans can vote online. We are confident that this is a goal that can be reached and that by using the Internet to cast ballots, the political process will become stronger, more secure, and more accessible for more Americans. Achieving this goal, however, will require a strong and lasting commitment from federal and state governments, extensive study by academics and researchers, and willingness to experiment and develop a gradual transition from today's disparate voting systems to Internet voting in the future.

Step 1: 2002–2004

The road to widespread Internet voting is under construction now, at the Federal Voting Assistance Program. There, staff are working on getting Internet voting services to one of the hardest-to-reach voting populations: individuals who live or serve in the armed forces overseas. This initiative—SERVE—will be in operation during the entire 2004 election cycle, providing valuable information on how overseas voters use the Internet to cast their ballots. One of the benefits of SERVE is that the government is funding an extensive evaluation component, which we are heading, to determine the factors that lead individuals to vote online and the issues encountered by election administrators. With these data, it will be possible to begin to develop a baseline for understanding the barriers and benefits of Internet voting. A key aspect of SERVE is that it also is a voter registration system, so for the first time there will be data on the use of the Internet to register voters.

SERVE is likely to play an important role in setting standards for the operation of future Internet voting systems. The FVAP is working closely with the Federal Election Commission (FEC) in order to use the process of developing and certifying the SERVE system as the basis for developing Internet voting system standards. SERVE and the FEC will work together closely during the development and implementation of SERVE. For example, members of the FEC standards-setting body will sit on the SERVE steering committee, providing guidance for conducting registration and voting over the Internet and offering advice on the features and functions that the systems should have and the way that the systems should be implemented. Thus the SERVE program is likely to play a key role in shaping the way future Internet elections are conducted.

While SERVE is being developed and conducted in the United States, a series of ongoing Internet voting experiments will be taking place in the United Kingdom. The United Kingdom's Office of the e-Envoy is planning to spend £10 million ($16.6 million) over the 2003–2005 period to support Internet voting experiments across the nation. Local election officials will be working with the e-Envoy to develop Internet voting experiments in local elections in 2003 and in other elections in 2004 and 2005. These experiments will be evaluated to provide another body of useful data about the impact of Internet voting on elections. If the results are similar to those found in previous U.K. elections, they are likely to show that Internet voting benefits voters and election administrators alike.

Moreover, all across the United States, states and counties are upgrading their existing voting systems, in most cases by purchasing new touch-screen machines. These purchases really represent a transition from the voting systems of the past to Internet voting in the future. The touch-screen systems should allow voters and election officials to become familiar with the use of computers in the voting process, and their use should provide a good deal of necessary data on Internet voting. By the end of the 2004 presidential elections, a lot will have been learned, for better and worse, about how voters and election officials respond to electronic voting, at least in the polling place.

Step 2: 2005–2006

By the 2004 election, the new federal election agency, the Election Assistance Commission, will be in place. Congress has given the commission the task of conducting a comprehensive review of Internet voting that includes an analysis of the critical issues we have discussed throughout the book:

—security requirements

—certification requirements

—online voter registration

—legal and regulatory barriers to Internet registration and voting

—the impact of Internet technology on voter participation rates, voter education, and public access

—data collection, storage, and processing

—the implementation cost of an online or Internet voting or voter registration system

—equity of access to online or Internet voting

—the impact of technology on the speed, timeliness, and accuracy of vote counts.

This reporting requirement provides a unique opportunity for the Election Assistance Commission to evaluate Internet voting in the United States. The commission will be able to conduct a thorough review of any laws or regulations that may serve as barriers to the implementation of Internet voting. For example, many states will not accept digital signatures on a voter registration form or an absentee Internet voting ballot, even though digital signatures are legal in most other situations. Other laws are more draconian: for example, some states will not allow ballots to be transmitted online. This study will be the first effort to catalogue the barriers to Internet voting. Its findings will allow Congress to determine whether the government should assist in making Internet voting a reality or in developing model state legislation to facilitate Internet voting.

However, even more exciting is the possibility that the commission will use this study as an opportunity to fund a series of Internet voting experiments in 2005 and 2006. In 2005, both Virginia and New Jersey will have elections for statewide offices, and many large cities—from Atlanta to Los Angeles, Seattle, and New York—will have mayoral elections. In addition, many smaller local governments will hold regular elections, and special elections will be called to fill various vacancies and vote in various referendums. These elections provide fertile ground for testing Internet voting following the scientific guidelines discussed earlier in this chapter. The Internet would supplement, not replace, traditional voting in these elections. Careful evaluation would provide critical data on what makes for a successful—or abysmal—Internet voting experience.

The results of the experiments in 2005 can serve as the benchmark for additional experiments in the 2006 midterm elections. Internet voting studies, using solid, scientific experimental methods, could be conducted in the primary and in the general elections, providing a wealth of data on the impact of these systems on both hardcore voters—the partisan types who typically vote in primary elections—and the more casual voters who turn out in general elections. Some jurisdictions could use Internet voting for up to three elections before the 2006 general election, providing a wealth of data about how well voters and election administrators alike adapt to the system over time. In addition, if the FVAP's SERVE experiment goes well in 2004, there may be pressure from Congress to continue the program for the 2006 election, which will provide another longitudinal test of the system. These experiments also would allow the commission to make truly meaningful recommendations to Congress about the future of Internet voting in the United States and the actions that the federal government can take to make it a reality. Moreover, the tests would also begin the process of phasing in Internet voting across the nation. Both local election officials and voters would be able to familiarize themselves with this new technology, creating a cadre of users who will be able to hit the ground running when Internet voting becomes broadly available.

While these field experiments of Internet voting are being conducted, the process of addressing security issues will already have begun. Through the Cyber Security Research and Development Act (CSRDA), Congress will have started to assist the Election Administration Commission in its effort to evaluate Internet voting. Congress wants to ensure that election reforms do not result in increases in voter fraud, and it is especially supportive of research to make Internet voting as secure as possible. The federal grants issued under CSRDA for cybersecurity research will directly benefit Internet voting. If Congress fully funds this program, by the 2008 election there should be a larger cadre of individuals with expertise in Internet security to work with local election officials to make sure that their systems have as few vulnerabilities as possible. Likewise, the process of disseminating better information about Internet security will have begun, which should help to increase the security of the Internet overall.

Step 3: 2007–2012

The small, early Internet voting experiments that could be conducted in 2005 and 2006 should be continued in 2007 and 2008. However, the second wave of experiments would benefit greatly from lessons learned from analyses of the earlier experiments. All too often, public policies are implemented incrementally, with "incremental" meaning only that more jurisdictions are included; no real consideration is given to how effective a policy is. Internet voting experiments in 2005 and 2006 could provide policymakers with important data on the factors that lead to successful implementation of Internet systems. These lessons can be acted on in the next phase of implementations, so that by the end of the 2008 presidential election cycle, a clear understanding will emerge of what makes for a successful Internet voting experience.

Step 4: 2009 and Beyond

By the end of 2008, market forces, possibly bolstered by government policies, should narrow the digital divide considerably, creating a nation in which the gap between the wired and unwired communities is much smaller. Similarly, new, lower-cost technologies such as wireless Internet and hand-held computers will bring in even more people, in a broader range of environments. It will have been fifteen years since the advent of the Internet as we know it, and voters and election administrators will have had five years of Internet voting experiments under their belts. Clear lessons will have been learned about who votes online and why and about what makes for a successful Internet voting experience. In addition, market pressures among competing Internet providers should bring the cost of voting services down—and the cost of election systems in general with it.

At the turn of the decade, the public will be well aware of the benefits and costs associated with the new election technology and policymakers will be in a position to expand Internet voting from the experimental stage—in small elections or among select populations of voters in larger elections—to the forefront of the election process. If policymakers use the experimental methods we describe, by the 2010 midterm elections and the 2012 presidential election, the business executive, the working parent, the college student, the person with a disability, and the technologically savvy all may find themselves voting for members of Congress and the president with the click of a mouse—assuming, of course, that computers still have them.

Notes

Chapter 1

1. The language from the consent decree can be found in Governor's Select Task Force on Election Procedures, Standards, and Technology, "Revitalizing Democracy in Florida" (Tallahassee: Collins Center for Public Policy, March 1, 2001), p. 59.

2. Paul Brinkley-Rogers, "Absentee Ballots: GOP Sues to Have Military Votes from Overseas Counted," *Miami Herald*, November 23, 2000, p. C12.

3. Paul Brinkley-Rogers, "Military Ballots: Rejected Votes Not Unusual," *Miami Herald*, November 21, 2000, p. A16.

4. Eric C.Newburger, *Home Computers and Internet Use in the United States: August 2000* (Census Bureau, 2001) (www.census.gov/population/www/socdemo/computer.html [July 28, 2003]).

5. Richard L. Berke, "Forbes Declares Candidacy on Internet and the Stump," *New York Times*, March 17, 1999, p. A19.

6. Don Van Natta, "The 2000 Campaign: The Money Game; McCain Gets Big Payoff on Web Site," *New York Times*, February 24, 2000, p. A24.

7. Walter Kirn, "The New Radicals: The People Who Brought Us Seattle Have Now Done Washington; Are They Dreamers or Sly Subversives?" *Time*, April 24, 2000, p. 42.

8. Jennifer Lee, "How Protesters Mobilized So Many and So Nimbly," *New York Times*, February 23, 2003, p. 3. See also George Packer, "Smart-Mobbing the War," *New York Times Magazine*, March 9, 2003, pp. 46–49.

9. Shanthi Kalathil, "Dot Com for Dictators," *Foreign Affairs* (March-April 2003), pp. 43–49; and William J. Drake, Shanthi Kalathil, and Taylor C. Boas, "Dictatorships in the Digital Age: Some Considerations on the Internet in China and Cuba," *iMP: The Magazine on Information Impacts* (October 2000)

(www.ceip.org/files/Publications/dictatorships_digital_age.asp?p=5&from=pub-
date [September 26, 2003]).

10. For an overview of e-government in the U.S., see Elaine Ciulla Kamarck
and Joseph S. Nye Jr., eds., *Governance.com: Democracy in the Information Age*
(Brookings, 2002). An international perspective can be found in J.E.J.S. Prins, ed.,
*Designing E-Government: On the Crossroads of Technical Innovation and Insti-
tutional Change* (The Hague: Kluwer Law International, 2001).

11. Kathy M. Kristof, "File Taxes Online, on Their Dime," *Los Angeles Times*,
January 19, 2003, p. C3. According to the IRS, 226,609,323 returns were filed in
fiscal year 2002 (www.irs.gov/pub/irs-soi/02db04nr.xls [September 26, 2003]) and
46,890,813 of them were filed electronically and accepted (www.irs.gov/pub/irs-
soi/02db03nr.xls [September 26, 2003]). Electronic tax returns were filed using a
touch-tone telephone (TeleFile) directly by a taxpayer using the online filing option,
or they were filed electronically by a tax preparer.

12. Hart-Teeter Research, *The New E-Government Equation: Ease, Engagement, Privacy, and Protection* (Washington: Council for Excellence in Government,
April 2003).

13. This directive resulted in a NSF-sponsored workshop on Internet voting in
October 2000, the results of which are reported in Internet Policy Institute, *Report
of the National Workshop on Internet Voting: Issues and Research Agenda* (Washington, March 2001).

14. A comprehensive definition of the varieties of Internet voting can be found
in the California Internet Voting Task Force's "A Report on the Feasibility of Internet Voting," January 2000 (www.electioncenter.org/voting/voting_report.html
[October 3, 2003]). We draw on their definitions here and, unless otherwise noted,
mean remote Internet voting when we use the term "Internet voting."

15. Despite our use of the term "Internet voting" to refer to an integrated Internet-based registration and voting system, it is, of course, possible that the Internet could be used for one but not the other. In particular, some states, like California,
currently have voter registration procedures that do use the Internet, although they
are not true Internet-based procedures; California has an online form that is filled
in by the applicant; the form is then submitted, printed, and sent to the applicant
to be signed and mailed to the appropriate county election office.

16. Caltech/MIT Voting Technology Project, *Voting: What Is, What Could Be*
(2001) (www.vote.caltech.edu/Reports/july01/July01_VTP_%20Voting_Report_
Entire.pdf [September 26, 2003]). This group found that between 1.5 and 3 million votes were "lost" in the 2000 election due to voter registration problems and
that up to 1 million votes were "lost" in the same election due to polling place
problems.

17. The Federal Voting Assistance Program found that online voter registration and status checking were both critical elements in their online voting system.

18. See, for example, the General Accounting Office report "Voting Assistance

to Military and Overseas Citizens Should be Improved," September 2001; Kosuke Imai and Gary King, "Did Illegally Counted Overseas Absentee Ballots Decide the 2000 U.S. Presidential Election?" Harvard University (http://gking.harvard.edu/files/ballots.pdf [September 26, 2003]).

19. General Accounting Office, "Voters with Disabilities: Access to Polling Places and Alternative Methods," October 2001.

20. A concise discussion of this can be found in Thomas Mann, *An Agenda for Election Reform*, Policy Brief 82 (Brookings, June 2001) (www.brook.edu/comm/policybriefs/pb082/pb82.htm [July 28, 2003]).

21. In five of the last six statewide elections in California (the 1998, 2000, and 2002 primary and general elections), at least 25 percent of ballots were cast by absentee voters. The exception was the 2000 primary election, when 23 percent of ballots were cast by absentee voters. See www.ss.ca.gov/elections/hist_absentee.htm [September 26, 2003]).

22. Ariana Eunjung Cha and John Schwartz, "More Big Web Sites Hit by Hackers," *Washington Post*, February 9, 2000, p. E1.

23. Nicole C. Wong, "'Code Red' Worm Likely to Return," *Washington Post*, July 31, 2001, p. E1.

24. Vernon Loeb, "Cyberwar's Economic Threat: U.S. Is Vulnerable to Foreign Attacks, Hill Panel Is Told," *Washington Post*, February 24, 2000, p. A19.

25. Ibid.

26. R. Michael Alvarez and Jonathan Nagler, "The Likely Consequences of Internet Voting for Political Representation," *Loyola of Los Angeles Law Review*, vol. 34, no. 3 (2001), pp. 1115–53.

27. National Telecommunications and Information Administration, "A Nation Online: How Americans Are Expanding Their Use of the Internet" (2001) (www.ntia.doc.gov/ntiahome/dn/anationonline2.pdf [September 26, 2003]), p. 39.

28. Caltech/MIT Voting Technology Project, "Residual Votes Attributable to Technology: An Assessment of the Reliability of Existing Voting Equipment" (www.hss.caltech.edu/~voting/CalTech_MIT_Report_Version2.pdf [September 26, 2003]).

29. Robert D. Putnam, *Bowling Alone: The Collapse and Revival of American Community* (New York: Touchstone Books, 2001).

30. Hearing 3, Panel 4: Perspectives of Political Parties (www.reformelections.org/data/transcripts/h3/hearing3_p4.php [July 28, 2003]). The same argument has recently been made by Norman H. Nie and Lutz Erbring, "Internet and Society: A Preliminary Report," Stanford Institute for the Quantitative Study of Society, 2000 (www.stanford.edu/group/siqss/Press_Release/Preliminary_Report.pdf [July 28, 2003]).

31. Federal Election Commission, *Performance and Test Standards for Punchcard, Marksense and Direct Recording Electronic Voting Systems* (1990).

32. Brad Hahn, "Goodbye Chad: Bush Signs Bill; Punch Cards Knocked Out,"

Sun-Sentinel, May 10, 2001, p. A1. Steven Thomma, "Ballot Reform Unlikely by 2002; Florida, Georgia Make a Start, but Disputes Rage over Many Points," *Pittsburgh Post-Gazette*, March 27, 2001, p. A9.

33. Jeannette Sanchez-Palacios and Greg Risling, "Early Voting Begins via Touch-Screen in County; Hundreds Take Advantage of the New System; Visually Impaired Voters and Those Who Use Foreign Language Ballots Can Also Participate," *Los Angeles Times*, October 18, 2000, p. B2. See also Conny B. McCormack, "The Challenge: Voting System Replacement," memorandum to the Los Angeles County Board of Supervisors, October 1, 2001 (http://regrec.co.la.ca.us/general/vs-replacement.htm [July 28, 2003]).

34. Section 1604 of the National Defense Authorization Act for Fiscal Year 2002 (PL 107-107) directed the secretary of defense to conduct a demonstration project allowing absent uniformed services voters to cast ballots in the regularly scheduled general election for federal office in the November 2002 elections by using an electronic voting system. However, it gave the secretary the authority to delay the project until the November 2004 federal general elections. Given the complexity of developing and implementing a reliable, usable, and secure Internet voting system, the project has been scheduled to be carried out during the 2004 federal elections.

Chapter 2

1. One important exception to this is Roy G. Saltman's report, *Accuracy, Integrity, and Security in Computerized Vote-Tallying*, NBS Special Publication 500-158 (Institute for Computer Sciences and Technology, National Bureau of Standards, 1988). Saltman discusses "on-line voting" in section 3.10 of his report, focusing on two technical problems: first, the possibility that election-day voting might overwhelm data networks; second, the problem of voter authentication in remote electronic voting. In section 6.5, he discusses political requirements for remote electronic voting, especially access and the trade-off between costs and benefits.

2. California Internet Voting Task Force, "A Report on the Feasibility of Internet Voting" (January 2000) (www.electioncenter.org/voting/voting_report.html [October 3, 2003]); Internet Policy Institute, *Report of the National Workshop on Internet Voting: Issues and Research Agenda* (Washington, March 2001) (www.electionline.org/site/docs/pdf/internet_policy_institute.pdf [October 3, 2003]).

3. National Telecommunications and Information Administration (NTIA), "A Nation Online: How Americans Are Expanding Their Use of the Internet," February 2002 (www.ntia.doc.gov/ntiahome/dn/index.html [July 3, 2003]).

4. Ibid. The NTIA report found that 22.3 percent of households had high-speed Internet access in the western United States; 22.2 percent in the Northeast; 17.6 percent in the South; and 15.3 percent in the Midwest. The report did not address state-by-state high-speed Internet use.

5. Public Policy Institute of California, "Californians and Their Government," statewide survey, December 1999 (www.ppic.org/publications/CalSurvey8/survey8.pdf [July 3, 2003]).

6. The technologists included David Jefferson (Compaq), Kaye Caldwell (Silicon Valley Software Industry Coalition), Jim Adler and Pete Adlerberg (Votehere.net), Sylvia Ahern (Sterling Software), Steve Cunningham (Cisco), Tim Draper (Draper, Fisher, Jurvetson), Thad Howard (the Howard Agency), Steve Knecht (Global Election Systems), Philip Mueller (Political Technologies Inc.), Cameron O'Rourke (Oracle), Mark Reynolds (iLumen Corp.), Joe Rodata (FAQvoter.com), Peter Schmidt (Cisco), and James Wayman (National Biometric Test Center). The three academics were Linda Valenty (San Jose State University), Michael Alvarez (Caltech), and Jonathan Nagler (University of California, Riverside). Kim Alexander (California Voter Foundation) and Jacquie Canfield (League of Women Voters) represented voting rights groups. Jim Cunneen (member of the state assembly), Stacy Morgan (from Cunneen's office), Rom Lopez (state assembly elections committee), and Larry Sokel (state senate elections committee), represented the state legislature. The ten election representatives were Alfie Charles, Brian Gangler, Pam Giarrizzo, Tom Hill, Bernard Soriano, and John Mott-Smith (all from the state secretary of state's office) and Dwight Beattie (Sacramento County), Roger Dao (Santa Clara County), Mikel Hass (San Diego County), and Warren Slocum (San Mateo County).

7. California Internet Voting Task Force, "Report on the Feasibility of Internet Voting," p. 2.

8. White House memorandum, "Electronic Government," December 17, 1999. Reprinted in Internet Policy Institute, *Report of the National Workshop on Internet Voting: Issues and Research Agenda*, p. 41.

9. Ibid, p. 42.

10. *Digital Democracy Study Act of 1999*, H.Rept. 3232, 106 Cong. 1 sess. (November 5, 1999). The bill was referred to the Committee on House Administration; no further action was taken, most likely because of President Clinton's order.

11. The participants in the NSF workshop included Paul Craft (Florida Department of State), David Elliot (Washington secretary of state's office), Sandra Steinbach (Iowa secretary of state's office), Patricia Hollarn (supervisor of elections, Okaloosa County, Florida), Thomas Mann (Brookings Institution), Paul Herrnson (University of Maryland), Frederic Solop (Northern Arizona University), Michael Alvarez (Caltech), David Brady (Stanford University), Richard Neimi (University of Rochester), Michael Traugott (University of Michigan), Raymond Wolfinger (University of California, Berkeley), Lorrie Faith Cranor (AT&T Research Labs), David Jefferson (Compaq Systems Research Center), Michael Fischer (Yale University), Dan Geer (@Stake, Inc), Lance Hoffman (George Washington University), Carl Landwehr (Mitretek Systems, Inc.), Ron Rivest (MIT),

Aviel Rubin (AT&T), Barbara Simons (Association for Computing Machinery), Roy Saltman (consultant), Erich Bloch (former head of NSF), Penelope Bonsall (Federal Election Commission), Polli Brunelli (FVAP), Craig Donsanto (Department of Justice), Lawrence Brandt (NSF Digital Government program), Valerie Gregg (NSF digital government program), Frank Scioli (NSF political science program), David Cheney (IPI), Richard Schum (IPI), and Adam C. Powell III (Freedom Forum).

12. These recommendations are summarized on page 2 of the workshop report.

13. For an overview of the NSF's priority areas and strategic goals, see "NSF Guide to Programs, Fiscal Year 2002," www.nsf.gov/od/lpa/news/publicat/nsf0203/nsf0203.pdf [July 3, 2003]).

14. See the archive of digital government projects at the University of Southern California, Information Sciences Institute (www.digitalgovernment.org/archive/projects.jsp [July 3, 2003]).

15. Aviel D. Rubin, "Security Considerations for Remote Electronic Voting over the Internet," TRPC2001, Twenty-Ninth Research Conference on Communication, Information, and Internet Policy, October 2001 (http://avirubin.com/e-voting.security.pdf [July 3, 2003]), p. 10.

16. Lorrie Faith Cranor, "Electronic Voting," *ACM Crossroads*, April 1996 (www.acm.org/crossroads/xrds2-4/voting.html [July 3, 2003]).

17. Lorrie Faith Cranor, "Voting after Florida: No Easy Answers," December 2000, rev. March 2001 (http://lorrie.cranor.org/voting/essay.html [July 3, 2003]).

18. Rebecca Mercuri, "Electronic Vote Tabulation: Checks and Balances," Ph.D. dissertation, UMI Microform 3003665, University of Pennsylvania, 2001, pp. 188–189.

19. Caltech/MIT Voting Technology Project, *Voting: What Is, What Could Be* (2001) (www.vote.caltech.edu/Reports/july01/July01_VTP_%20Voting_Report_Entire.pdf [September 30, 2003]), pp. 15–16.

20. This report went on to note that "[s]ome of the 2002 local election pilots are already experimenting with this multichannel approach and the process of piloting, testing and then introducing new approaches will become an increasing feature of electoral practice." Lawrence Pratchett, "The Implementation of Electronic Voting in the UK," May 2002 (www.electoralcommission.org.uk/files/dms/e-votingreport_6605-6192__E__N__S__W__.pdf [September 30, 2003]).

21. An Internet voting system could provide audio capacity for visually impaired voters. Alternatively, visually impaired voters could use programs that translate the text of an Internet voting website into audio. In either case, these voters should be able to cast more private ballots using an Internet voting system than they can now using any of the conventional mechanical or paper-based voting systems now in use in the United States.

Chapter 3

1. R. Michael Alvarez, D. E. "Betsy" Sinclair, and Catherine Wilson, "Counting Ballots and the 2000 Election: What Went Wrong?" in Ann Crigler, Marion Just, and Edward McCaffery, eds., *Rethinking the Vote* (Oxford University Press, 2003).

2. See the Caltech/MIT Voting Technology Project, *Voting: What Is, What Could Be* (2001) (www.vote.caltech.edu/Reports/july01/July01_VTP_%20Voting_ Report_Entire.pdf [September 30, 2003]), p. 11. Details of how the number of "lost" votes was estimated are given on pages 87 and 88 of the report. Note that the estimate of 4 to 6 million lost votes does not include any estimate of the number of votes that might not have been cast or counted due to problems with the absentee voting process.

3. For a comprehensive discussion, see Alexander Keyssar, *The Right to Vote* (New York: Basic Books, 2000).

4. At least five lawsuits were filed in the wake of the 2000 presidential election in California, Florida, Illinois, and Georgia. These cases are summarized in Richard L. Hasen, "*Bush* v. *Gore* and the Future of Equal Protection Law in Elections," *Florida State University Law Review*, vol. 29, no.2 (2001), pp. 393–94, note 85.

5. Recent legal scholarship also has noted that the U.S. Supreme Court's decision in *Bush* v. *Gore* might make "just about any disparity regarding the means of voting into a judiciable question": Hasen, "*Bush* v. *Gore* and the Future of Equal Protection Law," p. 378. Further discussion of this point is in Richard L. Hasen, "After the Storm: The Uses, Normative Implications, and Unintended Consequences of Voting Reform Research in Post–*Bush* v. *Gore* Equal Protection Challenges," in Crigler, Just, and McCaffery, eds., *Rethinking the Vote*.

6. See, for example, *Federalist 10* in Clinton Rossiter, ed., *The Federalist Papers* (New York: NAL Penguin Inc., 1961). See also *Federalist 63* for a discussion of the creation of the Senate as one way to ensure effective and varied representation in Congress.

7. *Federalist 35*, p. 216

8. This is deftly described by Morris P. Fiorina in *Congress, Keystone of the Washington Establishment* (Yale University Press, 1989).

9. John Stuart Mill, *Considerations on Representative Government* (New York: Liberal Arts Press, 1958), p. 44.

10. Robert A. Dahl, *On Democracy* (Yale University Press, 1998), p. 37.

11. Hanna F. Pitkin, *The Concept of Representation* (University of California Press, 1967).

12. The breadth of this debate can be seen in the work of scholars such as David T. Canon, *Race, Redistricting, and Representation* (University of Chicago Press, 1999); Claudine Gay, "The Effect of Minority Districts and Minority Representation on Political Participation in California" (San Francisco: Public Policy Insti-

tute of California, June 2001); David I. Lublin, *The Paradox of Representation* (Princeton University Press,1997); and Carol M. Swain, *Black Faces, Black Interests* (Harvard University, 1993).

13. See Swain, *Black Faces, Black Interests*; and Richard Fleisher, "Explaining the Change in Roll-Call Voting Behavior of Southern Democrats," *Journal of Politics*, vol. 55, no. 2 (1993), pp. 327–41.

14. See chart 4, "Revitalizing Democracy in Florida," Governor's Select Task Force on Election Procedures, Standards, and Technology, March 1, 2001 (www.collinscenter.org/ usr_doc/Revitalizing_Democracy_in_Florida.pdf [October 3, 2003]).

15. U.S. Census Bureau, *Statistical Abstract of the United States: 2001* (Government Printing Office), table 401, "Voting-Age Population, Percent Reporting Registered and Voted: 1980 to 2000."

16. Sidney Verba and others, "Citizen Activity: Who Participates? What Do They Say?" *American Political Science Review*, vol. 87, no. 2 (1993), pp. 303–18. Also see Sidney Verba, Kay Lehman Schlozman, and Henry Brady, *Voice and Equality* (Harvard University Press, 1995).

17. With the right Internet voting standards, it is possible to develop different Internet voting platforms—perhaps by different system vendors—that will look and operate identically across systems for voters. The underlying system architecture, and of course the computer code, may be radically different, as may the way the systems work for election officials. But the voter interface, method of operation, and the way the vote is cast could be highly standardized.

18. Anthony Downs makes this argument in *An Economic Theory of Democracy* (Harper & Brothers, 1957).

19. General Accounting Office, *Elections: Perspectives on Activities and Challenges across the Nation* (Government Printing Office, 2001). See especially appendix VI, Selected State Statutory Requirements for Elections, p. 397.

20. Keyssar, *The Right to Vote*. See pages 151–59 for an examination of voter registration requirements instituted between the Civil War and World War I and pages 227–29 for a discussion of the poll tax.

21. Steven Rosenstone and Raymond Wolfinger, "The Effect of Registration Laws on Voter Turnout," *American Political Science Review*, vol. 72, no.1 (1978), pp. 22–45.

22. A majority of states require individuals to register at least twenty-eight days before election day: General Accounting Office, *Elections: Perspectives on Activities and Challenges*, 373–75. Rosenstone and Wolfinger, "The Effect of Registration Laws on Voter Turnout," pp. 31–32.

23. Currently there are six states with same-day voter registration: Idaho, Maine, Minnesota, New Hampshire, Wisconsin, and Wyoming. Studies typically find that voter turnout in these states increased by between 3 and 6 percentage points following implementation of same-day registration. For further details

about the impact of same-day registration on voter turnout see Craig L. Brians, "Voter Registration Laws and Turnout in America: The Last Two Decades," Ph.D. dissertation, University of California–Irvine, 1997; Craig L. Brians and B. Grofman, "When Registration Barriers Fall, Who Votes? An Empirical Test of a Rational Choice Model," *Public Choice*, vol. 99 (1999), pp. 161–76; Mark J. Fenster, "The Impact of Allowing Day of Registration Voting on Turnout in U.S. Elections from 1960 to 1992," *American Politics Quarterly*, vol. 22, no.1 (1994), pp. 74–87; Benjamin Highton, "Easy Registration and Voter Turnout," *Journal of Politics*, vol. 59, no. 2 (1997), pp. 565–75; Stephen Knack, "Election-Day Registration: The Second Wave," *American Politics Quarterly*, vol. 29, no.1 (2001), pp. 65–78; Glenn E. Mitchell and C. Wlezian, "The Impact of Legal Constraints on Voter Registration, Turnout, and the Composition of the American Electorate," *Political Behavior*, vol. 17, no. 2 (1995), pp. 179–202; Staci Rhine, "Registration Reform and Turnout Change in the American States," *American Politics Quarterly*, vol. 23, no.4 (1995), pp. 409–26; Ruy A. Teixeira, *The Disappearing American Voter* (Brookings, 1992); Raymond E. Wolfinger and S. J. Rosenstone, *Who Votes?* (Yale University Press, 1980); Steven J. Rosenstone and J. M. Hansen, *Mobilization, Participation, and Democracy in America* (Macmillan, 1993).

24. Public Law No. 103–31, National Voter Registration Act of 1993. The text above was taken directly from a Congressional Research summary of the bill.

25. In testimony before the National Commission on Federal Election Reform, many witnesses noted that the NVRA has not made registering more easy for everyone. For example, it often is easy not to sign the voter registration forms issued by departments of motor vehicles because the signature lines for the driver's license and for voter registration are easy to confuse. Similarly, not all service providers seem to ensure that their clientele are offered voter registration forms when they visit.

26. The U.S. Census Bureau issues an annual report, *Geographical Mobility*, that examines the movement of the U.S. population for a one-year period. These reports can be found at www.census.gov/population/socdemo/migrate.html [July 14, 2003]).

27. Amy Friedlander has written two reports discussing the development of these industries and the divides: *Power and Light: Electricity in the U.S. Energy Infrastructure 1870–1940* (Washington: Corporation for National Research Initiatives, 1996) and *Natural Monopoly and Universal Service: Telephones and Telegraphs in the U.S. Communications Infrastructure, 1837–1940* (Washington: Corporation for National Research Initiatives, 1995).

28. U.S. Census Bureau, *Statistical Abstract of the United States: 2001*. Specifically, see table 1126, "Utilization of Selected Media: 1970 to 1999."

29. Ibid.

30. Data on computer ownership can be found in the occasional U.S. Census Bureau report by Eric Charles Newburger, *Home Computers and Internet Use in*

the United States (Government Printing Office, October 1997 and August 2000) (www.census.gov/population/www/socdemo/computer.html [July 14, 2003]). A broader perspective on the digital divide issue is in Pippa Norris, *Digital Divide: Civic Engagement, Information Poverty, and the Internet Worldwide* (Cambridge University Press, 2001), where she examines the digital divide using different sources of data and compares it across nations and technologies.

31. General Accounting Office, "Telecommunications: Characteristics and Choices of Internet Users," GAO-01-345 (2001). Quote is on page 5.

32. Ibid. The remaining 0.4 percent have wireless Internet access.

33. Ibid.

34. CBS Market Watch, CBS News Internet Poll (www.cbs.marketwatch.com [January 1999]).

35. A recent study found that 24 percent of twenty- to twenty-five-year-olds "always voted," in contrast to 72 percent of those age fifty-six or older. Some of the differences in voting can be attributed to differential registration rates between younger and older citizens, but much of what is argued to fuel active political participation is differences in individual resources (income and education), interactions with civic and political organizations (churches and political groups), and values. See Scott Keeter and others, "The Civic and Political Health of the Nation: A Generational Portrait," Center for Information and Research in Civic Learning and Engagement (CIRCLE), September 19, 2002 (www.puaf.umd.edu/CIRCLE/research/products/Civic_and_Political_Health.pdf [September 30, 2003]).

36. "Short-Term Impacts, Long-Term Opportunities," Center for Information and Research in Civic Learning and Engagement (CIRCLE), March 2002 (www.civicyouth.org/ research/products/National_Youth_Survey_outside2.htm [September 30, 2003]).

Chapter 4

1. Evan I. Schwartz, "Direct Democracy: Are You Ready for the Democracy Channel?" *Wired*, no. 2.01 (January 1994) (www.wired.com/wired/archive/2.01/e.dem_pr.html [July 15, 2003]).

2. Dick Morris, *Vote.com* (Los Angeles: Renaissance Books, 2001), pp. 26, 31. It is interesting to note how similar Morris's vision of how the Internet should be used to promote direct democracy is to Perot's vision from the 1992 campaign for the electronic town hall.

3. Cass Sunstein, *Republic.com* (Princeton University Press, 2001), p.16.

4. Alexander Keyssar, *The Right to Vote* (New York: Basic Books, 2000), p.142.

5. See, for example, Angus Campbell and others, *The American Voter*, unabridged ed., University of Chicago Press, 1960 (Midway reprint, 1976).

6. Arthur Lupia, "Shortcuts versus Encyclopedias: Information and Voting Behavior in California Insurance Reform Elections," *American Political Science Review*, vol. 88, no.1 (1994), pp. 63–76.

7. Ibid. Lupia provides an excellent analysis of the impact of endorsements in the 1988 elections in California on five different ballot measures regarding insurance reform. For an experimental study of the impact of candidate endorsements on election outcomes, see Richard D. McKelvey and Peter C. Ordeshook, "Information and Elections: Retrospective Voting and Rational Expectations," in John A. Ferejohn and James H. Kuklinski, eds., *Information and Democratic Processes* (University of Chicago Press, 1990), pp. 281–312.

8. Samuel L. Popkin, *The Reasoning Voter* (University of Chicago Press, 1991), pp. 1–3.

9. The literature is too large to cite adequately here. See R. Michael Alvarez, *Information and Elections* (University of Michigan Press, 1997), for a discussion of the literature.

10. Caroline J. Tolbert and Ramona S. McNeal, "Unraveling the Effects of the Internet on Political Participation?" *Political Research Quarterly* 56 (June 2003), pp. 175–85. Tolbert and McNeal estimate that in the 2000 presidential election, using online election news services could have increased the likelihood of voting by 12.5 percent, while having Internet access could have increased the likelihood of voting by 7.7 percent, holding a series of other variables constant.

11. Bruce Cain, "The Internet in the (Dis)service of Democracy?" *Loyola of Los Angeles Law Review*, vol. 34, no. 3 (April 2001), p. 1014.

12. See Sunstein, *Republic.com*, chapter 3; and Cain, "The Internet in the (Dis)service of Democracy?" p. 1018.

13. Cain, "The Internet in the (Dis)service of Democracy?" p. 1019.

14. Sunstein, *Republic.com*, chapter 3.

15. Schwartz, "Direct Democracy."

16. The term "deliberative democracy" is synonymous with "civic discovery," "discursive democracy," "strong democracy," and "unitary democracy." These concepts are discussed, respectively, in Amy Gutmann and Dennis Thompson, *Democracy and Disagreement* (Harvard University Press, 1996); Robert B. Reich, *The Power of Public Ideas* (Harvard University Press, 1988); John S. Dryzek, *Discursive Democracy: Politics, Policy, and Political Science* (Cambridge University Press, 1990); Benjamin Barber, *Strong Democracy: Participatory Politics for a New Age* (University of California Press, 1984); and Jane Mansbridge, *Beyond Adversary Democracy* (Basic Books, 1980).

17. See James S. Fishkin, *Democracy and Deliberation: New Directions for Democratic Reform* (Yale University Press, 1991).

18. Carmen Sirianni and Lewis Friedland, "Deliberative Democracy" (www.cpn.org/ tools/dictionary/deliberate.html [September 30, 2003]).

19. Edward Weeks, "The Practice of Deliberative Democracy: Results from Four Large-Scale Trials," *Public Administration Review*, vol. 60, no. 4 (2000), pp. 360–72.

20. The importance of public deliberation in a deliberative democracy is discussed by many scholars. Important examples include Barber, *Strong Democracy:*

Participatory Politics for a New Age; Gutmann and Thompson, *Democracy and Disagreement*; and Jurgen Habermas, *Between Facts and Norms: Contributions to a Discourse Theory of Law and Democracy* (MIT Press, 1996).

21. Edward Weeks of the University of Oregon was involved in both efforts; the following discussion is taken from "The Practice of Deliberative Democracy."

22. The participating sites were ABCNews.com, America Online, Excite, CNN.com, FOXNews.com, I-Village.com, MSN.com, MSNBC.com, Netnoia.com, MTV.com, NPR.com, NYTimes.com, Oxygen.com, PBS.com, Washington Post.com, USAToday.com, and Yahoo.com (www.webwhiteblue.org [July 15, 2003]).

23. Arthur Lupia, "Evaluation: The Web White and Blue Network," March 2001 (www.markle.org/news/WWBEvaluation.pdf [September 30, 2003]).

24. The volunteer survey was offered to visitors to the website; therefore the sample is not necessarily representative. The experimental study, on the other hand, cannot be generalized. The sample of UCSD undergraduates used is not likely to represent the larger population of American voters who have access to the Internet.

25. Knowledge Networks has developed an innovative Internet survey technique: it attempts to construct a representative sample of households by promising to give a household a computer and Internet access in exchange for the household's periodic participation in Internet surveys (www.knowledgenetworks.com [July 15, 2003]). Knowledge Networks samples are panels, and many if not most respondents have participated in previous Internet surveys.

26. National Initiative for Democracy. See specifically the First Principles section (www.ni4d.org/ [July 15, 2003]).

27. Davis S. Broder, *Democracy Derailed: Initiative Campaigns and the Power of Money* (Harcourt, 2000), p. 37.

28. Ibid., p. 44.

29. For futher information about these ballot measures and the general history of the initiative process in California, see John M. Allswang, *California Initiatives and Referendums, 1912–1990: A Survey and Guide to Research* (Los Angeles: Edmund G. "Pat" Brown Institute of Public Affairs, 1991); John M. Allswang, *The Initiative and Referendum in California, 1898–1998* (Stanford University Press, 2000).

30. These data come from *A History of California Initiatives* (California Secretary of State, 2001) (www.ss.ca.gov/elections/init_history.pdf [July 15, 2003]).

31. The data on county measures come from *Report on County Initiatives During 1999-2000* (California Secretary of State) (www.ss.ca.gov/elections/init_county_99-00.pdf [July 15, 2003]). The municipal initiative data come from *Report on Municipal Initiative Measures During 1999–2000* (California Secretary of State) (www.ss.ca.gov/elections/ init_muni_99-00.pdf [July 15, 2003]).

32. See the *Supplemental Voter Information Guide: March 7, 2000 Primary Election* (California Secretary of State) (http://Primary2000.ss.ca.gov/Voter-Guide/pdf/FinalSupp.pdf [July 15, 2003]).

33. See Broder, *Democracy Derailed*, pp. 163–64. Broder notes that there are no good figures on the amount of money that is spent on local initiative campaigns.

34. There is debate in the academic literature over the extent to which the initiative process empowers interest groups; see Elisabeth R. Gerber, *The Populist Paradox: Interest Group Influence and the Promise of Direct Legislation* (Princeton University Press, 1999) and Frederic J. Boehmke, "Beyond the Ballot: The Effect of Direct Democracy on Interest Group Behavior," Ph.D. dissertation, California Institute of Technology, 2000.

35. See, for example, Lupia, "Shortcuts versus Encyclopedias," pp. 63–76.

36. Mark Baldassare, *California in the New Millennium* (University of California Press, 2000), table 2.4, p. 30.

37. Cain, "The Internet in the (Dis)service of Democracy?" p. 1015.

38. James Madison, "Federalist 10," in Alexander Hamilton, James Madison, and John Jay, *The Federalist Papers* (New American Library, 1961), p. 81.

39. An excellent example of the social choice literature on the new institutionalism is in Kenneth A. Shepsle, "Institutional Arrangements and Equilibrium in Multidimensional Voting Models," *American Journal of Political Science*, vol. 23, no. 1 (1979), pp. 27–59; see the citations within this article for other research in the social choice literature. For a less formal introduction, see William H. Riker, *Liberalism against Populism: A Confrontation between the Theory of Democracy and the Theory of Social Choice* (New York: W. H. Freeman and Co., 1982).

40. Sunstein, *Republic.com*. The idea of "The Daily Me" is discussed in chapter 1. The original conception comes from Nicholas Negroponte, the cofounder and director of the MIT Media Laboratory.

41. Diana Mutz and Paul Martin, "Facilitating Communication across Lines of Political Difference," *American Political Science Review* (March 1, 2001).

Chapter 5

1. California Internet Voting Task Force, "A Report on the Feasibility of Internet Voting" (January 2000) (www.electioncenter.org/voting/voting_report.html [October 3, 2003]); Internet Policy Institute, *Report of the National Workshop on Internet Voting: Issues and Research Agenda* (Washington, March 2001) (www.electionline.org/site/docs/pdf/internet_policy_institute.pdf [October 3, 2003]).

2. See, for example, Ed Iwata, "Digital Trail, Chat Room Boasts Led to Teen Hacker," *USA Today*, February 16, 2000, p. B3.

3. Bruce Schneier, *Secrets and Lies: Digital Security in a Networked World* (John Wiley and Sons, 2000).

4. Of course, all of these access attempts might not have been attempts to hack the author's computer. However, these data show that even a computer system of little interest is potentially vulnerable once the network cable or modem connection is activated unless steps are taken to monitor and block unwanted attempts by others to access the system over the Internet. The irony is that shortly after these sentences were originally written, the laptop was infected by an e-mail–borne virus that disguised its presence by disabling the firewall and virus-checking software in such a way that both appeared to be working but were not. The virus then essentially hijacked Internet connections when it could to send spam. This was detected only when the system administrator noticed changes in e-mail volume and began to receive complaints about the spam (a matter of a week or so).

5. Barton Gellman, "Cyber-attacks by al Qaeda Feared," *Washington Post*, June 27, 2002, p. A1.

6. Business Software Alliance, U.S. Business Cyber Security Study, July 24, 2002 (www.bsa.org/usa/ [July 18, 2003]).

7. Ibid.

8. "2002 CSI/FBI Computer Crime and Security Survey," *Computer Security Issues & Trends* (Spring 2002) (www.gocsi.com/forms/fbi/pdf.jhtml [September 30, 2003]).

9. This report, "Common Sense Guide for Senior Managers: Top Ten Recommended Information Security Practices," can be accessed at www.isalliance.org [July 18, 2003]).

10. "2002 CSI/FBI Computer Crime and Security Survey."

11. "Riptech Internet Security Threat Report," Riptech Corporation, January 2002. The reports can be ordered from the Riptech website (www.riptech.com [October 3, 2003]).

12. Cybersource.com, Recent Fraud Statistics (www.cybersource.com/promo/2002fraud/ [September 30, 2003]).

13. Ibid.

14. "VeriSign Adopts a New E-Commerce Anti-Fraud System," *USA Today*, September 4, 2002 (www.usatoday.com/tech/news/internetprivacy/2002-09-04-verisign-mastercard_x.htm [September 30, 2003]).

15. Simson Garfinkel and Gene Spafford, *Web Security & Commerce* (Cambridge, Mass.: O'Reilly & Associates, 1997).

16. For example, in Los Angeles County, law enforcement helicopters commonly are used to ferry the fire-proofed bags containing completed ballots from remote areas of the county to the central tabulation facility. Both authors were on hand to observe the June 5, 2001, Los Angeles city elections, in which helicopters from the fire department were used for the same purpose; officials from the fire department explained to the authors that providing such assistance gave their staff invaluable logistical training!

17. In Aviel D. Rubin, "Security Considerations for Remote Electronic Voting

over the Internet," AT&T Labs–Research, Florham Park, N.J. (http://avirubin.com/e-voting.security.html [July 21, 2003]).

18. Deborah Solomon and Kevin Johnson, "FBI Launches Cyberhunt: Reno Vows to Pin Down Hackers; Two More Web Sites Knocked Out," *USA Today*, February 10, 2000, p. A1; and Deborah Solomon and Kevin Johnson, "Online Boasting Leaves Trail—FBI: Teen a Schoolboy by Day, Brazen Hacker by Night," *USA Today*, April 20, 2000, p. A1.

19. Manny Frishberg, "A Star Wars Defense to Hackers," wired.com, November 21, 2000 (www.wired.com/news/technology/0,1282,40297,00.html [July 21, 2003]).

20. Schneier, *Secrets and Lies*, 46–47. See also Walt Bogdanich, "Stealing The Code: Con Men and Cash Machines; Criminals Focus on A.T.M.'s, Weak Link in Banking System," *New York Times*, August 3, 2003, p. A1.

21. Barton Gellman, "Cyber-Attacks by Al Qaeda Feared," *Washington Post*, June 27, 2002, p. A1.

22. All information in this paragraph comes from Gellman, "Cyber-Attacks by Al Qaeda Feared."

23. This issue was discussed on *CNN Live Today*, 10:00 a.m., EST, on January 28, 2002. A rush transcript of the discussion is available through www.nexis.com.

24. This critique is well summarized, with links to related articles, in Brendan I. Koerner's "Bush's Cyberstrategery: The Administration's War against a Bogus Threat," March 3, 2003 (http://slate.msn.com/id/2079549/ [July 21, 2003]).

25. Joshua Green, "The Myth of Cyberterrorism," *Washington Monthly*, November 2002.

26. Joseph R. Daughen, "Anonymous Warning Tries to Scare Voters," *Philadelphia Daily News*, April 21, 2003 (www.philly.com/mld/dailynews/news/local/5680078.htm [July 21, 2003]).

27. Schneier, *Secrets and Lies*, pp. 6–7.

28. A comprehensive report about the 2002 election problems in Miami-Dade County was issued by the county's inspector general (www.miamidadeig.org/reports/Sept102002election.pdf [July 21, 2003]).

29. For example, Hispanic voters are more likely to vote later in the day than are other populations of voters. This is discussed in Mark Hansen's report in *To Assure Pride and Confidence in the Electoral Process: The National Commission on Federal Election Reform* (Brookings, 2002), pp. 212-13.

30. Whether such an attack would lead to the actual invalidation of the election is an open question, as it would depend on the extent of the attack as well as local, state, and federal election laws.

31. See the report of Conny McCormack, Registrar-Recorder/County Clerk, "March 5, 2002, Primary Election: Problems, Solutions, and Resources Needed for Improvement," April 9, 2002 (http://regrec.co.la.ca.us/general/3-5-02PSR/ [July 21, 2003]).

32. "Special Report: Florida, Broward and Miami-Dade County Election Problems and Solutions," *Election Administration Reports*, vol. 32, no. 19 (September 30, 2002). Also, poll sites in Florida have between 600 and 1,000 more voters per precinct, on average, than is the case in Los Angeles.

33. John Zebrowski, "Irked County Council Asks State for Audit of Election Foul-Ups," *Seattle Times*, December 10, 2002. The Washington secretary of state's report was produced by the Election Certification and Training Program, "Election Procedures Review of King County, State of Washington," February 2002 (www.secstate.wa.gov/elections/pdf/KingCounty.pdf [July 21, 2003]).

34. The 1998 and 1999 absentee voting rates were the most recent available. See www.secstate.wa.gov/elections/absentee_stats.aspx [July 21, 2003]. The participation data come from the Washington secretary of state; see www.secstate.wa.gov/elections [July 21, 2003].

35. These concerns are discussed thoroughly in Caltech/MIT Voting Technology Project, *Voting: What Is, What Could Be* (2001), pp. 38–39 (www.vote.caltech.edu/ Reports/july01/July01_VTP_%20Voting_Report_Entire.pdf [September 30, 2003]).

36. This story can be found on the NPR website (http://discover.npr.org/features/feature.jhtml?wfId=1147255 [September 30, 2003]).

37. R. Michael Alvarez, "How Widespread Is Voting Fraud?" California Institute of Technology, 2002.

38. See, for example, Rebecca Mercuri and Peter Neumann, "System Integrity Revisited," *Communications of the ACM*, vol. 44, no. 1 (2001), p. 160; and "Rebecca Mercuri's Statement on Electronic Voting" (www.notablesoftware.com/RMstatement.html [July 21, 2003]).

39. Caltech/MIT Voting Technology Project, *Voting: What Is, What Could Be.*

40. The same issue can be raised in regard to "provisional" ballots used (as of 2002) in only about one-third of the states. Provisional ballots are used when for some reason polling place workers have doubts about whether a person is eligible to vote in a precinct, typically because his or her name does not appear on the voter registration rolls; the provisional ballot allows the voter to cast a ballot and the voter's eligibility to be verified later by election personnel. Recently passed federal legislation will require all states to adopt provisional procedures.

41. See the Internet Fraud Complaint Center's "IFCC 2001 Internet Fraud Report" (www.ifccfbi.gov/strategy/2002_IFCCReport.pdf [July 21, 2003]). The National Infrastructure Protection Center's website (www.nipc.gov [July 21, 2003]) has a wealth of quantitative information about computer security threats.

42. Various solutions to some of these problems have been advanced by researchers. See Dimitris A. Gritzalis, ed., *Secure Electronic Voting* (Boston: Kluwer Academic Publishers, 2003).

43. As we noted previously, Internet security companies such as Riptech tout their monitoring capabilities in their reports. Bruce Schneier also discusses the

importance of monitoring and physical security in *Secrets and Lies*.

44. This is evidenced by the existence of organizations such as the National Association of State Chief Information Officers (www.nascio.org [July 21, 2003]).

45. This recommendation was included in the Technical Committee Recommendations of the California Internet Voting Task Force (www.electioncenter.org/voting/voting_report.html [October 3, 2003]).

46. A complete description of the FROG modular voting architecture can be found in the Caltech/MIT Voting Technology report, *Voting: What Is, What Could Be*, pp. 58–64. The "voter-verified paper trails" recently proposed for electronic voting systems are really just one form of the FROG voting system architecture, wherein the independent recording of the vote is done on paper. A thorough discussion of the voter-verified paper trail issue can be found in the California secretary of state's "Ad Hoc Touch Screen Task Force Report" (www.ss.ca.gov/elections/taskforce_report.htm [September 30, 2003]).

47. President's Critical Infrastructure Protection Board, *National Strategy to Secure Cyberspace*, February 2003 (www.whitehouse.gov/pcipb/cyberspace_strategy.pdf [September 30, 2003]).

48. Charles Mann, "Homeland Insecurity," *Atlantic Monthly* (September 2002); the article can be found online at www.theatlantic.com/issues/2002/09/mann.htm [July 21, 2003]).

49. Brendan I. Koerner, "In Computer Security, A Bigger Reason to Squirm," *New York Times*, September 7, 2003.

50. See the Trusted Computing Group's website for additional information (www.trustedcomputinggroup.org [September 30, 2003]).

Chapter 6

1. Replacing most of the temporary employees with full-time employees to provide services to citizens makes the elections system more professional.

2. Eugene Meyer, "Easier Voting Could Boost Turnout, Study Says," *Washington Post*, March 2, 2003, p. C4. See also James G. Gimpel and Jason E. Schuknecht, "Political Participation and the Accessibility of the Ballot Box," *Political Geography*, vol. 22 (2003), pp. 471–88.

3. A comprehensive history of absentee voting from the nation's founding through World War II can be found in George F. Miller, *Absentee Voters and Suffrage Laws* (Washington: Daylion Company, 1948), especially chapter 2.

4. B. A. Martin, "The Service Voting in the Elections of 1944," *American Political Science Review*, vol. 39, no. 1 (1945), p. 721.

5. Miller, *Absentee Voters*, p. 29.

6. Alexander Keyssar, *The Right to Vote* (New York: Basic Books, 2000), pp. 150–55, and P. O. Ray, "Military Absent-Voting Laws," *American Political Science Review*, vol. 13, no. 2 (1918), pp. 264–74. See also Miller, *Absentee Voters*,

and Thad. E. Hall and R. M. Alvarez, "The History of Military Voting," California Institute of Technology, 2001.

7. Martin, "Service Voting," pp. 723–24. He estimates that about 2 million eligible American voters were overseas during the 1918 election but does not estimate the number who attempted to vote in that midterm election.

8. See Miller, *Absentee Voters*, p. 45.

9. The variety of state procedures is discussed in detail by Martin, "Service Voting," p. 724.

10. It is interesting to note that this appears to be the historical origin of the current Federal Post Card Application (FPCA) for overseas voters. In the contemporary FPCA process, overseas citizens complete the postcard application as required by their state and county regulations and send it to the appropriate election office. The FPCA serves a dual role, both to register the citizen as an eligible voter and to process an absentee ballot request.

11. Martin, "Service Voting," p. 731.

12. Ibid., p. 732.

13. J. Eric Oliver, "The Effects of Eligibility Restrictions and Party Activity on Absentee Voting and Overall Turnout," *American Journal of Political Science*, vol. 40, no. 2 (1996), pp. 498–513.

14. According to data from the office of the California secretary of state (www.ss.ca.gov/elections/hist_absentee.htm [July 22, 2003]).

15. This issue came up repeatedly when one of the authors, Hall, interviewed voters at polling sites during the June 5, 2001, Los Angeles mayoral election.

16. Oliver, "Effects of Eligibility Restrictions."

17. D. E. "Betsy" Sinclair and R. Michael Alvarez, "Who Overvotes, Who Undervotes, Using Punchcards? Evidence from Los Angeles County," 2002, unpublished manuscript, California Institute of Technology.

18. The Caltech/MIT report (July 2001) recommended that liberalized absentee voting procedures be replaced with expanded early-voting opportunities. It states, "We have no systematic measures of fraud, but fraud appears to be especially difficult to regulate in absentee systems. In-precinct voting or 'kiosk' voting is observable. Absentee voting is not. The prospect for coercion is increased with absentee voting on demand" (p. 41).

19. The best overview of early voting is Robert M. Stein's "Introduction: Early Voting," *Public Opinion Quarterly*, vol. 62, no. 1 (1998), pp. 57–69. See Sidney Verba, Kay Lehman Schlozman and Henry Brady, *Voice and Equality* (Harvard University Press, 1995) for more discussion of demographic factors and voter participation rates.

20. See the center's August 30, 2000, press release "Mobilization Propels Modest Turnout Increase; GOP Out Organizes Democrats; Registration Lower, Parties in Trouble; Reforms Fail to Boost Turnout" (www.gspm.org/csae/cgans9.html [July 22, 2003]).

21. Oliver, "Effects of Eligibility Restrictions."

22. "Judge Orders New Miami Mayoral Election," CNN, March 4, 1998 (www.cnn.com/ALLPOLITICS/1998/03/04/miami.mayor [July 22, 2003]).

23. R. Michael Alvarez, "How Widespread Is Voting Fraud?" California Institute of Technology, November 2002. Alvarez also examines other data on absentee voting fraud and finds little evidence of it.

24. Miller, *Absentee Voters*. See especially chapter 5.

25. "The Dangers of Voting outside the Booth," *New York Times*, August 3, 2001 (www.aeipoliticalcorner.org/NO%20Articles/no010803.pdf [July 22, 2003]).

26. From the office of the Oregon secretary of state. The 2000 data can be found at www.sos.state.or.us/elections/nov72000/other.info/g00byday.htm [July 22, 2003] and the 2002 data at www.sos.state.or.us/elections/nov52002/g02byday.pdf [July 22, 2003].

27. See the Oregon election laws, chapter 251 (www.leg.state.or.us/ors/251.html [July 22, 2003]).

28. This history comes from Priscilla L. Southwell and Justin Burchett, "Survey of Vote-by-Mail Senate Election in the State of Oregon," *PS: Political Science and Politics* vol. 91, no. 1 (March 1997), pp. 53–57.

29. Adam J. Berinsky, Nancy Burns, and Michael W. Traugott, "Who Votes by Mail? A Dynamic Model of the Individual-Level Consequences of Voting-by-Mail Systems," *Public Opinion Quarterly*, vol. 65, no. 2 (2001), pp. 178–97.

30. Ibid.

31. "Statistical Examination of Ballot Types in Oregon General Elections: 1992–2000" (www.sos.state.or.us/executive/policy-initiatives/vbm/pcstudy.PDF [July 22, 2003]).

32. Only ten counties used punch cards at the beginning of the 1990s, and only seven do so today.

33. It would be expected that there would be higher error rates in off-year elections, since that is when Oregon has most of its statewide elections for state office—governor, secretary of state, and treasurer. An increase in the number of races increases the likelihood that there will be more true undervoting, that is, accidentally not voting in every race. See Jack Walker, "Ballot Forms and Voter Fatigue: An Analysis of the Office Block and Party Column Ballots," *Midwest Journal of Political Science*, vol. 10, no. 4 (1966), pp. 448–63, for a discussion of what political scientists refer to as "ballot roll-off."

34. Priscilla L. Southwell and Justin I. Burchett, "The Effect of All-Mail Elections on Voter Turnout," *American Politics Research*, vol. 28, no. 1 (January 2002), p. 76.

35. The following discussion is taken from the Electoral Commission, "Pilot Scheme Evaluation, West Wiltshire District Council, 13 June 2002," August 2002 (www.electoralcommission.gov.uk/files/dms/westwiltshire_6751-6296__E__N__S__W__.pdf [October 3, 2003]).

36. Electoral Commission, "The Shape of Elections to Come," July 2003, pages 5–6 (www.electoralcommission.gov.uk/about-us/may2003pilots.cfm [October 3, 2003]).

Chapter 7

1. Of all Alaskan households, 68.7 percent had computers in 2001 and 64.1 percent had Internet access, according to a report by the National Telecommunications and Information Administration (NTIA), "A Nation Online: How Americans Are Expanding Their Use of the Internet," February 2002 (www.ntia.doc.gov/ntiahome/dn/index.html [July 23, 2003]).

2. A quote attributed to Christy Adkinson, director of marketing for Vote-Here.net, in "Alaska Outposts Vote Online," *Federal Computer Week*, February 7, 2000. This assessment was echoed, however, in comments by Jim Adler, Vote-Here.net's president and CEO in an interview by James Ledbetter in *Industry Standard*, "Net Voting Experiment Leaves Alaskans Cold," January 26, 2000.

3. "Net Voting Experiment Leaves Alaskans Cold."

4. NTIA, "A Nation Online."

5. Thirteen percent of Arizona's population but only 5.7 percent of Alaska's population is older than sixty-five. In Arizona, 81.5 percent of the population has a high school degree or better; in Alaska, 87.9 percent of the population does. The median household income in Arizona is $38,830; in Alaska, it is $52,894. All these figures come from the 2000 U.S. Census except those for the rural population, which are from the 1990 U.S. Census.

6. In 1996, Governor Fife Symington scheduled the Arizona presidential primary for February 27, picking a date early in the 1996 primary season in an attempt to boost Arizona's national political profile and to help the chances of his and Senator John McCain's favored candidate for president, Senator Phil Gramm. See Rhodes Cook, *United States Presidential Primary Elections, 1968–1996* (Washington.: CQ Press, 2000), p. 60. However, at that time national Democratic Party rules did not permit states to hold Democratic presidential primary elections before March 1. The Democratic party therefore held a privately run primary on March 9, 1996. See Ballot Access News, "Arizona Primary," vol. 11, no. 7 (September 21, 1995), available at www.ballot-access.org/1995/0921.html#08 [September 30, 2003].

7. This is just one hypothesis that could have been tested in Arizona. Virtually any hypothesis could have been examined, from the relative costs of different voting mechanisms, to the accessibility of each mechanism, to questions about security and reliability.

8. The Democratic voter registration statistic comes from the February 15, 2000, registration report of the Arizona secretary of state (www.sosaz.com/election/VoterReg/2000-02-15.pdf [July 23, 2003]).

9. Frederic I. Solop, "Digital Democracy Comes of Age: Internet Voting and the 2000 Arizona Democratic Primary Election," *Political Science and Politics* (June 2001), p. 290.

10. See Rhodes Cook, *United States Presidential Primary Elections, 1968–1996* (Washington: CQ Press, 2000). Cook discusses the Democratic preference "primaries" in Arizona on page 60. Interestingly, Solop (" Digitial Democracy," pp. 289–90) also discusses the history of preference primaries in Arizona but does not acknowledge that the 1996 Democratic presidential nomination was uncontested nor that the Democratic party conducted a very limited preference "primary" in that year, making it a poor baseline from which to assess the interest of Arizona Democratic voters in Internet voting.

11. The same argument, and the same comparison, is made in R. Michael Alvarez and Jonathan Nagler, "The Likely Consequences of Internet Voting for Political Representation," *Loyola of Los Angeles Law Review* vol. 34, no. 3 (2001), pp. 1139–1141.

12. This question also has been considered by Alvarez and Nagler in "The Likely Consequences of Internet Voting," and we will discuss more of their research results. Like Alvarez and Nagler, we study the nonwhite populations of each county, not the fraction of the Democratic electorate in each county that is nonwhite. While the latter can be estimated—as Alvarez and Nagler attempted to do—like any statistical estimate it includes some error. Also, the population statistics are, of course, easier for researchers to collect and use. Unlike Alvarez and Nagler, we use racial data from the 2000 U.S. Census; Alvarez and Nagler used population estimates from the Arizona Department of Commerce in their study.

13. Alvarez and Nagler, "Likely Consequences of Internet Voting."

14. Solop, in "Digital Democracy," presents survey results that he argues demonstrate that race had no bearing on the choice to vote on the Internet. Solop's research, however, is based on three telephone surveys, two apparently conducted before the election and one conducted afterward. Solop does not report when these surveys were conducted, nor which surveys his analysis in tables 2 and 3 of his report are drawn from. Also, he does not report the percentages of survey respondents who stated that they would, or did, use the Internet to vote. Without additional information about the survey methodologies, it is difficult to determine why Solop's results are at odds with those reported by Alvarez and Nagler.

15. Deborah M. Phillips and Hans A. von Spakovsky, "Gauging the Risks of Internet Elections," *Communications of the ACM*, vol. 44, no. 1 (January 2001), p. 80. These authors also point out that the Internet voting system used in this election was not accessible by blind voters.

16. Solop, "Digital Democracy," p. 291.

17. The act covers four categories of citizens: those who are in the uniformed services on active duty (Army, Navy, Air Force, Marine Corps, Coast Guard, the

Commissioned Corps of the Public Health Service and the National Oceanic and Atmospheric Administration, and students of the armed forces academies); members of the Merchant Marine; the dependents of uniformed service personnel or Merchant Marine members; and all other overseas citizens who are qualified to vote at their last place of residence. The UOCAVA (42 U.S.C. § 1973) allows these citizens to use absentee registration procedures and to vote by absentee ballot in federal general, special, primary, and run-off elections. The Help America Vote Act (2002) amplifies the UOCAVA provisions.

18. General Accounting Office, *Elections: Voting Assistance to Military and Overseas Citizens Should Be Improved*, GAO-01-1026, September 2001; General Accounting Office, *Elections: Issues Affecting Military and Overseas Absentee Voters*, GAO-01-704T (2001).

19. GAO, *Elections: Voting Assistance*, pp. 40–41.

20. Federal Voting Assistance Program, "Voting Over the Internet Pilot Project Assessment Report" (Department of Defense, June 2001), pp. 1–6.

21. Ibid., 1–14 through 1–15.

22. Ibid., 1–15.

23. Ibid., ES-1.

24. These efforts are detailed in "Voting Over the Internet Pilot Project Initial Assessment Report," 1–13 through 1–14.

25. Caltech/MIT Voting Technology Project, *Voting: What Is, What Could Be* (2001) (www.vote.caltech.edu/Reports/july01/July01_VTP_%20Voting_Report_Entire.pdf [September 26, 2003]), pp. 51–52.

26. See "Voting Over the Internet Pilot Project," 1–15 through 1–16.

27. Voters in Arizona who could not reach a technical support person were likely deterred from voting.

28. A description of CyberVote and of the three trials discussed here can be found online at www.eucybervote.org/main.html [July 23, 2003].

29. "Germany Seeks to Introduce Online Voting in Elections," Agence France Presse, May 3, 2001.

30. See Alison Langley, "Geneva Suburb Casts Ballots on the Internet in Test Project," *New York Times*, January 12, 2003; "Switzerland: Internet Votes Make History," *Ottawa Citizen*, January 20, 2003, p. A7. The discussion of the security procedures used in the Geneva case, including the discussion of "white-hat" hacking, was found at www.nexis.com, BBC Worldwide Monitoring, "E-Voting Brings New Potential to Swiss Elections," January 21, 2003.

31. Electoral Commission, "Modernising Elections: A Strategic Evaluation of the 2002 Electoral Pilot Schemes," August 2002 (www.electoralcommission.org.uk/files/dms/Modernising_elections_6574-6170__E__N__S__W__.pdf [September 30, 2003]).

Chapter 8

1. There is a large and very accessible academic literature on experimental and quasi-experimental design in science. One of the best studies is Donald T. Campbell and Julian Stanley's 1966 classic, *Experimental and Quasi-Experimental Designs for Research* (Boston: Houghton Mifflin Company, 1966).

2. The classic is Campbell and Stanley's *Experimental and Quasi-Experimental Designs for Research*, but there is an enormous literature on the experimental method, especially as it relates to social science research. There also are many variations on what we have called a classic experimental design, because in many contexts a true experiment is difficult to conduct, is impractical or unethical, or is too expensive. These issues are discussed in Campbell and Stanley's work.

3. The NSF proposal for the IRIS project defines the DHT concept clearly: "DHTs enable data-centric networking by allowing requests for data to be sent without requiring any knowledge of where the corresponding items may be stored. One way of using the DHT abstraction would be to associate a name with each object of interest, and hash that name to a 'key' in an m-bit virtual address space. The virtual address space is partitioned into cells, which form contiguous regions of this address space. Depending on the design of the specific DHT algorithm, either a single host or a set of hosts is assigned to each cell of the virtual address space. Each host is assigned to one or more cells, and maintains copies of those key-value bindings whose key values lie within its assigned cells. The partitioning of the address space and the assignment of hosts to cells is dynamic and, in particular, changes whenever a node enters, departs or fails, or whenever load balancing is required to match the capabilities of nodes with the bandwidth, storage and processing requirements assigned to them." "IRIS ITR Proposal Summary" (http://project-iris.net/proposal.html [October 1, 2003]).

4. See "DHS Secretary Ridge Creates New Division to Combat Cyber Threats" (www.ncs.gov/n5_hp/Customer_Service/XAffairs/NewService/2003/2003-036.htm [October 1, 2003]).

5. *The National Strategy to Secure Cyberspace* (www.whitehouse.gov/pcipb/ [October 1, 2003]).

6. See "Cybersecurity Today and Tomorrow" (www.nap.edu/html/cybersecurity/ [October 1, 2003]).

7. H. Asher Bolande, "Watch Out 3G, Wi-Fi Is Here," *Far Eastern Economic Review* (February 27, 2003), 36–39; Alan S. Kay, "Wi-Fi Promise vs. Reality: The Wireless Technology Gets Put to the Speed Test," *Washington Post*, April 20, 2003, H-9; Yuki Noguchi, "A New Wave of Wireless: 'Wi-Fi' Networks Are Expanding Internet's Reach, Profit Opportunities," *Washington Post*, April 20, 2003, H-1; Rob Pegoraro, "Better Security for Wireless Access," *Washington Post*, April 20, 2003, H-7.

8. National Science Board, *Science and Engineering Indicators: 2002*, NSB-02-1 (Arlington, Va.: National Science Foundation, 2002), pp. 5–10.

9. See Federal Election Commission, *Voting System Standards* (www.fec.gov/pages/vssfinal/vss.html [July 25, 2003]). The revised standards clearly allow for electronic voting systems that are in some way networked, but the systems as defined in the standards are what we have called kiosk Internet voting systems, which are in a polling place or another location controlled by election officials.

10. See Benjamin M. Compaine, "Declare the War Won," in Bejamin M. Compaine, ed., *The Digital Divide: Facing Crisis or Creating a Myth?* (London: MIT Press, 2001); John Simons, "Cheap Computers Bridge the Digital Divide," *Wall Street Journal*, January 27, 2000.

11. Cheskin Research, "The Digital World of the U.S. Hispanic," 2000 (www.cheskin.com/p/ar.asp?mlid=7&arid=11&art=0 [October 2, 2003]).

12. Norman H. Nie and Lutz Erbring, "Internet and Society," Stanford Institute for the Quantitative Study of Society, 2000 (www.stanford.edu/group/siqss/Press_Release/Preliminary_Report.pdf [October 2, 2003]).

13. Compaine, "Declare the War Won."

14. A statistical analysis in the most recent Commerce Department study on the digital divide concluded that when computers and the Internet were first introduced to Americans, "inequality (in access) based on income and education was substantial. Over time, however, declining prices, increased availability in schools and libraries, and wider applications in many occupations have combined to reduce inequality in both computer and Internet use" (U.S. Department of Commerce, "A Nation Online," February 2002, p. 88) (www.ntia.doc.gov/ntiahome/dn/ [October 3, 2003]) . Under the assumption that current trends in household computer ownership continue, the Commerce Department's analysis indicates that the digital divide could be eliminated as early as the end of this decade (see figure 9-3 and project the trend from 1997 to 2002 forward), perhaps sooner.

15. Marc Lacey, "Clinton Enlists Top-Grade Help for Plan to Increase Computer Use," *New York Times*, February 3, 2000, p. A25.

16. Communications Act of 1934, Title 1, page 1 (www.fcc.gov/Reports/1934new.pdf [July 25, 2003]).

17. This FCC program is called informally the "E-rate" program. For details of the study of the impact of the E-rate program on California public schools, see Austan Goolsbee and Jonathan Guryan, "The Impact of Internet Subsidies in Public Schools," University of Chicago, 2002 (http://gsbwww.uchicago.edu/fac/austan.goolsbee/research/erate.pdf [July 25, 2003]).

18. Department of Commerce, "A Nation Online," p. 3.

19. Budget of the U.S. Government, Fiscal Year 2003 (http://w3.access.gpo.gov/usbudget/fy2003/budget.html [July 25, 2003]).

20. "McCain Targets $5.2 Billion of Pork Barrel Projects in Defense Spending Bill," August 1, 2002 (www.senate.gov/~mccain/index.cfm?fuseaction=Newscenter.ViewPressRelease&Content_id=431 [October 2, 2003]).

21. This successful initiative was fully discussed in Michel Marriott, "A Barn-Raising for the Internet Age," *New York Times*, December 19, 2002, p. E1.

22. For a more complete assessment of community computing, see Donald A. Schön, Bish Sanyal, and William J. Mitchell, eds., *High Technology and Low-Income Communities: Prospects for the Positive Use of Advanced Information Technology* (MIT Press, 2001).

Index

Absentee voting: comparison table, 104–05; denial-of-service problem, 88–89; eligibility standards, 107–08; historical overview, 105–07; as model for Internet voting, 19; participation barriers, 5–6; privacy/fraud concerns, 89–92, 111–12; turnout statistics, 108–09, 112–13. *See also* overseas voters

Access arguments. *See* digital divide; turnout/participation

African Americans, 35, 36, 45–46, 48–50. *See also* minorities

Age levels: and democratic representation, 34–35; early voting, 110; participation statistics, 38, 42, 72; potential Internet voting impact, 6, 10, 28, 48–50, 52; vote-by-mail systems, 116–17

Alaska, Internet straw polling, 124–27

"All-postal elections," United Kingdom, 119–21

Alvarez, R. Michael, 133–34

Anonymity issue. *See* fraud/privacy concerns

Apache County, Arizona, 129–30, 131

Arizona, 113, 127–35
Arkansas, 107
Assembly Bill *44*, 18
ATM fraud, 84

Baldassare, Mark, 71–72
Ballot errors (voter-caused): absentee voting, 109, 112; Internet advantages, 6, 40; Oregon's study, 118–19. *See also* lost-vote problem (system-caused)
Beck, Juliette, 3
"Black box" problem, 90–91
Bremen, Germany, Internet voting trial, 144
Britain. *See* United Kingdom
Broadband access rates, 46, 48
Broder, David, 68–69
Broward County, Florida, 88
Burchett, Justin, 119
Bush, George W., 125–26

Cable modem technology, socioeconomic comparisons, 8, 46, 48
Cain, Bruce, 60, 73
California: absentee voting, 102–03, 108, 109, 111–12, 113; as candidate for Internet voting, 17–18;

Presidential election (2000): deliberative democracy field test, 65–68;
lost-vote statistics, 31–32; overseas
ballots, 1–2; voting system differences, 36–37
Privacy arguments. *See* fraud/privacy
concerns
Propositions *30* and *31,* 70–71
Public Law *712,* 107
Public opinion surveys, Internet voting, 17
Punch card voting, 118–19
Putnam, Robert, 9

Question of the Day project, 65–67

Registration systems: and democratic
representation, 36; historic purposes, 41–42; Internet benefits, 5,
43–44; NVRA legislation, 42–43;
overseas Internet project, 137–38;
as voting barriers, 37, 42
Remote Internet voting, defined, 4
Representation. *See* democratic representation
Republicans: absentee/early voting,
109, 110; Alaska's straw poll,
124–27; Internet voting impact,
51; vote-by-mail systems, 117
Republic.com (Sunstein), 55–56, 74
Research needs, security problems,
92–93, 154–58. *See also* trials/pilot
testing
Research review: California task
force, 17–21, 99–100;
Caltech/MIT project, 27; framing
limitations, 26–27; independent
scientists, 23–26; IPI workshop,
21–23; United Kingdom report,
27–28. *See also* trials/pilot testing
Rhode Island, 106
Riptech Corporation, 81
Rolling Cyber Debate, 65, 66–67
Ross, Ron, 85
Rubin, Avi, 24, 25, 83

Sacramento, California, 64–65, 74–75
Santa Cruz County, Arizona, 129–30
Schneier, Bruce, 78, 87
Schools, 3, 162–63, 164–65
Schum, Richard, 22
Script kiddies, 78, 84
Secrets and Lies (Schneier), 78
Secure Electronic Registration and
Voting Experiment (SERVE), 146,
148–49, 165–66
Security problems: criticisms summarized, 7–9; data inadequacies, 25;
incentives for solutions, 96–99;
online potential, 78–82, 83–87; as
opposition argument, 7–9, 24; pre-
vention strategies, 82, 90, 91–92,
93–96; public perceptions, 78, 79;
research proposals, 92–93,
154–58; traditional elections compared, 76–77, 82, 87–92. *See also*
identity verification; research
review
September *11* impact, 84–85, 96–97,
155–56
Server security, 93, 94
SERVE (Secure Electronic Registration
and Voting Experiment), 146,
148–49, 165–66
Socioeconomic comparisons: Alaska-
Arizona populations, 127;
Arizona's Internet voting trial,
132–33; California voting population, 71–72; computers/Internet
access, 8, 45–48; early voters, 110;
participation in voting process,
38–40; potential impact of Internet
voting, 48–50; vote-by-mail sys-
tems, 116–18
Solop, Frederic I., 130, 134
Source code, 160
South Carolina, 137, 139
Southwell, Priscilla, 119
Spafford, Gene, 81
Spectrum auction fees, 164
Spoofing, 84